'And I, betwixt them both, to please them both
And yet to give the story as it rose,
I moved as in a strange diagonal,
And maybe neither pleased
myself nor them."

· TENNYSONIAN LOVE ·
THE STRANGE DIAGONAL

by Gerhard Joseph

UNIVERSITY OF MINNESOTA PRESS · MINNEAPOLIS

Library of Congress Catalog Card Number: 68-57204

For Eileen, Lise, Miriam, and Elaine

Acknowledgments

I WISH to express my gratitude to the persons who have generously aided me in the task of completing this study. During the early stages of composition Raymond Reno of George-
town University read the entire manuscript and his comments
helped shape its initial form. Colleagues at the University of Minnesota who offered sound criticisms include Samuel Holt Monk,
Martin Roth, James Scoggins, Gordon O'Brien, Toni McNaron,
and, especially, Ted Zorn. James Kissane of Grinnell College read
and made suggestions for the improvement of Chapters VIII and
IX. My primary intellectual debt, however, is to G. Robert Stange
of Tufts University, a teacher and friend who first exposed me to
serious study in the Victorian period. His counsel and encourage-
ment have provided crucial support throughout the writing of this
book.

A grant from the Graduate School of the University of Minnesota made possible a visit to several libraries. And I thank the editors of *Modern Philology* and *Victorian Newsletter* for allowing
me to reprint in Chapters VIII and IX, respectively, material that
originally appeared in their journals.

G. J.

Bronx, New York

Table of Contents

TENNYSONIAN LOVE

FOR MARK YOU, Phaedrus, beauty alone is both divine and visible; and so it is the sense way, the artist's way, little Phaedrus, to the spirit. But, now tell me, my dear boy, do you believe that such a man can ever attain wisdom and true manly worth, for whom the path to the spirit must lead through the senses? Or do you rather think . . . that it is a path of perilous sweetness, a way of transgression, and must surely lead him who walks in it astray?

Thomas Mann, *Death in Venice*

IT HAS BEEN sometimes said that art is a means of escape from "the tyranny of the senses." It may be so for the spectator: he may find that the spectacle of supreme works of art takes from the life of the senses something of its turbid fever. But this is possible for the spectator only because the artist, in producing those works, has gradually sunk his intellectual and spiritual ideas in sensuous form. He may live, as Keats lived, a pure life; but his soul, like that of Plato's false astronomer, becomes more and more immersed in sense, until nothing which lacks the appeal to sense has interest for him. How could such an one ever again endure the greyness of the ideal or spiritual world? The spiritualist is satisfied as he watches the escape of the sensuous elements from his conceptions; his interest grows, as the dyed garment bleaches in the keener air. But the artist steeps his thought again and again into the fire of colour.

Walter Pater, "Winckelmann," *The Renaissance*

CHAPTER I

Tennysonism

AT THE climax of "Enoch Arden," Enoch, the protagonist in one of Alfred Tennyson's most popular domestic idylls, returns to England, having at last been rescued from ten years of solitude on a desert island. To his intense sorrow he learns of his wife's marriage to his childhood friend and rival for her hand, Philip. Although he will not reveal himself to the couple, he cannot forbear stealing up to their cottage to see if his wife and children are content with their new lot. The stylized, mawkish scene that confronts Enoch as, hidden by the darkness, he peers through the window into the brightly lit parlor may well serve as a classical instance of Tennysonian and indeed "Victorian" love:

> For cups and silver on the burnish'd board
> Sparkled and shone; so genial was the hearth;
> And on the right hand of the hearth he saw
> Philip, the slighted suitor of old times,
> Stout, rosy, with his babe across his knees;
> And o'er her second father stoopt a girl,
> A later but a loftier Annie Lee,
> Fair-hair'd and tall, and from her lifted hand
> Dangled a length of ribbon and a ring
> To tempt the babe, who rear'd his creasy arms,
> Caught at and ever miss'd it, and they laughed;
> And on the left hand of the hearth he saw

The mother glancing often toward her babe,
But turning now and then to speak with him,
Her son, who stood beside her tall and strong
And saying that which pleased him, for he smiled.

(ll. 738–753) [1]

The frozen moment contains all the properties of a "Tennyson-ism" [2] that was anathema to those writers and social commentators in the late nineteenth century who were trying to shatter the mold of a stultifying Victorian domesticity. Most of the attitudes that constitute the Victorian family tintype manage to reveal them-selves. The children are carefully disposed according to size, sex, and the demands of symmetry. Poised in their innocence, charm-ingly devoted to one another and to their parents, they are starched exemplars of a harmony that is sanctioned by and proof of a bene-ficent God. Annie, the satisfied wife and all-protecting mother, oversees a domain of polished furniture and gleaming cutlery. John Ruskin has apotheosized the type — such a woman is "enduringly, incorruptibly good; instinctively, infallibly wise — wise, not for self-development, but for self-renunciation: wise, not that she may set herself above her husband, but that she may never fail from his side: wise, not with the narrowness of insolent and loveless pride, but with the passionate gentleness of an infinitely variable, because infinitely applicable, modesty of service — the true changefulness

[1] Unless otherwise indicated, all references to Tennyson's poetry are from W. J. Rolfe's one-volume *The Poetic and Dramatic Works of Alfred Lord Tennyson* (Boston and New York, 1898) — hereafter cited as *Works*. There will also be occasional references to notes of the six-volume Eversley *Works of Tennyson*, ed. Hallam Tennyson (London and New York, 1908).

[2] Henry Seidel Canby's *American Memoir* (Boston, 1947), pp. 88ff., con-tains an extended definition of what the term meant to an American at the turn of the century: "No, the trouble was the Tennysonism of the sexular attitude, the Longfellowism of our morality. The only possible relationship between men and women that is as vital as the relationship between men or be-tween women is the one in which even the married and the bechildrened, and the faithful to their spouses, still feel a permanent possibility of sexual awaken-ing. It does not have to be mutual, it is enough that the most settled should know that their nature is still tender, and inflammable by nature if not by will. We, in our middle age, talked to middle-aged women as if they were cinders — agreeable, yes, admirable often, interesting often, yet cinders, good for home walks and garden beds, but long emptied of fire — and like cinders they re-sponded."

of woman." [3] And "stout, rosy" Philip is Tennyson's version of the Victorian husband presiding over a hearth whose glow provides sufficient refuge from a threatening universe. Here the *paterfamilias* can avoid, if only for a time, the cash-payment nexus of the larger society and the intellectual shock waves that are battering at his traditional values; here he can forget "a world alien, not your world . . . not a home at all, of hearts and faces who are yours, whose you are." [4]

The least promising avenue to a sympathetic reading of Tennyson would seem to be a prolonged consideration of such scenes, such cloying images of that most subtle of phenomena, human love, which he served up to his age. In the pendulum swing away from a Victorian idolatry of Tennyson that began in the 1860's the shallowness of the domestic love idylls — along with the dogmatism of his verse sermons on religion and politics — has borne the brunt of criticism. The most intemperate of the twentieth-century outbursts against Tennyson would seem to be a thing of the past. A new generation of readers, while rejecting the exaggerated claims of the Victorian audience for its *sacer vates*, has insisted in subdued but generous tones upon the imaginative depth and intelligence of his best work. As a result the Edwardian ridicule and the Bloomsbury smirk at Tennyson's expense seem facile and dated. Still, despite this gradual rehabilitation of critical reputation the modern reader probably finds Tennyson's view of love somewhat irrelevant if not imperceptive. The narrative paeans to chaste romantic courtships must strike a post-Freudian generation as embarrassingly vapid and more than a bit naive; the tributes to idyllic marriages may well seem artificial period pieces, social documents of service primarily to those intent upon beating, somewhat belatedly and even unfashionably, the dead horse of Victorian "prudery" and "hypocrisy."

If, then, human love is not a subject that always inspired Tenny-

[3] "Of Queens' Gardens," *Sesame and Lilies, Works* (London, 1902–1912), XVIII, 142. Outside of Tennyson, this essay and Coventry Patmore's various works may serve as the two representative and full Victorian statements on the edifying destiny of woman.

[4] Thomas Carlyle, *Past and Present* (London, 1897), p. 274.

son's best poetry, what justification is there for this study of Tennysonian love? In the first place Tennyson's adjustment to and reflection of his age were in such felicitous balance that, as George Saintsbury observed, "no age of poetry can be called the age of one man with such critical accuracy as the later Nineteenth Century is, with us, the Age of Tennyson." [5] A systematic exploration of a concept that made Tennyson the immensely admired secular prophet he became ought to imply a good deal about Victorian social attitudes and the spirit of the middle and late nineteenth century. Secondly, what Tennyson meant by love deserves study in its own right as the subject of some of his most interesting work. The complexities of mood evidenced when he writes of love — the uncertainties of motive and anguished half-repressions that his imagery reveals — account for the richness of his best poetry and the provocative angularities of his less than best. The gloomy failures of love in Tennyson's work also suggest a skein far more intricate than that which the turn of the century simplified and excoriated as Tennysonism. His lifelong delight in sensuous detail can shatter the cozy idyll before the hearth in strange and creative ways; his praise of secure domesticity is often contained within a context of melancholia and deathlike grief.

Thus, the cheerful "little pictures" both early as in "Supposed Confessions of a Second-Rate Sensitive Mind" (1830) and late as in the homecoming scene from "Enoch Arden" (1864) may strike a modern reader as unbearably saccharine. But the delights of familial calm occur against a backdrop of frustration, defeat, and impending death. We come to know the human felicity that Tennyson describes not through the consciousness of those who experience it but through the eyes of a despairing exile. Enoch stands outside the human family whose composure is projected onto the very landscape: behind Philip's cottage

> Flourish'd a little garden square and wall'd,
> And in it throve an ancient evergreen,

[5] Quoted in G. M. Young, "The Age of Tennyson," *Proceedings of the British Academy*, XXV (London, 1939), p. 127, which essay takes Saintsbury's remark as its thesis; reprinted in John Killham, *Critical Essays on the Poetry of Tennyson* (London, 1960), p. 26.

> A yew-tree, and all around it ran a walk
> Of shingle, and a walk divided it.   (ll. 730–733)

Shut out from the warmth and joy he observes but cannot share,
Enoch is tortured for the rest of his life by a memory and desire
which hasten his death. Such a memory recalls not only the domes-
ticated *locus amoenus* in which the love forbidden to him can grow
but also another, more unsettling vision of nature. His mind must
continually wander back to the seductively luxuriant, rococo landscape of his desert island, a wilderness sublimely indifferent to his
yearning for human contact:

> The mountain wooded to the peak, the lawns
> And winding glades high up like ways to heaven,
> The slender coco's drooping crown of plumes,
> The lightning flash of insect and of bird,
> The lustre of the long convolvuluses
> That coil'd around the stately stems, and ran
> Even to the limit of the land, the glows
> And glories of the broad belt of the world, —
> All these he saw. . . .
> The myriad shriek of wheeling ocean-fowl,
> The league-long roller thundering on the reef,
>
> . . . .
>
> The blaze upon the waters to the east;
> The blaze upon his island overhead;
> The blaze upon the waters to the west;
> Then the great stars that globed themselves in heaven,
> The hollower-bellowing ocean, and again
> The scarlet shafts of sunrise — but no sail.   (ll. 568–595)

Perhaps Walter Bagehot and Gerard Manley Hopkins were justified in condemning the uninspired ornamentation of these lines,[6]
and perhaps their mild infusion of naturalism does not redeem the
poem from its prevailing sentimentality. But the juxtaposition of
these lines and the picture that Enoch, standing in the garden, sees

[6] For representative examples of the beginning of the reaction against
Tennyson idolatry, see Walter Bagehot, "Wordsworth, Tennyson, and
Browning; or Pure, Ornate, and Grotesque Art in English Poetry," in *Liter-
ary Studies*, ed. Richard Holt Hutton, II (London, 1895); and Gerard Man-
ley Hopkins' letter to W. M. Baillie in *Further Letters of Gerard Manley
Hopkins*, ed. C. C. Abbott (London, 1938), p. 68.

through the window suggests a creative tension that Tennyson had not finally relieved even by the time of his personal maturity and the professional success of the 1864 volume. The static images of secure married love framed within the cultivated Tennysonian garden are surrounded by a wild, fecund nature — by coiling convolvuluses, by myriad shrieks of birds, by the bellowing ocean. The sensuous landscape, symbolic as it is for Tennyson, constantly threatens to pass into a humanly sensual one. Even this late in his life one feels the uncertainty of the poet's response to an unbridled eroticism that releases the terrified vehemence of "Lucretius," "The Vision of Sin," or "The Ancient Sage." The precarious balance between sense and spirit in Tennysonian love thus deserves investigation both as a characteristic Victorian tension and as a perspective on Tennyson's poetry.

A prolonged discussion of love in the works of a Victorian poet, particularly if his treatment of the emotion is to be called "typical," presents a difficult task of focusing. Love for Tennyson represents several things. It is, first of all, a phase both of a historical idea and of an ever-changing literary convention whose strands are as twisted and difficult to disentangle as the intellectual and emotional history of Western man. It is, secondly, a peculiarly Victorian phenomenon, for it both reflects and helps to consolidate a Victorian social assumption: the romantic erotic union of man and woman should occur within the confines of a sacramental and contractual marriage. Finally, Tennysonian love arises out of his own unique temperament and experience, and is most profitably examined in what is known about his life and, more important, in the poetry itself. To capture, necessarily in outline form, the intellectual and literary tradition out of which Tennysonian love evolved, to do justice to it as a Victorian response to that tradition, and to consider it as a personal and idiosyncratic poetic expression of a powerful complex of feelings — this is the threefold purpose of the study that follows.

The last of these purposes would seem to call for a criticism that borrows from the insights of modern psychological analysis. But principles of agreement among critic and reader are hard to come

by in such an amorphous and still disputed area. Furthermore, as
W. H. Auden has said, "no other poetry is easier, and less illumi-
nating, to psychoanalyze" than Tennyson's.[7] For such reasons I
have usually avoided reference to current theories and findings
about sexual repression, projection, sublimation, and the like. It is
true that much has been added in recent times to an objective understanding of sexual feelings, and their role in character formation
and, consequently, their function in fantasy making and art. But,
on the whole, it has seemed more tactful and more relevant to ad-
here to the language of a nineteenth-century faculty psychology
and of a traditional ontology that Tennyson and his contemporaries found natural — to see Victorian love in the light of a confrontation of "sense" and "soul," "body" and "spirit" (simplistic
and outdated as that opposition may strike some readers). Such
diffidence may facilitate the reading of Tennyson's poetry in a way
that does not completely distort or debase his intentions, while an
occasional lifting of reserve may allow for implications that are
meaningful to a modern reader's different mode of perception.
Through an eclecticism that moves between a Victorian and a
modern psychology we can best disentangle the stylistic complex
that is the poem, the intention the poet seems to announce, and the
shrouded effects he sometimes achieves.

[7] *Selected Poems of Tennyson* (New York, 1944), p. x.

CHAPTER II

The Divided Heritage

IF THERE is truth to Alfred North Whitehead's assertion that all of Western philosophy is but a series of footnotes to Plato, something of the sort may also be said of Western ideas about love. Certainly the ladder the soul must climb in order to achieve once more the forms of the True, the Good, and the Beautiful which she remembers from a previous existence is a conceptual metaphor that has had a long life. Caught within the body's prison she must begin her ascent by a sensate attachment to "the beauties of the earth and mount upwards for the sake of that other beauty, using these as steps only, and from one going on to two, and from two to all fair forms, and from fair forms to fair practices, and from fair practices to fair notions, until from fair notions she arrives at the notion of absolute beauty, and at last she knows what the essence of beauty is." [1] During this climb the conversion from an attachment to the sensate "beauties of the earth" to the super-sensible "essence of beauty" accounts for Plato's absolute distinction between the two goddesses who correspond to these separate loves, a "common" and a "heavenly" Aphrodite.

The Platonistic Fathers of the Church insisted upon a similar profound division in their contraposition of a fleshly *cupiditas* and

[1] *Symposium, Five Great Dialogues*, trans. Benjamin Jowett (New York, 1942), p. 202.

spiritual *caritas*. Jerome and Augustine agree with Plato that the soul's conversion from a carnal to a spiritual love is not gradual but rather requires the step from one discrete cognitive realm into a higher one: one must leave the City of Flesh behind before entering into the City of the Spirit. Indeed the early Church was obsessive in its distaste for the lowly sensate rungs of Plato's ladder. The Marcionites, the Basilideans, the Saturninians, the Gnostics, and the Manichaeans who preached complete avoidance of physical contact between the sexes testify to the early Church's extreme aversion to man's carnal nature. While these sects were eventually declared heretical, the medieval Church incorporated much of their antipathy toward the sensuous and the sensual into its view of love. Although the married state gradually gained respectability after the fifth-century doctrine of marriage as a sacrament was dispersed throughout Europe, the early Church's bias against sexuality, even when legitimized by marriage, expressed itself officially as late as the mid-sixteenth century. The Council of Trent's condemnation with anathema of the doctrine that the married state was as good as, or superior to, celibacy indicates the continuing repugnance toward man's physical nature, and the insistent separation of a carnal love from a spiritualized agape. When throughout Western history this sexual puritanism has periodically asserted itself, it has done so by redefining with a renewed vigor and precision the dualism which received its classic statement in the works of Plato.

But alongside this tradition there has existed another that has denied — or at any rate tended to mitigate — the emphatic separation of body and spirit. The Christian notion of Incarnation and of the body's resurrection, for instance, allows to man's fleshly nature a dignity lacking or muted in the asceticism of the early apologists. Relatively modern theological statements about the relationship of a pagan eros and a Christian agape tend to avoid the attribution of sinfulness to every sexual act since the Fall, to blur the clear-cut dualism of a Paul or Tertullian.[2] The sources of this blurring — the

[2] See, for instance, Martin D'Arcy, *The Mind and Heart of Love* (New York, 1947); Ronald Knox, *Enthusiasm* (Oxford, 1950); and Anders Nygren, *Agape and Eros*, trans. Philip Watson (Philadelphia, 1953).

Provençal invention of courtly passion, the revived classical inter-
fusion of the sensual with the ideal during the Renaissance, and the
attempts of the Church to triumph over such heresies through an
adaptation of their outward trappings — have been thoroughly explored in a specialized scholarship. It is sufficient here to say that
the Neoplatonism of Dante's *Vita Nuova* and the romantic idealism
of the Renaissance poet that have crucially set the course of love
in post-Renaissance literature are serious departures from Platonic
asceticism. Dante's apotheosis of Beatrice in all her bodily splendor,
the lush reunion of Spenser's Scudamore and Amoret, the freshly
moving account of Arthur's meeting with Gloriana, the frank sensuality of Milton's Adam and Eve before the Fall — all suggest the
inruption of the fleshly into the spiritual in a way antithetical to
Platonic and early Christian dualism. The rungs of Plato's ladder,
as C. S. Lewis has suggested, are no longer distinct: "Those who
call themselves Platonists at the Renaissance may imagine a love
which reaches the divine without abandoning the human and becomes spiritual while remaining also carnal; but they do not find
this in Plato." [3]

Western love in the broadest sense, then, can be seen as a continuing dialectic between a tradition that has allowed for the interpenetration of the physical and the spiritual and one that has insisted on a wide and definable gap between them. Walter Pater,
like Tennyson a nineteenth-century witness to that dialectic, recognized the continuing hostility of these traditions toward one another in Western art: "Dante's belief in the resurrection of the
body, through which, even in heaven, Beatrice loses for him no
tinge of flesh-colour, or fold of raiment even; and the Platonic
dream of the passage of the soul through one form of life after another, with its passionate haste to escape from the burden of bodily
form altogether; are, for all effects of art and poetry, principles
diametrically opposite." [4]

It is the contention of this study that in the Victorian period the
antipathy between these rival views of love was especially intense,

[3] *The Allegory of Love* (Oxford, 1936), p. 5.
[4] "The Poetry of Michelangelo," *The Renaissance* (London, 1910), p. 86.

and that a poet so characteristic of his age as Tennyson was torn between them.

He was to an important degree the heir of a Christian pietism that was militantly reasserting a distinction between a despicable carnal passion and a "love" which was the manifestation of spirit. A temperamental and ideological uneasiness in the presence of man's physical nature had become a pronounced determinant in the English ethical scale during the years of Tennyson's adolescence, largely as the expression of a broadly based religious revival. On the lower levels of English society, particularly among agricultural laborers, the Methodist movement had encouraged an extreme distrust of the senses. John Wesley's resolution "to avoid all manner of passion" had gone so far as to make him abstain from meat and wine on his way to Georgia, and George Whitfield, the Methodist evangelist, had boasted that "if I know anything of my own heart, I am free from that foolish passion the world calls love." [5] This habit of asceticism and of attack upon sensual indulgence of all sorts gradually drifted upward; the religious fervor of laboring-class Methodists began to color the tastes of their social betters (even on the highest rungs of English society) who detected a moral flaccidity in eighteenth-century latitudinarianism. The social distance may have been great between field preachers' calls for rectitude and the Blue Stocking vehemence of Mrs. Vesey, Mrs. Montague, and Hannah More. Nevertheless, the need to improve the moral tone and the manners of what the reformers in common considered a decadent and irreligious country united them in a way that mitigated class differences. The evangelical fire spread by Wilberforce's party, combining with the earlier reforming zeal of the Methodists, was a paramount influence in forging Victorian puritanism.

Not that the passion for reform was entirely devoid of self-seeking motives. Eighteenth-century assaults upon license began as, and in some measure continued to be, maneuvers in a class conflict. Middle-class commentators tended to ascribe extraordinary sexual appetites to aristocratic practitioners of base seductions —

[5] Quoted in Arnold Lunn, *John Wesley* (London, 1929), pp. 27, 254.

witness the enormous popular success Samuel Richardson and his many imitators achieved in using that stereotype. One of the ways that the middle class sought its share in the political and social establishment was through a literary assault upon upper-class snobbery and sexual irresponsibility.[6] During the years of Tennyson's adolescence this antipathy toward aristocratic license was intensified by the Regency scandals that were as notorious as they were colorful. Perhaps the flamboyant libertinism that Thackeray raked so scathingly in his lecture on George IV did go underground at the accession of Victoria who rendered more respectable the outward appearance of court life. Still, throughout the middle Victorian years the dark reputation of the London demimonde and the corruption attributed to aristocratic rakes were continually disturbing motes in the public eye. It was thus, to simplify, the common front of a Dissenting moral fervor, an upper-class penchant for self-reform, and a disguised middle-class upward thrust that was fostering changes in taste and decorum at the beginning of the century.

To be sure, the religious revival had already passed its most exalted stages by the time that Tennyson was growing up in Somersby. It was not long before Dissenters were to become stock hypocrites in Victorian novels. Moreover, the larger currents of the developing Victorian ethos must have touched the young Tennyson in his remote Lincolnshire village only faintly. There the direct forces that shaped his "common sense" about love, his middle way between mystical idealism and doctrines of fleshly mortification that smacked of Dissenting enthusiasm, must have been his immediate family. Few members of the Tennyson household altogether avoided the tendency toward "black bloodedness." Alfred's grandfather, George Clayton Tennyson, the elder, the crusty patriarch of Bayons Manor, could be driven to "an extreme pitch of irritation and morbid sensibility" should his will be challenged or thwarted. The streak was most apparent in Tennyson's father, George Tennyson, the younger, whose propensity for fits

---

[6] See Ian Watt, "Love and the Novel: *Pamela*," *The Rise of the Novel* (Berkeley, 1959), pp. 135–173.

of severe depression was aggravated by his father's early decision to make Charles, a younger brother, the heir to the family fortune and estate. Alfred's father was consequently relegated to the comparative poverty of a church living. The difficulty of life in the Somersby rectory that was to become his home and prison; the occasional need to house "three and twenty in a family and sleep five or six in a room"; the nagging sense of the injustice that his father had done him; the consciousness of his considerable speculative and scholarly talents rotting away ingloriously in the Lincolnshire wilds — these cast a darkness over George Tennyson's life and over that of his family. In the umbra of his father's malaise Alfred Tennyson cultivated his own sense of all-pervading loss.[7]

Alfred, the fourth of George Tennyson's eleven children, seemingly inherited his father's capacity for gloomy reverie as well as his sensitive intelligence. Cut off from frequent contact with polite society, left to roam through the countryside or to devour the extravagant romances and mythical works of his father's library, the young Tennyson came to nourish a talent for poetic expression in the course of his rather solitary existence.

Tennyson's adolescence was a trying time, for his father had taken to serious drinking and could become violent with the children and especially with Mrs. Tennyson. It was during such times that Tennyson perhaps came to know the melancholia, the longing for death and retreat from activity that became important themes in his poetry. While Tennyson clearly had a real affection for his sick-souled father, he learned early from his father's negative example the need for self-control in order to tame within himself the unruly drives that had ruined his father's life. One senses as one reads the poetry a terror of extreme passion and a continual need to assert the moderation that his father shunned.

To judge from the model of woman as wife and mother that Tennyson forged for a receptive Victorian audience, Elizabeth

[7] Sir Charles Tennyson, *Alfred Tennyson* (London and New York, 1949), pp. 4–46. See, however, Hallam Tennyson's lightening of what from the evidence of the poetry and the family circumstances would seem to have been a fairly unhappy childhood: *Alfred Lord Tennyson: A Memoir by His Son*, 2 vols. (London and New York, 1897), I, 5 — hereafter cited as *Memoir*.

Tennyson, the poet's mother, was the counterbalancing force to the negative model of the father. In large part because she supplied her erratic, volatile sons with a center of emotional stability, Tennyson throughout his life seemed to value woman as a guide and support and to upbraid her when she failed in so lofty a calling.

It was the simple pietism of Tennyson's mother more than the intellectualized Anglicanism of his father that determined the son's religious sentiments and his conception of love. Some inkling of Elizabeth Tennyson's fervor and simplicity of faith emerges in a letter that she wrote at eighty to her son upon the publication of the *Idylls of the King*:

O dearest Ally, how fervently have I prayed for years that our merciful Redeemer would intercede with our Heavenly Father, to grant thee His Holy Spirit to urge thee to employ the talents He has given thee, by taking every opportunity of endeavouring to impress the precepts of His Holy Word on the minds of others. My beloved son, words are too feeble to express the joy of my heart in perceiving that thou art earnestly endeavouring to do so. Dearest Ally, there is nothing for a moment to be compared to the favour of God: I need not ask thee if thou art of the same opinion. Thy writings are a convincive proof that thou art. My beloved child, when our Heavenly Father summons us hence, may we meet, and all that are dear to us, in that blessed state where sorrow is unknown, never more to be separated.[8]

There were several doctrines that his mother's evangelical creed gave to Tennyson which remained with him and reinforced themselves in later life: the conviction that the ultimate reality is not material but spiritual; the belief in the immortality of the human soul; and the strong persuasion that the central principle in the universe is Love. The most important of these for the purposes of this study, the trust in a God of Love, finds its earliest expression in the unfinished play, *The Devil and the Lady*, that Tennyson wrote in his adolescence:

> O thou omnipotent Love, whose boundless sway
> And uncontroll'd dominion boweth down
> The Spirits of the Mighty, thou great Despot,

[8] *Memoir*, I, 452. Other representative letters are included in *Letters to Frederick Tennyson*, ed. Hugh J. Schonfield (London, 1930), pp. 133–136.

Who bindest in thy golden chains the strong
And the imbecile, thou immortal Pan-Arch
Tyrant o' th' earth and sea whose sunless depth
And desolate Abyss is vivified
And quicken'd at thy bidding — thou vast link
Of the Creation — thou deep sentiment!
Thou only to be understood by those
Who feel thee and aid thy purpose. . . .[9]

In contrast to his mother's gentle pietism Tennyson was exposed early in his life to the severe Dissenting fervor of his Calvinistic Aunt Mary Bourne who lived five miles away from the Somersby rectory. The effects of her gloomy preachments show through in certain youthful Tennyson poems, filled with allusions to the doctrine of the Elect and with speakers who consider themselves damned from birth (see "Remorse," "Armageddon," and "The Coach of Death" in *Unpublished Early Poems*). Tennyson soon outgrew whatever temporary impression Mary Bourne may have had upon his religious sensibility; he was rather amused in later years at her violent Calvinistic outbursts during his youth. Nevertheless, the most important influences Tennyson underwent both in Somersby and later at Cambridge were in the direction of an intense moralism that was one of the characteristic emanations of Victorian thought.

On one of his sides, then, Tennyson was a trustworthy mirror of an evangelical age. A serious religiosity, an earnestness, a distaste for gestures blatantly sexual, a growing abhorrence of license in any form — such attitudes were moving through the larger London world and reaching the Lincolnshire countryside in which Tennyson was growing up.

What complicated the pietism developing within Tennyson was its mingling with the sensate temperament of the artist. The religious revival to which Tennyson was, however indirectly, exposed tended to strengthen the orthodox moralist's suspicion of a sense

[9] *The Devil and the Lady*, ed. Charles Tennyson (London, 1930), p. 1. Indiana University Press has recently combined the play and Tennyson's *Unpublished Early Poems*, also edited by Charles Tennyson, into a single volume (Bloomington, 1964).

that could all too easily degenerate into sensuality. But Tennyson was not merely a Christian with a conviction that the ultimate reality was spiritual not material; he was also a poet with powerful appetites (even if those appetites did not take a particularly sexual direction).[10] Tennyson throughout his life was passionately absorbed in the sensuous beauties of the natural world. As an unrebellious child of his time he might agree that sensuality and license were perils to be shunned; but the early stirrings within him of a volatile emotional sensibility implied a denial that poetic indulgence in sense must inevitably lead to such evils. The moralist in him only gradually began to suspect under the incessant proddings of his age that the way of the senses was full of snares. But before those proddings could touch him he was exposed to a romantic tradition of erotic idealism that along with the legacy of evangelical Christianity helped to shape the Victorian artist.

Periodicals and pulpits during the early years of the century were outraged by the "last age in France" whose profligate "literature of prostitution" had contributed to the present moral decay of English life. The most eminent and influential Victorian prophets were one in their denunciation of the French "goddess of Lubricity," of this "*new* astonishing Phallus-Worship, with universal Balzac-Sand melodies and litanies."[11] But guardians of English virtue did not have to look across the channel for literary productions that insulted the emerging Victorian ethos. In the popular mind as well as in the thought of many critics, the behavior and poetry of the Romantics, especially the second generation, created an impression of erotic irresponsibility. Just as the seventeenth-century Puritans had directed an indiscriminate wrath against the sensuous and the sensual, so too did their Victorian descendants

[10] Charles Tennyson (*Six Tennyson Essays* [London, 1954], p. 102) and more extensively Ralph Wilson Rader (*Tennyson's "Maud": The Biographical Genesis* [Berkeley, 1963]) have argued, however, that Tennyson's passion for Rosa Baring "was one of the most important episodes of his life, leaving its mark not only on the 'Locksley Hall' poems but on other major works as well" (Rader, p. 22).

[11] Matthew Arnold, "Numbers," *Discourses in America* (London, 1885), pp. 40–41 and 56–57; and Thomas Carlyle, *Latter-Day Pamphlets, Works*, Centenary Edition (London, 1907), pp. 81–82.

insist upon an intimate connection between the two. The unseemly display of intense passion among the native poets, popular journals of the day intimated, was bound to besmirch even the most innocuous subject matter. The romances of Scott and Byron, for instance, illustrated the degenerate condition of contemporary imaginative literature and its unhealthy effect upon the impressionable youth of the day.

Literature has, of late years, been prostituted to all the purposes of the bagnio. Poetry, in particular, arrayed in her most bewitching colours, has been taught to exercise the arts of the *Leno*, and to charm only that she may destroy. The Muse, who once dipped her hardy wing in the chastest dews of Castalia and spoke nothing but what had a tendency to confirm and invigorate the manly ardour of a virtuous mind, now breathes only the voluptuous languishings of the harlot, and, like the brood of Circe, touches her charmed chord with a grace, that, while it ravishes the ear, deludes and beguiles the sense.[12]

But the sensuous absorption which social reformers from their various perspectives found debilitating was frequently the foundation of Romantic conceptions of poetry and love. The second generation of Romantic poets, the immediate models for the youthful Tennyson, were either in their lives or in their work — and certainly in popular reputation — tinged by an eroticism whose appeal was to plague Tennyson throughout life. Shelley and Keats loom especially large in the background of Tennyson's art, although it was not until 1829 and his association with the Apostles at Trinity College that he came to know their work intimately and to identify himself with their techniques.[13] We might glance briefly at Arthur Hallam's famous review of Tennyson's first independent volume, *Poems, Chiefly Lyrical* (1830), for a precise description of what it was in Shelley and Keats that Tennyson was consciously trying to emulate:

They are both poets of sensation rather than reflection. Susceptible of the slightest impulse from external nature, their fine organs

[12] *Remains of Henry Kirke White*, 10th ed. (London, 1823), I, 218–219; as quoted in Richard Altick, *The English Common Reader: A Social History of the Mass Reading Public 1800–1900* (Chicago, 1957), p. 112.
[13] Charles Tennyson, *Tennyson*, p. 34.

trembled into emotions at colors, and sounds, and movements, unperceived or unregarded by duller temperaments. Rich and clear were their perceptions of visible forms; full and deep their feelings of music. So vivid was the delight attending the simple exertions of eye and ear, that it became mingled more and more with their trains of active thought, and tended to absorb their whole being into the energy of sense. Other poets *seek* for images to illustrate their conceptions; these men had no need to seek; they lived in a world of images. . . .[14]

While Tennyson followed Shelley and Keats in recognizing the aesthetic primacy of the senses, he was no less their disciple in his insistence upon spiritual love as a proper metaphor of the soul's quest for the ideal. The crystallization of woman into a goddess of spiritual love which is so much a part of both the Neoplatonic and the courtly love tradition found its characteristic Romantic expression in the Cynthias and Asias of Keats and Shelley. Tennyson's early reading in Eastern mythological works and his interest in Dante (see Chapter IV) undoubtedly contributed to his adaptation of this tradition. Tennyson's idealization did not derive solely from his Romantic predecessors, and Shelley's adaptation of Platonism that makes woman a symbol of intellectual beauty is foreign to the less theoretical Tennyson. Still, Shelley's dependence on woman for guidance, for influence — that "universal thirst for a communion not merely of the senses, but of our whole nature, intellectual, imaginative, and sensitive"[15] — must have been a component in Tennyson's own idealization of woman. The works of Shelley that he read and admired at Cambridge explored both the glories and the dangers of romantic love with special intensity. The infinite passion of "Epipsychidion" (a work that with "Alastor," "Adonais," and *Prometheus Unbound* Tennyson especially prized)[16] shunned all restraint.

[14] "On Some Characteristics of Modern Poetry, and on the Lyrical Poems of Alfred Tennyson," Moxon's *Englishman's Magazine*, August 1831, pp. 616–628; reprinted in *The Writings of Arthur Hallam*, ed. T. H. Vail Motter (New York and London, 1943), pp. 182–198. The quotation appears on pp. 187–188 of the latter volume.

[15] *Shelley's Collected Prose Work, Works*, ed. Roger Ingpen and W. E. Peck (London, 1926–1930), VII, 228.

[16] *Memoir*, II, 285.

But Shelley — and certainly Tennyson after him — recognized the pitfalls of such universal thirsts "in which ideas . . . assume the force of sensations through the confusion of thought with the object of thought" and in which "excess of passion animates the creations of the imagination." [17] It was possible, Shelley knew and Tennyson's Lancelot was to discover, to delude oneself about the individual women that the psyche insisted upon deifying as prototypes of human excellence. Shelley himself was notoriously tempted into such "pleasing delusions" by the likes of Harriet Westbrook, Elizabeth Hitchener, Cornelia Turner, Mrs. Boinville, and Mary Godwin. Certainly the "crystallizations," to use Stendhal's term for the same process, that Shelley undertook in his life and dramatized in his poetry led to some rather audacious, morally suspect behavior. While the Emilia of "Epipsychidion" was one more emblem of what Shelley meant by intellectual beauty ("that part of the inmost soul which participates in the world soul"), the poem was read by some contemporaries as a veiled justification of adulterous elopement.

The threat of Shelley's Neoplatonism and of the Romantic doctrine of infinite aspiration to established morality was thus an old one. The mystical visions, the obsessive drives of the poet in "Alastor" were heroic and invited the young reader's enthusiastic participation. A youthful Tennyson must have found it difficult not to identify himself with the Shelleyan wanderer's search for

> the mighty portal,
> Like a volcano's meteor-breathing chasm,
> Whence the oracular vapour is hurled up
> Which lonely men drink wandering in their youth,
> And call truth, virtue, love, genius, or joy,
> That maddening wine of life, whose dregs they drain
> To deep intoxication; and uplift,
> Like Maenads who cry loud, Evoe! Evoe!
> The voice which is contagion to the world.
>
> (*Prometheus Unbound* II.iii.2–10)

The abstractions — "truth, virtue, love, genius, or joy" — are inseparable from a "deep intoxication." If, as "The Poet" of Tennyson's

---

[17] *Letters, Works*, VIII, 98.

1830 volume would suggest, Tennyson was attracted to a Shelleyan aesthetic wherein the poet's task is to bring such abstract truths into the world, the riot of the maenads that the Victorian moralist within Tennyson heard in Shelley's life and works could only lead to the reservations that he clearly held about Shelley's greatness.

If Shelley's contemporaries were dismayed by his extraordinary domestic entanglements and by his search for the epipsyche which seemed an invitation to untrammeled promiscuity, their objections to John Keats were addressed more exclusively to the sensuous effect of his poetry than to the excesses of his personal life. Keats' idealism, the climbing of what in a letter to John Taylor (Jan. 30, 1818) he labels the "Pleasure Thermometer," approximates the eros of Shelley's wanderer. The lover's soul, beginning in the world of sense, moves through a series of mounting intensities toward divine essence, toward what Keats called Abstractions. But the eros of Keats never leaves the world of sense experience behind. The metaphysical "fellowship with essence" that engages the passion of his speakers is incompletely realized, while the particular objects of sense that they contemplate are suffused with erotic life.

The revulsion against Keats' "fine excess" occasionally carried over into Victorian reservations about his life, especially after the publication of the Fanny Brawne letters in 1878. Matthew Arnold read them as "the love letters of a surgeon's apprentice, full of relaxed self-abandonment. . . . The sensuous man speaks out in [them], and the sensuous man of a badly bred and badly trained sort." [18] By and large the Victorians carved out for themselves a simplified and distorted image of Keats; they saw him preeminently as one who preferred "a life of Sensations rather than of Thoughts." The irony of his reputation is that this most fastidious, morally balanced man was hypersensitive to the perils of sensuous abandon, especially when it threatened human love. Keats' attack on Robert Burton's account of love — "the old plague spot; the pestilence, the raw scrofula" wherein it is difficult to separate the "goatish, whinnyish, lustful love" from "the abstract adoration of the de-

[18] Essays in Criticism, 2nd series, 1888 (London, 1891), p. 74.

ity" [19] — illuminates an almost puritanical vigilance. The aesthetic struggle that Keats underwent was thus not very different from the one Tennyson came to identify during the 1830's as *the* dilemma of the poet: both writers were torn between a penchant for sensuous self-exploration and a commitment to a socially responsible morality. The stentorian prophet that Tennyson became in his later years would frequently mask the languorous melancholic sorely tempted by a Keatsian "magic," by the possibilities of a soft withdrawal into easeful death. Even in his last years Tennyson revered his Romantic predecessors and understood the fundamental similarity of his struggle and theirs. Keats, he felt, "would have been among the very greatest of us had he lived. There is something of the innermost soul of poetry in almost everything he ever wrote." [20] Characteristically, as generously as he admired the Romantics, Tennyson, like Arnold, came to distinguish them from poets who were wise in addition to being creators of sensation: "One must distinguish Keats, Shelley, and Byron from the great sage poets of all, who are both great thinkers and great artists, like Aeschylus, Shakespeare, Dante, and Goethe." [21]

But this is an older Tennyson speaking. For the young poet of Cambridge the attraction of the Romantic vision was irresistible. It is this subversive vision that coalesced with the moralism of Tennyson's pietistic upbringing to send forth his notion of love. To the degree that Tennyson counseled spiritual aspiration at the expense of "the reeling Faun, the sensual feast" (*In Memoriam*, CXVIII) and portrays the struggle of "Sense at war with Soul" ("To the Queen," l. 37), what he means by love grows out of a recurring English puritanism. It is the nineteenth-century version of an orthodox dualism that has habitually subordinated a rigorously delimited "body" to "spirit," "sense" to "essence," "eros" to "agape," and the infinite aspiration of passionate adultery to the self-control of contractual marriage.

But this nineteenth-century dualism was continually being chal-

[19] *The Complete Works of John Keats*, ed. M. B. Forman (Glasgow, 1900–1901), III, 286.
[20] *Memoir*, II, 286.
[21] *Ibid.*, p. 287.

lenged by an antithetical force — a Romantic art, frequently Neo-platonic in its theories of love, that tended to blur distinctions because of its insistence upon a vibrantly sensuous response to the beauties of the world. Insofar as Tennyson's conception of love is shaped by his early commitment to a disinterested exploration of the senses and to the erotic idealism of his Romantic forebears, it belongs to a tradition in which sense and soul are not readily separable. The resulting poetic anomaly we can now begin to examine in detail.

CHAPTER III

Lord of the Five Senses

"IT IS the distance," Tennyson maintained to his friend James Knowles late in life, "that charms me in the landscape, the picture and the past, and not the immediate today in which I move."[1] The remark provides the authority of Tennyson's own voice for a truism of Tennyson criticism, the certainty that the addiction to the distant in time, the remote in landscape, and the exotic in subject matter is the central impulse of his poetry. It is this inclination that he tended either to war against in order to escape the censure of his critics and his own conscience or to indulge.

What Tennyson came to call his "passion of the past" determined his conception of love and art. He saw time past as an attractive realm of erotic allurement, of quiescent falling away from an unappealing present; and he was temperamentally inclined to clothe a love and art associated with this past in a sensuousness that he considered both creative and harmless. But Tennyson gradually developed some reservations about his preference for the "far, far away," for he came to recognize how easy it was for man to become trapped within a cloying, hypnotic trance as he wandered through the past. The allegorical speculations about the relation of time, sense, and conscience in Tennyson's juvenilia and in his con-

[1] James Knowles, "Aspects of Tennyson, II: A Personal Reminiscence," *The Nineteenth Century*, XXXIII (1893), 170.

tributions to *Poems by Two Brothers* (1827) reveal that for both lover and artist the past can become a magic avenue of escape from an unbearable present or a perilous thicket through which one moves at considerable moral risk.

"Sense and Conscience," [2] an unfinished allegory, outlines the sense-soul conflict that in less abstract forms will occupy Tennyson throughout life and that will receive its epic treatment in the *Idylls of the King*. At the opening of the fragment the speaker's Soul shows itself unwilling to make proper use of Time's treasure and to take possession of a Spirit which has been "ridden over by the exulting *Sense*" (ll. 15–18). Rather, the speaker has used all of Time's "most precious ore" to give himself over to Sense which thereupon "grew large and prosper'd at the court of Time." In order to bar the speaker's return to Spirit, Sense gives Conscience, "the boldest of the warriors of Time," a potion which puts Conscience to sleep (to sleep only — Conscience can never be entirely obliterated). The shades within which Conscience dallies prepare for the Lotos-land in which the mariners of Ulysses will welcome their languorous intoxication in "The Lotos-Eaters"; the "delicious dreams" of Conscience are filled with "a gloom monotonously musical/ With hum of murmurous bees," "the constant moan/ Of waterfalls i' th' distance," and "voices of doves,/ Which ever bowing cooed and cooing bowed/ Unto each other as they could not cease" (ll. 45–51). Finally Memory and Pain rouse the speaker to seize a "wondrous blade" with which he lays a bloody waste to the "deep shades" of Sense:

> The ivy from the stem
> Was torn, the vine made desolate; his feet
> Were crimson'd with its blood, from which flows joy
> And bitterness, first joy from bitterness,
> And then again great bitterness from joy.
>
> (ll. 94–98)

While the speaker, through the agency of Memory, launches this strenuous attack upon Sense in defense of Spirit, the language of

[2] *Unpublished Early Poems*, ed. Charles Tennyson (London, 1931), pp. 42–46.

the assault insinuates its futility. The impression the allegory intends to convey is that Sense ought to be and eventually will be
overwhelmed by Conscience. Yet the imagery renders doubtful
the certainty of Conscience's final triumph; the very act of smoth-
ering Sense initiates an erotic immolation which in its Keatsian
ambivalence comprehends both "joy" and "bitterness." As in
Keats' "Ode on Melancholy" the two emotions melt into one
another. The repression of desire — the combined "joy" and "pain"
of this attempted control is the inspiration of Tennyson's early
poetry — will make Conscience suffer all the more. Tennyson's
best work will always suggest the pained interpenetration or the
unresolved duel of Conscience and Sense and of the lyric, dramatic,
and mythic transformations these abstractions will undergo. (The
union of Arthur and Guinevere will be both a "marriage" and a
"war.") This uncertainty will be evident even when Tennyson's
moral intention would seem to posit the complete and unequivocal
victory of Conscience.

Memory, "Sense and Conscience" would suggest, is an ally of
Spirit, an enemy of Sense; it can recall to the soul rapt in dalliance
the necessary tasks of contemporary existence. Thus in the early
"Memory"[3] the poet apostrophizes a "Blesséd, curséd, Memory"
which has become "a conscience dropping tears of fire/ On the
heart, which vain desire/ Vexeth all too bitterly" (ll. 1–6). But
just as frequently in Tennyson's work, memory and the dream
state which facilitates its operation are conducive to the workings
of the creative imagination. In the Prologue to "The Day Dream"
(published in 1842) the dream state is directly equated with the
poetic act; it is a languorous "brooding warm" that releases the "re-
flex of a legend past" and allows it "loosely" to settle into aesthetic
form (ll. 1–12). Memory, we see, can move the soul in contradictory directions: as an agent of Conscience, it reminds the soul
dallying in the thickets of the past of its present responsibilities; as
an agent of Sense it stimulates the creative brooding of dream.

This contradiction is less apparent in Tennyson's juvenilia because he rather frequently hides behind a Byronic "mask of great

[3] *Ibid.*, p. 33, ll. 5–10.

age," a melancholic pose that he adopted as a young man in an attempt to embrace as well as to fend off experience.[4] The speakers of "Darkness and Sorrow," "The Old Sword," and "And Ask Ye Why These Sad Tears Stream?" are aged, broken figures who look back remorsefully on a blighted youth. "Memory"[5] presents a speaker who is typically theatrical in his avoidance — through distancing — of the sense–conscience opposition outlined above:

> Memory! dear enchanter!
>   Why bring back to view
> Dreams of youth, which banter
>   All that e'er was true?
>
> Why present before me
>   Thoughts of years gone by,
> Which like shadows o'er me,
>   Dim in distance fly?
>
> Days of youth, now shaded
>   By twilight of long years,
> Flowers of youth, now faded,
>   Though bathed in sorrow's tears. . . .
>   (ll. 1–12)

For the young Tennyson the "magic cirque" of memory is a device that projects his present failures and future desires into a past recapturable by memory. The anxious striving of youth is transformed into a pose of disillusioned age. This mask of age gives the poet imaginative space in which to maneuver, making it possible for him to mute the conflict of sense and conscience and to disguise the vaguely autobiographical sorrow out of which that conflict no doubt arose.

The movement into the past will always hold moral dangers for Tennyson; dream and memory allow him psychic release from present pain and provide the aesthetic foundation of his highly sensuous art. But the withdrawal into the dream of the middle dis-

---

[4] W. D. Paden describes this strategy in *Tennyson in Egypt: A Study of the Imagery in His Earlier Work* (Lawrence, Kansas, 1942), pp. 53–56.

[5] From *Poems by Two Brothers* in the Cambridge *Works*, p. 755; to be distinguished from the "Memory" of *Unpublished Early Poems*, though the former is clearly derived from the latter and both prepare for the 1830 "Ode to Memory."

tance, the mountain height of "The Palace of Art," the sea journey of "Ulysses," and the past of Eastern fairy tales is in part a guilty retreat, one constantly cut off by what Tennyson calls "Conscience" or "Soul." When Tennyson allows his lyrical voice free play in the early works, he composes his finest poetry, but only because he comes increasingly to believe in the subversive nature of such dominance. The strictures of conscience insist that the indulgence in sensuous lyricism be tempered by melancholia and guilt.

Tennyson's view of love and his resultant conception of women in *Poems by Two Brothers* are extensions of the struggle between sense and conscience. He can praise love as an idea or even describe a sensuous passion, especially if he is experimenting with the styles of his Romantic predecessors. In "Love" the personified abstraction is "almighty," the one force whose "nameless power" holds sway over all beings from the "glittering fly" to the "crafty elephant." Such a rapturous apostrophe of a love in which all the speaker's senses are wrapped becomes the lyrical evocation of a specific if vaguely identified woman in two poems. In "Thou Camest to Thy Bower, My Love, Across the Musky Grove" a Keatsian maiden wins her lover with her "blooming charms within the coolness of the shade." A Wordsworthian equivalent of her "youthful passion" is the simple grace of "The Maid of Savoy" whose eyes are filled with "the look of love" as she gambols with noiseless tread down the hills of her native province.

But such blissful celebrations of sensuous women are rare in the youthful Tennyson, who makes full use of his mask of age to surround a dangerous eroticism with an aura of death and loss and to render most of his women inaccessible. Not only does this device work to disguise the poet's inexperience in love, it also serves as a brake to the erotic abandon whose dangers Tennyson had examined in the earlier allegorical works and in the *The Devil and the Lady* (see Chapter VII). The particular ways in which the women are inaccessible foreshadow the major separations between lover and beloved in Tennyson's later work. Typically, some disaster has blasted the love which exists in the bitter past of the narrator's memory: (1) The beloved has died — the woman in "And Ask Ye Why These Sad Tears Stream?" appears to the speaker from beyond the grave, sweeping her lyre with angel-hand and leading the speaker to tears as he learns that he cannot follow her. (2) The woman has betrayed her lover and turned toward another — the disloyal maiden of "Did Not Thy Roseate Lips Outvie" deceives "still with practis'd look/ With fickle vow, and well feign'd sigh." (3) The woman is lost to the speaker, although the exact cause of the parting, whether death, a shattered vow, or parental disapproval is unclear — Ellen of "We Meet No More" has deserted her lover for some obscure reason. (4) An appropriate mythical or legendary mold encases a private grief brought on by the loss of a beloved — Cleopatra of "Antony to Cleopatra" eludes a dying Antony, while Berenice takes a fatal potion which frees her from the degrading prospect of Roman slavery but also separates her from her beloved Mithridates ("Mithridates Presenting Berenice with the Cup of Poison").

Thus while two of Tennyson's contributions to *Poems by Two Brothers* glorify a happy love, most dramatize its frustration. The blending of love and death, the *Liebestod* of romantic passion, is a key element in the convention within which the young Tennyson is working. While Tennyson's view of love had not yet matured by the time of *Poems by Two Brothers*, some of the traditional difficulties of Romantic love have already intruded into his poetry in aggravated forms. It is already possible to sense a hardening division between the exaltation of soul and the flight from sense. To be sure, Tennyson does not yet pay obsessive attention to the traditional pitfalls of sense. One can read his hesitations into these early poems largely in the light of his subsequent development.

The *Poems, Chiefly Lyrical* of 1830, Tennyson's first independent volume, abandons the mask-of-age strategy for the most part and gives extended scope to the penchant for the "far, far away" in time and space. Fully indulging his Keatsian and Eastern strain, Tennyson constructs an aesthetic that continually turns away from the outer world and the present. But as the Eastern luxuriance achieves full play, the poems develop hints of suspicion concerning the senses as a foundation for love and art.

"Recollections of the Arabian Nights" establishes a motif which is to become more threatening to the protagonists of subsequent poems, the movement into an ominous grove of sense. Characteristically, the speaker falls into a dream which draws him back into the erotic past of Tennyson's childhood reading in Arabian history and myth, into the "golden prime/ Of good Haroun Alraschid." After a phantasmagoric sea journey down the Tigris through tangled, fragrant vegetation, the speaker arrives at the garden of Haroun Alraschid, "a realm of pleasance" filled with exotic flowers and shrubbery. Within the thicket he comes upon a Persian girl,

> Serene with argent-lidded eyes
> Amorous, and lashes like to rays
> Of darkness, and a brow of pearl
> Tressed with redolent ebony,
> In many a dark delicious curl,
> Flowing beneath her rose-hued zone.
>
> (ll. 135–140)

The speaker must steal up into the Pavilion of the Caliphat to gain his climactic sight of the girl. Just how perilous the trip down the Tigris or the piercing of the harem has been is difficult to establish. Enthralled by the lush scenes, the speaker seems largely to have ignored the possible dangers and the reader is only vaguely exposed to their existence by the context, the literary convention of a harem which it is death to enter. The Persian girl, partially because she is the property of Haroun Alraschid, offers no threat to the dreamer, and the poem, once the girl has been described, trails off into a final stanza of praise for Haroun Alraschid and his Pavilion. The woman locked within such "garden-bowers and grots" is a recurrent figure in Tennyson's poetry; the male journey inward can in later poems become quite self-destructive in a way made exotic by lushness of image.

An interesting inversion of the dramatic situation in "Recollections of the Arabian Nights" appears in "Anacaona," a poem Tennyson composed at Cambridge sometime between 1828 and 1831.[6] Developing the perspective of the pursued maiden rather than of the pursuing wanderer, the poem once more displays Tennyson's persistent indulgence of a hidden and frail eroticism. Anacaona and her maidens exult in an Edenic harmony with a beneficent nature:

> A dark Indian maiden,
> Warbling in the bloom'd liana
> Stepping lightly flower-laden,
> By the crimson-eyed anana,
> Wantoning in orange groves
> Naked, and dark-limb'd, and gay,
> Bathing in the slumbrous coves,
> In the cocoa-shadow'd coves,
> Of sunbright Xaraguay,
> Who was so happy as Anacaona,
> The beauty of Espagnola,
> The golden flower of Hayti?   (st. i)

"Naked, without fear," she welcomes white "fair-faced and tall" men to her island. What happens to Anacaona and the men next is rather mysterious:

> Following her wild carol
> She led them down the pleasant places,
> For they were kingly in apparel,
> Loftily stepping with fair faces.
> But never more upon the shore
> Dancing at the break of day,
> In the deep wood no more, —
> By the deep sea no more, —
> No more in Xaraguay
> Wander'd happy Anacaona,
> The beauty of Espagnola,
> The golden flower of Hayti!   (st. vi)

The reader does not know how to react to Anacaona. Is she in this last stanza the prototype of Oenone or Vivien? Given the probable

---

[6] "Anacaona," which appears in *Memoir*, I, 56, is prefaced by Hallam Tennyson's explanation: "My father liked this poem but did not publish it, because the natural history and the rhymes did not satisfy him. He evidently chose words which sounded well, and gave a tropical air to the whole, and he did not then care, as in his later poems, for absolute accuracy."

Keatsian allusions (especially the carol reminiscent in its "wildness" of "La Belle Dame sans Merci"), one might possibly see Anacaona as an early instance of the Tennysonian siren who lures men to their doom before disappearing. More likely, the obscure, unstated betrayal is perpetrated by the emissaries from the outside world who in their colonial exploitation of the island manage to blast the peace of Hayti and its "golden flower." Tennyson, that is, converts the Romantic convention of the noble savage corrupted by civilization to his own thematic purposes. While the reverse may be true in later poems, when the sensuous woman becomes a distinct threat, in the "Eastern flowers" of the 1830 volume it is rarely the Persian maidens or the Anacaonas who destroy. Rather, it is the intruders from the active world who threaten the serenity of an exotic Western garden.

Though one is tempted to attribute to this poem an intentional duplicity which would allow to "Anacaona" the equivocal response that "La Belle Dame" and "Lamia" elicit as sorrowing succubi, such a reading is probably not justified. That Anacaona is little more than a stock noble savage is suggested by the context of another poem from the Cambridge period. "The Hesperides" of the 1833 volume,[7] another of Tennyson's suppressed early works and an early instance of his use of classical subject, also concerns a secluded Eden and an aggressive intruder. In both poems despoilers from the East come to upset a Western sanctuary. While the terror of the Hesperidean Sisters at the impending approach of Heracles, the "one from the East" who will try to steal the golden apples, conveys none of the charm of Anacaona's "Warbling in the bloom'd liana," the apparent openness of the Sisters to the vigorous rapine of Heracles is reminiscent of Anacaona's vulnerability. But, again, Tennyson is ambiguous about whether to portray the Sisters as victims or as potential victimizers. While they may be helpless to withstand the coming theft by Heracles, the poem hints that they in their turn threaten the equanimity and life of mankind. Their song of woe and loss may be seductive to passing ships. In a

[7] The work was originally published in the *Poems* of 1833 and thereafter suppressed until its publication in the *Memoir*, I, 61–65.

blank verse Prologue to the poem the Carthaginian commander Hanno passing between the southern and the western Horn hears the Sisters' song "like the voices in a dream,/ Continuous, till he reached the outer sea" (ll. 12–13). These are not quite "The Sea Fairies" of the 1830 volume, the sirens who lure weary sailors into an enchantment with their sweet faces and shrill music. But one can hear in the melody of the Sisters an echo of the earlier siren song. Tennyson's commitment to them is hesitant; one can already feel in his uneasy praise of their private sensuous garden an indistinct preparation for his equally ambiguous rejection of Lotosland and the Palace of Art.

To represent this vacillation, Tennyson in the course of his early poetry fashions both a horizontal and a vertical spatial symbolism. "Anacaona" and "The Hesperides" give narrative expression to a recurrent East-West movement and countermovement. On balance Tennyson commits himself in his early poetry to a Western past of sensuous art as against an Eastern present of energy and social responsibility. And the overripe sea vegetation of "The Hesperides" with its suggestion of erotic death indicates his preference for a Western quiescence.[8]

The symbolic pattern of verticality, the exact height or depth at which activity takes place, is, however, not as evident in "The Hesperides" as it is in "The Mermaid," "The Merman," and "The Kraken" of the 1830 volume.

In "The Merman" and "The Mermaid" the quasi-human lovers of the ocean sport in voluptuous freedom near the water's surface. True, they are both "singing alone," but the imagery tracing their gambols conveys a light, diaphanous joy. The merman describes mermaids who

> would pelt me with starry spangles and shells,
> Laughing and clapping their hands between,
> All night, merrily, merrily,

[8] G. Robert Stange, "Tennyson's Garden of Art: A Study of *The Hesperides*," *PMLA*, LXVII (1952), 735–738, summarizes the manner in which both the West and the submarine world, places of twilight, secrecy, and guilt, are set up in a lifelong antithesis to the East, the land of activity, of everyday life, and — in the 1842 "Move Eastward, Happy Earth" — of married love.

> But I would throw to them back in mine
> Turkis and agate and almondine.   (ll. 28–32)

Because the merman and mermaid are at the same time "lovers" and "singers," Tennyson combines in them two of his major poetic concerns — the creative role of sense in love and in art. The merman "would sit and sing the whole of the day" and "fill the sea-halls with a voice of power." Only at night, and Tennyson's night is a time both of death and of creative sensuality, would he "roam abroad and play/ With mermaids in and out of the rocks." The innocent merriment of the merman's love is the source of his joyous art.

But the portrayal of the mermaid — like the Persian Maiden, Anacaona, and the Hesperidean Sisters — intimates a growing circumspection on Tennyson's part. While the mermaid spends her time in the same careless abandon as her companion, the merman, she releases a monstrous force which, though it does not disturb her, surely has sinister associations for the reader. Combing her hair "till my ringlets would fall/ Low adown, low adown," she would look like "a fountain of gold" whose beauty should rouse the beasts of the deep:

> . . . that great sea-snake under the sea
> From his coiled sleeps in the central deeps
> Would slowly trail himself sevenfold
> Round the hall where I sate, and look in at the gate
> With his large calm eyes for the love of me.
>
>   (ll. 23–27)

In later poems (notably "Merlin and Vivien") as well as in the juvenilia the embrace of various undulating creatures crushes their victims, even as the sweet delirium such lamias offer has its charm. The mournful asp of "Memory" clings to a palm tree, souring its "bright fruit"; and in the earlier fragment with the same title the serpentine trope is elaborated by a speaker who, intoxicated by his nocturnal memories, compares himself to

> a hungry serpent coiled
> Round a palm tree in the wild,
> When his bakéd jaws are bare

> Burning in the burning air,
> And his corky tongue is black
> With the raging famine-crack,
> If perchance afar he sees
> Winding up among the trees,
> Lordly-headed buffaloes,
> Or but hears their distant lows,
> With the fierce remembrance drunk
> He crushes all the stalwart trunk
> Round which his fainting folds are prest,
> With delirium-causing throes
> Of anticipated zest.[9]

Such passages once more suggest how dangerous the creative act of "fierce remembrance" can be for the Tennysonian dreamer; the nocturnal visions, productive as they are of "anticipated zest," also release images of drought in a barren waste and of envenomed delirium. And these ambiguous reptiles in the juvenilia are preparations for the great sea-snake of "The Mermaid." The sevenfold coiling about the mermaid's hall recalls the sinuous lubricity of "Memory's" asp and the intoxicated crushing of a tree trunk by the "hungry serpent" of the earlier fragment. That the sea-snake of "The Mermaid" has "large calm eyes for the love of me" disguises through coyness the possibility of a monstrous passion. One cannot help suspecting that the deeps from which he rises are more than physical, that they are the uncharted recesses of the mind itself.

The depth out of which the sea-snake has erupted becomes in "The Kraken" an area "Far, far beneath in the abysmal sea," the submarine equivalent of the "far, far away" that Tennyson preferred in time and setting. But while the ocean floor, like the Tennysonian past, is ripe and softly quiescent, its attractiveness is the offer of oblivion; it gives off a "sickly light":

> Below the thunders of the upper deep,
> Far, far beneath in the abysmal sea,
> His ancient, dreamless, uninvaded sleep
> The Kraken sleepeth: faintest sunlights flee

[9] Again, "Memory" appears in the Cambridge *Works*, p. 755, and the fragment "Memory" in *Unpublished Early Poems*, pp. 33–34.

About his shadowy sides; above him swell
Huge sponges of millennial growth and height;
And far away into the sickly light,
From many a wondrous grot and secret cell
Unnumber'd and enormous polypi
Winnow with giant arms the slumbering green.

(ll. 1–10)

Spawned in a primeval past, the Kraken will rise to the surface only when "the latter fires shall heat the deep," on the Day of Judgment when it will for a single apocalyptic moment be seen by man. In this gradual descent from the upper deep, the playground of the frolicking mermaid and merman to the "abysmal sea" of the Kraken, Tennyson establishes a spatial trope, an inverted Platonic ladder: innocent and creative sensuousness can decline rapidly into an ugly, prolix menace. The multitudinousness, the uncontrolled spawning of the Kraken's "unnumber'd and enormous polypi" was for Tennyson always a special horror. As he told his son, "The lavish profusion . . . in the natural world appals me, from the growths of the tropical forest to the capacity of man to multiply, the torrent of babies. I can almost understand some of the Gnostic heresies. . . ." [10]

In his review of *Poems, Chiefly Lyrical* (see Chapter II) Arthur Hallam tried to justify Tennyson's imitation of his Romantic predecessors, Shelley and Keats. But a thorough examination suggests that Hallam — and Tennyson — were not as unequivocally committed to an "aesthetic" poetry as the later reputation and influence of the review might lead us to believe. If this truculent introduction of Tennyson to his early audience can be taken as a reflection of Tennyson's own thinking, it already implies the limits of a Keatsian eroticism in both art and love. Like "The Merman" and "The Mermaid" Hallam's review tends to undermine the very sensuousness it seems to be celebrating.

Hallam begins by distinguishing the two streams of Romantic poetry — the poetry of reflection represented by Wordsworth and the Lake poets; and the poetry of sensation exemplified by the

[10] *Memoir*, I, 314.

works of Keats and Shelley, whom the young Tennyson is trying to follow in the 1830 volume. While advocating the latter tradition, Hallam announces a theory of English literary history. In the infancy of any literature, specifically in England during the time of Shakespeare and Milton, poets have a "clearer and larger access to the minds of their compatriots than can ever open to those who are circumscribed by less fortunate circumstances." And surely the early Victorian period, an age which comes late in English cultural history, has long since left behind "that first raciness and juvenile vigor of literature" which was the effulgence of the Elizabethan era. Hallam then skims over the "French contagion and the heresies of the Popian school" to bring his capsule history down to the beginning of the nineteenth century:

With the close of the last century came an era of reaction, an era of painful struggle to bring our over-civilised condition of thought into union with the fresh productive spirit that brightened the morning of our literature. But repentance is unlike innocence; the laborious endeavor to restore has more complicated methods of action than the freedom of untainted nature. Those different powers of poetic disposition, the energies of Sensitive, of Reflective, of Passionate Emotion, which in former times were intermingled, and derived from mutual support an extensive empire over the feelings of men, were now restrained within separate spheres of agency. The whole system no longer worked harmoniously, and by intrinsic harmony acquired external freedom; but there arose a violent and unusual action in the several component functions, each for itself, all striving to reproduce the regular power which the whole had once enjoyed.

Hence the melancholy which so evidently characterizes the spirit of modern poetry; hence that return of the mind upon itself and the habit of seeking relief in idiosyncrasies rather than community interest.[11]

Hallam enunciates here a dissociation of sensibility which looks forward to T. S. Eliot's more famous description in "The Metaphysical Poets" of the Romantic poets' revolt "against the ratiocinative, the descriptive; they thought and felt by fits, unbalanced;

[11] *Writings of Arthur Hallam*, p. 190. In a footnote to the word "Sensitive," Hallam allows for the substitution of "sensuous," "a word in use amongst our elder divines, and revived by a few bold writers in our own time."

they reflected." [12] But while Eliot's unified sensibility encompasses "thought" and "feeling," Hallam suggests that what Eliot was to call "feeling" must be further subdivided into the "Sensitive" and "Passionate Emotion." Because Shelley and Keats live in a world of images, their emotions "are immediately conversant with sensation." There is for Hallam, then, a recognizable chasm between "the *usual* passions of the heart" (the emotions among which he includes love) and the "colors and sounds" of the sensational poets whose "fine organs trembled with emotions."

Hallam's essay implies a difficulty for any poet who would treat the subject of love. The Victorian dissociation of the faculties aggravates in the poet's mind the unhealthy divorce between sense and "the *usual* passions of the heart" as they reveal themselves in art or love. In his celebration of the "Sensitive" faculty Hallam restates the dilemma of Keats and Shelley: the ladder of the senses may lead to the "usual" emotion of love with all the mystical and idealistic associations that word had for the Romantics; it may also lead to a wallowing in sense or to the "sickly light" of the Kraken's ocean floor.

Tennyson in his years at Cambridge was surrounded by friends who continually addressed themselves to such a danger. Richard Trench's famous warning to Tennyson that "we cannot live in art" which led to the composition of "The Palace of Art" has usually been interpreted as evidence of the moralistic impact of the Apostles, while F. D. Maurice's endorsement of a poetry of moral urgency (which perhaps influenced "The Poet") [13] was also directed against a tendency toward excessive eroticism in Tennyson's work. Hallam himself, while he championed the aesthetic mode of his friend, was not unaware in his 1831 review of risks that a poetry of sense involved:

We do not deny that it is, on other accounts, dangerous for frail humanity to linger with fond attachment in the vicinity of sense. Minds of this description are especially liable to moral temptations;

[12] *Selected Essays of T. S. Eliot* (New York, 1932), p. 248.
[13] The account of Trench's conversation may be found in *Memoir*, I, 118–119. W. D. Paden argues in "Tennyson's 'The Poet,'" *The Explicator*, II (1944), Items 5 and 6, that Maurice's ideas are the foundation of "The Poet."

and upon them, more than any, it is incumbent to remember, that their mission as men, which they share with their fellow-beings, is of infinitely higher interest than their mission as artists, which they possess by rare and exclusive privilege. But it is obvious that, critically speaking, such temptations are of slight moment. Not the gross and evident passions of our nature, but the elevated and less separable desires, are the dangerous enemies which misguide the poetic spirit in its attempts at self-cultivation. That delicate sense of fitness which grows with the growth of artist feelings, and strengthens with their strength, until it acquires a celerity and weight of decision hardly inferior to the correspondent judgments of conscience, is weakened by every indulgence of heterogeneous aspirations, however pure they may be, however lofty, however suitable to human nature.[14]

For Tennyson surely the "gross and evident passions" offered few serious temptations. But for a poet who was inordinately aware of the division between sense and emotion, perhaps it is just when he approaches what he considers "the elevated and less separable desires" that the leap to be made seems a frightening one. The translation becomes a terrible gamble and a constant source of anxiety. More and more it would tend to result in two distinct subjects: the poet might indulge in the celebration of the "usual passion" of love and the celebration or, increasingly, the denigration of an eroticism that has little to do with the usual passion. In such a condition of disjunction the leap would not be necessary.

But the awareness of such a dilemma comes upon Tennyson gradually. As early as *The Devil and the Lady* and "Sense and Conscience" Tennyson seems to be conventionally aware of the dangers of sense. As Hallam's essay suggests, however, he tends to minimize such dangers in the creative process, insisting that the poet must test his responses in his sensations. "An artist ought to be lord of the five senses," Hallam quotes Tennyson as habitually saying. Characteristically Hallam adds, "But if he lacks the inward sense which reveals to him what is inward in the heart, he has left out the part of Hamlet in the play."[15]

Even if Tennyson throughout these early volumes begins to

---

[14] *Writings of Hallam*, pp. 186–187.
[15] *Memoir*, I, 500–501.

question the wisdom of sense in the abstract, he does not yet associate its destructive potential with women. In his first works Tennyson is unrealistic in his portrayals of women, whose primary function seems to be a definition of man. His experiments with female
portraits in the 1830 and 1833 volumes suggest that for the mask of
age in the juvenilia he has substituted the strategy of mechanical
abstraction. The occasional lushness of imagery used to describe
these women is rendered harmless by a recurring formula that is
unpoetically rigid and systematic. It is no wonder that the keep-
sake portraits of Lilian, Madeline, Adeline, Margaret, Rosalind,
Eleänore, and Kate have struck readers as pallid and artificial. In
each case Tennyson merely wishes to decorate, almost axiomati-
cally, some quality of mind — he does not respond to the concrete
presence of a real woman which leads him to the type. Perhaps
these figures contain a veiled threat to the speaker in the light of
what they can become in the later poetry; mostly they project the
charming peril of a mermaid to a lover as yet unacquainted with
the depths of human personality.

In these portraits certain distinct qualities of the lover and the
beloved that are particularly Tennysonian do emerge. While these
women are more accessible than many of the lost ladies in *Poems
by Two Brothers*, they are still beyond the imaginative reach of
the speaker for one reason or another. More than courtly tradition
creates the speaker's relative passivity: he is an asker of questions,
and it is the women who either are asked to approach the lover or
move to avoid his grasp. "Airy, Fairy Lilian" in her frolicsomeness
plays the mermaid to the narrator's merman; the will o' the wisp
Madeline, a phantom of mercurial moods and desires, is a Victorian version of the Renaissance lady toying with her lover; both the
melancholy Margaret and the "frolic falcon" Rosalind as they
elude the impassioned suits of their lovers foreshadow later Tennysonian "high-born maidens" (the Lady of Shalott, the soul in "The
Palace of Art," and Princess Ida of "Come down, O maid, from
yonder mountain height") who move in isolation far above ordinary humanity. Margaret, whom the speaker asks to "Come down,
come down, and hear me speak," loves "to hear the murmur of the

strife,/ But enter[s] not the toil of life." And Rosalind, a "gay young hawk" who keeps to the upper skies, also listens disdainfully to her lover's request that she "Come down, come home, my Rosalind." In such highly charged, unrealistic portraits of "moonshine maidens" (John Lockhart's denigrating phrase) Tennyson endows his women with a Keatsian luxuriance that is quite harmless; he does not yet turn them into the "fatal women" of later works. (The single exception, Eleänore, is discussed in Chapter VII.)

"Isabel" is the most successful of these portraits perhaps because, according to a note appended to the Eversley edition, it is the description of a real woman, Elizabeth Tennyson. The speaker's conventional wooing of fair ladies in the other early lyrical portraits here becomes a direct, "parasitical" dependence. The maternal and wifely Isabel is

> The mellow'd reflex of a winter moon;
> A clear stream flowing with a muddy one,
> Till in its onward current it absorbs
>   With swifter movement and in purer light
>   The vexed eddies of its wayward brother;
>   A leaning and upbearing parasite,
>   Clothing the stem, which else had fallen quite
> With cluster'd flower-bells and ambrosial orbs
>   Of rich fruit-bunches leaning on each other.

(ll. 29–37)

One of Tennyson's first maternal heroines, Isabel combines the virtues of chastity, female fortitude, and golden charity to reflect Tennyson's adoration of his mother. Her saintly image, which in large measure accounted for the piety of his life and the decorousness of his tastes, rules Tennyson's notion of what is best in woman from the early "Isabel" through *The Princess* of the middle years and into the late "Demeter and Persephone."

That Tennyson fused the roles of wife and mother as ministering angels is evident from both his life and poetry. If we look ahead momentarily to "The Miller's Daughter" of the 1833 *Poems* and "The Two Voices" of the 1842 volumes, we encounter instances of the recuperative balm the Tennysonian wife-mother can offer. In "The Miller's Daughter," Tennyson's first extended account of a happy love affair, a speaker addresses his aged wife with whom he has been contented and remembers how he wooed her. The speaker had been a squire's son, and his mother had objected to his marrying below his station. Once she had met her future daughter-in-law, however, the obvious love that the miller's daughter felt for the son pacified the mother with remarkable dispatch. In the novels of the period questions of class difference are hardly reconciled with such ease. But the emphasis of "The Miller's Daughter" is on the extent to which the protagonist is girded round by the representatives of two generations of women; the happiness of the young lover depends upon the harmony of his wife and mother.

"The Two Voices" mounts a variation of the same theme. Throughout the major portion of the poem the speaker has been overpowered by the first voice's intimation that any suggestion of special significance to man's existence is undercut by the certainty that in a universe of pure matter, "thy peculiar difference/ Is cancell'd in a world of sense" (ll. 41–42). As in "Sense and Conscience," "Memory," and "Ode to Memory" of the juvenilia, the speaker resorts to dream and memory as implements with which to shoot "a random arrow through the air" to recover a belief in man's spiritual dignity, in his "naked essence." The speaker finally realizes that memory alone cannot fend off the intellectual onslaughts of despair's voice. But while failing to relieve him, the speaker's reliance on dream and memory precipitates the crucial turn of the poem, preparing him for the redemptive, idyllic scene that strikes his eye. Opening the window after his dark night of suffering, he contemplates a framed family portrait in the street below:

> One walk'd between his wife and child,
> With measured footfall firm and mild,
> And now and then he gravely smiled.

> The prudent partner of his blood,
> Lean'd on him, faithful, gentle, good,
> Wearing the rose of womanhood.

> And in their double love secure,
> The little maiden walk'd demure,
> Pacing with downward eyelids pure.

> These three made unity so sweet,
> My frozen heart began to beat,
> Remembering its ancient heat.

(ll. 412–423)

The speaker sees in the husband of this scene his own double. Like the speaker the husband requires support, and the wife on one side and the child on the other shelter him. The protection is, to be sure, reciprocal: the wife is herself leaning on the husband, while the child is secured by the "double love" of her parents. And this "little picture," so characteristic of Tennyson's English idylls in the 1842 volumes and thereafter, releases a memory that has been bottled up within the speaker; this image of man upheld — as in "The Miller's Daughter" — by women from two different generations frees the speaker from his despondency. He goes out into the fields where "Nature's living motion" sends forth the second voice of the poem whose "Rejoice! Rejoice!" restores to him the confidence of which the first voice had tried to strip him.

It is perhaps difficult for readers brought up on the fashionable idea of woman as castrating female or Terrible Mother to approach the angelic woman of Tennyson's poetry with absolute sympathy, but Tennyson is nowhere as representative of his age as in this unreserved conviction of woman's high, redemptive destiny: "She must train herself to do the large work that lies before her, even though she may not be destined to be wife or mother, cultivating her understanding not her memory only, her imagination in its highest phases, her inborn spirituality and her sympathy with all that is pure, noble and beautiful, rather than mere social accomplishments; then and then only will she further the progress of humanity, then and then only men will continue to hold her in reverence."[16] In Tennyson's dealings with women he constantly alluded to this "large work." Jane Carlyle, noting the diffidence of his response to most women, attributes it to just such an elevated regard for their potential: "Alfred is dreadfully embarrassed with women alone — for he entertains at one and the same moment a feeling of almost adoration for them and an ineffable contempt!

[16] *Ibid.*, p. 250.

adoration I suppose for what they *might be* — contempt for what they *are*! The only chance of my getting any right good of him was to make him forget my womanness. . . ." [17]

From what he himself says, Emily Sellwood became for Tennyson the kind of support he felt woman ought to be. A letter written during their engagement indicates his future reliance upon a wife who had much in common with Elizabeth Tennyson, so much so that they were the complementary models for Ida in *The Princess*: "I need thy assurances to make up the deficiencies in my own strength: thence most likely comes my preaching. If thy love for me is a strengthening influence to thyself, so shall mine for thee be to myself — if thy love makes thee discomforted, I pine in discomfort, and if thou dost, oh wherefore should I live? How should this dependence on thy state coexist with my flying from thee? ask not. Believe that it does." [18] And it was partly Emily's reservations about the orthodoxy of Tennyson's religion that made her hesitate for years before agreeing in 1850 to the marriage. Only after reading *In Memoriam* were her suspicions and those of her father quieted. Tennyson was even swayed by her in professional matters. Hallam Tennyson testifies that his father sent his mother two versions of the song "Sweet and Low" to be inserted in the third edition of *The Princess* in 1850, asking her to choose the one he should use. [19]

Thus, Tennyson's idealization of woman is projected onto the maternal wife of his poetry, a figure who dominates several of the poems in the 1830 and 1833 volumes. Whether the woman is a wife guiding her husband as in "Isabel" or the mother comforting her child as in "Supposed Confessions of a Second-Rate Sensitive Mind," the dependent personality of the male does not change. The "infant crying in the night" (*In Memoriam*, LIV) radiated a nameless fear which Tennyson understood well. As Tennyson grew older, the distillation of this anxiety into the ideological doubt of

[17] Letter of Jan. 31, 1845, *Jane Welsh Carlyle: A New Selection of Her Letters*, ed. Trudy Bliss (New York, 1950), p. 158.
[18] From a letter of Dec. 1839, quoted in Charles Tennyson, *Tennyson*, p. 181.
[19] *Ibid.*, p. 239; and *Memoir*, I, 328–332.

"Supposed Confessions," "The Two Voices," and, at its most powerful, *In Memoriam* made a refuge necessary. His concept of a woman whether mother or wife offering a sheltering love against a hostile world was the natural consequence of a terror that his age apparently understood and shared in indistinct but palpable ways.

But while Tennyson does present such ministering angels who supply a physical sense of well-being and a metaphysical shelter, they are not typical of the mood of Tennyson's early poems. There are few contented human lovers in the 1830 and 1833 volumes. When Tennyson's women are not merely extravagant, exotic fantasies of desire such as Oriana, the Mermaid, the Persian Maiden, and Fatima, they are characteristically deserted, dead, or dying maidens. The most memorable of Tennyson's creations in *Poems, Chiefly Lyrical* and *Poems* — Mariana, Oenone, and the Lady of Shalott — are beset by the same terrors as are Tennyson's men. The sexual distinction set up in the previous paragraph does not really hold up among these figures. As a matter of fact, for reasons that deserve exploration, the plight of the deserted woman seems to strike the poet with a greater urgency than that of the despairing male in the early work.

Certainly the peculiarly Tennysonian talent, that ability to charge the landscape with the psyche of a speaker, controls the structure of "Mariana." As he is to do frequently in his later mythic poems, Tennyson lets the story alluded to, in this case Angelo's desertion of Mariana in Shakespeare's *Measure for Measure*, provide the narrative framework for his own lyric cry. Examining the full implications of the poem's epigraph ("Mariana in the moated grange"), Tennyson embellishes Shakespeare's one-line glance at Mariana's imprisonment so imaginatively that one of Shakespeare's insignificant figures, introduced toward the end of *Measure for Measure* to resolve a plot complication, takes on a heightened individuality of her own. Her plight, unexplored by Shakespeare, finds its elaborate trope in the monotony and desolation of the grange that Tennyson evokes, a place of weeds and blackened sluice water, rusted nails, broken sheds, of mice shrieking in the wall, of footsteps on the upper floors. The landscape — the shadow of an ominous poplar aslant her bed at night as the wind rustles the white curtains — becomes the measure of Mariana's growing hysteria and dark inner solitude; it is the landscape that forces from her the choric cry of despair, the wish for death, that ends each stanza of the poem.

"Oenone" too explores the anxiety of the deserted maiden, this time in the context of classical mythology. As in "Mariana" Tennyson projects the disturbance within the human psyche onto a crumbling landscape and once more uses a melancholy refrain to achieve a ballad effect:

> O mother, hear me yet before I die.
> They came, they cut away my tallest pines,
> My tall dark pines, that plumed the craggy ledge
> High over the blue gorge, and all between
> The snowy peak and snow-white cataract
> Foster'd the callow eaglet — from beneath
> Whose thick mysterious boughs in the dark morn
> The panther's roar came muffled, while I sat
> Low in the valley. (ll. 203–211)

Oenone complains to her mother, Ida, decrying the loss to Helen of her "playmate on the hills," Paris. Several of Tennyson's lovers — the couples in "Locksley Hall," "Lady Clara Vere de Vere," and "Maud" — are childhood sweethearts or cousins. While such long acquaintance of lovers is as old a convention of legend and fairy tale as the romantic love-at-first-sight device that Tennyson also employs, the former has additional, purely Tennysonian connotations. Lovers who have been casual friends since childhood may be exempt from the excesses of the "sensual feast." At the same time the severing of a felicitous bond, enveloped in a cloud of childhood innocence and approved by the process of slow ripening, is especially grievous. Perhaps for this reason when Paris is faced with his choice (shall he award the Pelian apple to Hera, Athene, or Aphrodite?), Oenone instinctively feels that Athene's offer of "self-reverence, self-knowledge, self-control" approximates the love she and Paris share.

But Oenone's cry to Paris to award the apple to Athene goes unheeded. The temperate offering of Athene has for Paris none of the surface attraction of Aphrodite's voluptuous temptation, and her glitter is immediately irresistible:

> Idalian Aphrodite beautiful,
> Fresh as the foam, new-bathed in Paphian wells,
> With rosy slender fingers backward drew
> From her warm brows and bosom her deep hair
> Ambrosial, golden round her lucid throat
> And shoulder; from the violets her light foot
> Shone rosy-white, and o'er her rounded form
> Between the shadows of the vine-bunches
> Floated the glowing sunlights, as she moved.
>
> (ll. 170–178)

With her "subtle smile" this Aphrodite — in place of the "maiden love" that Athene-Oenone proffers — extends to Paris the fatal gift of Helen, "the fairest and most loving wife in Greece." Here for the first time in his work Tennyson arranges an overt narrative confrontation between a passionate adultery and the self-control of marriage or "maiden love." Helen and her appeal to Paris embody the vital link between eros and adultery so crucial to the myths of romantic love since its beginnings in Provence. It is presumably the illicitness of the projected affair with Helen, who is the wife of Menelaus, that appeals to Paris. As Oenone's own words suggest (ll. 192–202), she is not at all cold or sensually inferior to Helen, but unlike Helen she is a known quantity, Paris' childhood companion. Against both the mystery and the tempting illegality of forbidden fruit, Oenone's garden variety of legitimate love has little chance.

The Lady of Shalott is as alone as both Mariana and Oenone, though in the poem bearing her name the lady has not specifically been deserted. Her isolation receives little narrative elaboration: just as *Measure for Measure* supplies only attenuated hints about the origin of Mariana's predicament, so the reason for the curse upon the Lady of Shalott by which she will die if she tries to enter the real world is unstated. Again one has little more than the landscape of exile: the lady is separated from the world both by water and by height; she is imprisoned on a "silent isle" within "four gray walls, and four gray towers" that "overlook a space of flowers."

Tennyson's own description of the poem stresses the lady's epistemological confusion: "The new-born love for something, for someone in the wide world from which she has been so long secluded, takes her out of the region of shadows into that of realities." [20]

But the lady may also illustrate Tennyson's early parabolic treatment of the artist cut off from meaningful contact with the world.[21] In destroying herself as she attempts to enter the world through the "mirror blue," she reflects what Tennyson at this time felt to be the dilemma of the artist. The creation of a sensuous art necessitates the artist's separation from normal activity, especially from the common experience of love:

> But in her web she still delights
> To weave the mirror's magic sights,
> For often thro' the silent nights
> A funeral, with plumes and lights
>   And music, went to Camelot;
> Or when the moon was overhead,
> Came two young lovers lately wed.
>
> (ll. 64–70)

The sight of the lovers, framed as in "The Two Voices" and the "Enoch Arden" to come, suddenly makes her "half sick of shadows" and prepares her for the coming of Lancelot. As he moves across her crystal mirror, she hurries to her window to look out upon the rock of reality rather than at its image only. This insistence

---

[20] Memoir, I, 117.

[21] Such a way into the poem was first briefly suggested by Joyce Green, "Tennyson's Development during the 'Ten Years' Silence (1832–1842)," PMLA, LXVI (1951), 666, but was, I believe, anticipated by the character of Sybil Vane in Oscar Wilde's Picture of Dorian Gray. Like the Lady of Shalott, Sybil Vane is quite successful as an artist (of sorts) until she falls in love with her "Prince Charming," Dorian Gray. It is when she tries to descend from her tower of art that she destroys herself; her magic web flies apart, her mirror cracks, and Dorian will have nothing more to do with her, a fact that precipitates her suicide. That Wilde was alluding to Tennyson's lady in his portrait of the music hall actress is clear from her cry to Dorian, "My love! my love! Prince Charming! Prince of life! I have grown sick of shadows. You are more to me than all art can ever be" (The Picture of Dorian Gray, [New York, 1927], p. 164). This seems to be an echo of the Lady of Shalott's "I am half sick of shadows."

on a direct encounter with human substance rather than a voyeur-istic contemplation of its shadow disintegrates the magic "web with colors gay" and cracks the mirror. Immediately the promised curse descends upon her and precipitates her death, as she floats down the river to Camelot.

Tennyson may thus be dramatizing an opposition that has been emerging throughout his early poetry — an antagonism between art and love that is irresolvable. We have seen that the mermaid and merman affirm the creative role of sense in both art and love — they are at the same time "singers" and "lovers." But the Lady of Shalott finds that the life devoted to the spinning of her magic web of sense is unbearably sterile and that the attempt to loosen the spell and to enter into Hallam's "usual passions of the heart" leads to death. The distance between Hallam's — and Tennyson's — "Sensitive [or Sensuous]" and "Passionate Emotion" looms greater than ever, but now there seems to be no way for the soul of the artist to reconcile the two energies. Tennyson's earlier certainty that the artist must be lord of the five senses and must cultivate his talent secretly within the sacred garden of his mind (see "The Poet's Mind" of 1830) has been undermined, if it has not com-pletely disappeared. The Lady of Shalott is even willing to sacri-fice her creative imagination, her mirror and her web, to enter into a human feeling for Lancelot. But she cannot find a meaningful life in either direction; she can neither be satisfied with her magic web nor enter into a circle of ordinary humanity because the "curse" of the artist is upon her. Caught between two worlds to neither of which she can commit herself, she prefigures one of the central themes of the artist in our time.

It would be possible to extend this catalogue of doomed maidens in the volumes of 1830 and 1833. One could examine in detail a dreamer's movement in sleep through the familiar symbolic forest in "A Dream of Fair Women." There he confronts several classical exemplars of "Beauty and anguish walking hand in hand/ The downward slope to death" (ll. 15–16). Or we could chart Tenny-son's transposition of the despairing Mariana of the 1830 volume into an Italian setting in the 1833 volume ("Mariana in the South").

But it does not seem necessary to belabor what is clear: the type is a projection of Tennyson's deepest anxieties in the early 1830's. While the figure reappears in the two-volume *Poems* of 1842, in every case she is a revision (to be sure, frequently a substantial one) of the woman as she first emerged in earlier poems. The deserted woman never completely vanishes from Tennyson's poetry, but after the 1833 volume she is not the obsessive figure she seems to have been in Tennyson's youthful work.

The reason for her fading may be connected to the "solution" Tennyson evolved in "The Palace of Art," a famous enough watershed in his aesthetics but a poem that is equally significant in his changing view of love and women. Repudiating the celebration of sense in his earliest work, Tennyson in "The Palace of Art" also relieves the dilemma of the artist-lover adumbrated in "The Lady of Shalott." He does so by denying that it *is* a dilemma.

The speaker has built for his soul (once more a "she" raised above common humanity) a lordly pleasure house. Convinced of the need for an egoistic withdrawal, the speaker proceeds to describe the splendors of the palace's four courts — a series of paintings, tapestries, and landscapes all of which reveal the plenitude of the poet's imagination. Once the palace is complete, the soul, "Lord over Nature, lord of the visible earth,/ Lord of the senses five," revels in her godlike isolation. Where the Lady of Shalott yearned to enter into a world of activity, even if with trepidation, the soul of "The Palace of Art" is haughtily disdainful of the "swine" she contemplates below.

But after three years of increasing hallucinations and boredom brought on by the absence of human voices, the soul breaks down and recognizes the need for some human contact to shatter the "One deep, deep silence all." She suddenly feels the claustrophobia of a Mariana, the suffocation that both Oenone and the Lady of Shalott knew. In contrast to the trapped Lady of Shalott, however, the soul in "The Palace of Art" can merely change her mind. She finds no difficulty in journeying down from the palace to a "cottage in the vale" where she may "mourn and pray." The predicament of "The Lady of Shalott" in which the poetic soul can neither be content in its splendid isolation nor live in the world of Camelot's well-fed wits seems to have been solved with remarkable ease. Not only, moreover, can the soul discard her royal robes and enter the world of men and sober purpose without dying; she also plans to return "with others" once she has purged herself of guilt.

It is this unconvincing resolution of Tennyson's problem that has opened the poem to a good deal of criticism. The ending does seem a contrived reversal, considering the wealth of loving detail which the soul has had lavished upon her palace. As so frequently happens in Tennyson, the sensuous drift of a poem's imagery modifies and even contradicts a morally energetic theme. But to the extent that the soul's decision indicates Tennyson's conscious intention to muffle his sensuous voice and to give his didactic, socially responsible one the best possible hearing, the soul's movement into the valley signals the descent of the deserted maiden into a Victorian domesticity. She can come down from her isolated mountaintop to reside by the hearth in the valley. Gone are the morbid anxiety of the deserted grange, the chilly isolation of a palatial retreat; and muted is the evocation of lush surroundings.

Lionel Stevenson in an important and generally persuasive essay has advanced an explanation of how the fate of such maidens reflects Tennyson's psychological development.[22] Briefly, Stevenson argues that the maiden cut off from the world in her palace tower is derived from Tennyson's reading of Shelley at Cambridge. The maiden had not appeared in such detailed physical isolation before this time in Tennyson's juvenile poems. In "To a Skylark" Shelley associates two related figures in successive stanzas:

> Like a Poet hidden
>   In the light of thought,
> Singing hymns unbidden,
>   Till the world is wrought
> To sympathy with hopes and fears it heeded not:
>
> Like a high-born maiden
>   In a palace-tower,

[22] "The 'High-Born Maiden' Symbol in Tennyson," *PMLA*, LXIII (1948), 234–243.

> Soothing her love-laden
> Soul in secret hour
> With music sweet as love, which overflows her bower.

Tennyson, presumably exposed to Shelley for the first time during his stay at the university, fell under the spell of this "high-born maiden" as a correlative to the "Poet hidden/ In the light of thought." Thus the 1830 and 1833 volumes abound with explorations of this Shelleyan type. Gradually, as Tennyson was raked over by his critics for the derivative and artificial quality of his verse — as well as for its "cockney" luxuriance — he attempted to transcend this literary convention. The process of becoming "the master of his symbol instead of its thrall" had three distinct stages: (1) the vaguely evoked phantom of melancholy submerged in her landscape ("Mariana") became (2) an abstract representation of the poet in "The Lady of Shalott" and "The Palace of Art" until (3) finally the high-born maiden emerged as an objectified stock literary character in the 1842 volumes in general and in "Lady Clara Vere de Vere" in particular. In the third stage Tennyson for the first time transformed an intellectualized concept into an objective portrait "to bring his high-born maiden from the cloudy realms of legend and allegory to the noonday of contemporary England." [23]

Stevenson then suggests that this persistent recourse to a single female figure conforms with startling consistency to Carl Jung's archetypal *anima*, the symbol of the unconscious self which is always of the opposite sex. As he was maturing, Tennyson initially projected his *anima* upon a shadowy woman (as in "Mariana"); as he approached emotional stability he came to recognize this woman almost consciously as a personified abstraction of unconscious processes (the female soul in "The Palace of Art"); and finally he was able to thrust her from him completely and transform her into the typical heroine of the Victorian idylls.

As Stevenson presents this thesis, his language implies a general approval of the process, especially since the subsequent examples of the type (Amy of "Locksley Hall," Maud, and Princess Ida) manage to lose the cold pride of Lady Clara Vere de Vere. He

[23] *Ibid.*, p. 241.

quotes Jung to show that the process Tennyson is undergoing leads
to "maturity" and to "emotional stability"; he speaks of the "more
rational relationship" that the third stage suggests and the "psychological completeness" of Tennyson when he can make "a bland
objective use of the theme for its narrative value." But aside from
all questions of the declining aesthetic power of the later portraits
and whatever the truth of the Jungian correlative, Stevenson does
not, it seems to me, pay sufficient attention to the fact that the more
"emotional stability" Tennyson evinces in the 1842 volumes, the
nastier, more arrogant, and more destructive some of his women
can become. Finally, Stevenson does not choose to consider a parallel change in Tennyson's men which surely deserves mention in
a full account of Tennyson's psychic and literary development. For
there is an evolution in both the Tennysonian male and female figures after the 1842 volumes; and any description of that change
must expressly take into account, as Stevenson's essay does not, the
impact upon Tennyson's work of Arthur Hallam. Tennyson's
"complete maturity" and the concomitant transformation of his
art must, one suspects, be obscurely dependent on the crucial event
in his poetic life, the death of Hallam.

CHAPTER IV

Arthur Hallam and Erotic Devotion

To ——" which introduces "The Palace of Art" assures
Richard Trench, to whom both poems are addressed,

> That Beauty, Good, and Knowledge are three sisters
> That doat upon each other, friends to man,
> Living together under the same roof,
> And never can be sunder'd without tears.
>
> (ll. 10–13)

Tennyson has apparently resolved all doubts: the thirst for Beauty
and Love can now be reconciled with each other as they could not
in "The Lady of Shalott" and "Oenone." Whereas in "Oenone"
three goddesses, three contending urges in man, competed for the
golden apple in a bitter psychomachy, these three sisters "doat
upon each other" in harmonious balance. But "The Palace of Art"
itself implies a distinct hierarchy of values in this new sisterhood.
Whatever the imagery of the poem may betray, on the level of
conscious intention Tennyson is gradually moving away from a devotion to the "Beautiful" and toward a singleminded embrace of
the "Good" by the time of the 1833 volume, a shift of allegiance
that is reinforced by the poems of the 1842 volumes.

Such a drift is usually attributed to the coming together of several influences: the moral didacticism that was a pronounced strain among the Apostles at Cambridge; the unfriendly critical response to Tennyson's first two volumes that tended to denigrate his work as little more than a derivative extension of the cockney school of Keats and Shelley; and the success of his Apostle friends, especially Henry Alford and Richard Trench whose pietistic verse received a more enthusiastic public welcome than was accorded his own.[1] Furthermore when *Philip Van Artevelde*, a closet drama by Henry Taylor, a young poet of Tennyson's age, won the kind of immediate critical approval that Tennyson himself coveted, he was attracted to the principles that Taylor announced in his famous Preface to the play. In it Taylor censured the tendency of the second-generation Romantics (and by implication such of their disciples as Tennyson) to exalt a sensuous imagery over subject matter and reflection:

They wanted, in the first place, subject-matter. A feeling came more easily to them than a reflection, and an image was always at hand when a thought was not forthcoming. Either they did not look upon mankind with observant eyes, or they did not feel it to be any part of their vocation to turn what they saw to account. It did not belong to poetry, in their apprehension, to thread the mazes of life in all its classes and under all its circumstances, common as well as romantic, and, seeing all things, to infer and to instruct: on the contrary, it was to stand aloof from everything that is plain and true; to have little concern with what is rational or wise; it was to be, like music, a moving and enchanting art, acting upon the fancy, the affections, the passions, but scarcely connected with the exercise of the intellectual faculties.[2]

Tennyson's response both to the Preface and to *Philip Van Artevelde* itself indicates a willingness to view circumspectly the techniques and poetic inspirations of his youth. As he says in a letter to James Spedding, "I close with him [Taylor] in most that he says of modern poetry, tho' it may be that he does not take sufficiently

[1] Edgar F. Shannon, *Tennyson and the Reviewers: A Study of His Literary Reputation and of the Influence of the Critics upon His Poetry* (Cambridge, Mass., 1952), pp. 33–59.
[2] *Philip Van Artevelde* (London, 1843), pp. x–xiii.

into consideration the peculiar strength evolved by such writers as Byron and Shelley, who however mistaken they may be, did yet give the world another heart and new pulses, and so are we kept going. . . . But 'Philip is a famous man' and makes me 'shamed of my own faults.'" [3] And indeed a way of defining Tennyson's weaknesses in later years is to see that he fully accepted the dissociation between emotion and understanding both Hallam (see pp. 38–39) and Taylor from their opposed vantage points insisted on.

Yet, once allowance is made for such influences as the foregoing, it is important not to overemphasize them. Except for "The Palace of Art," and "Oenone," there is little in the early volumes to suggest that Tennyson had as yet been overwhelmed by the moralism of the Apostles. Their monolithic effect on Tennyson, moreover, is easy to exaggerate; their advice could be contradictory. Richard Trench is frequently cited as the Apostle who most explicitly calls for "objective foundations," deploring the subjective bent of Shelley, Keats, and Wordsworth that Tennyson is striving to follow in his poetry of the early 1830's:

When, except in our times, did men seek to build up their poetry on their own individual experiences, instead of some objective foundations, common to all men? Even we, who inhabit their own age, suffer by their error. Their poems are unintelligible to us, till we have gone through that very state of feeling to which they appeal; as, for instance, none can entirely comprehend "Alastor" who has not been laid waste by the unslaked thirst for female sympathies; and so with the rest.[4]

At the same time that Tennyson is being warned away from excessive woman worship, something like this "unslaked thirst for female sympathies" is being urged upon him by his times and, more specifically, by Arthur Hallam. The most dazzling of the Apostles to his university friends, Hallam left a lasting imprint on the uncertain, malleable youth Tennyson was at Cambridge.

A brilliant conversationalist, Hallam combined an intellectual and a personal attractiveness. Both his speculative audacity and the

---

[3] *Memoir*, I, 141.
[4] *Richard Chevenix Trench: Letters and Memorials*, ed. Maria Trench (London, 1888), I, 73.

charm of his character drew Tennyson in important ways, nowhere more so than in his influence on the poet's conception of love. While this influence shows through most clearly in *In Memoriam* which was not published until 1850, it would seem best to consider the impact of Hallam upon both Tennyson and his masterwork at this point. For Hallam's views and the fact of his death in 1833 throw light on Tennyson's psychic and aesthetic development, especially on his changing conception of love and woman in the 1830's.

Hallam's speculations about human love appear in four connected works: the "Theodicaea Novissima," an essay read to the Apostles on October 29, 1831, to show "that there is ground for believing that the existence of moral evil is absolutely necessary to the fulfillment of God's essential love for Christ"; a youthful autobiographical poem, "A Farewell to the South," completed by June 1828, in which Hallam describes his devotion as a seventeen-year-old Etonian to Anna Mildred Wintour during his travels through Italy in the winter of 1827–1828; "The Influence of Italian upon English Literature," a prize-winning declamation he delivered on Trinity College Commemoration Day in December 1831, in the course of which he traces romantic love back to its diverse sources; and "Remarks on Professor Rossetti's 'Disquisizioni Sullo Spirito Antipapale,'" part of his critical response to Gabriele Rossetti's *Analytic Commentary* on the *Divine Comedy*, which the latter singled out as an especially perceptive critique of his work.[5]

The "Theodicaea," Hallam's most impressive piece of undergraduate writing, illustrates his intellectual range, his ability to synthesize in an original, trinitarian way ideas taken from Bayle, Leibnitz, Jonathan Edwards, and William Ellery Channing (199–200).[6]

[5] *Writings of Hallam*, pp. 198–213, 8–27, 213–234, and 237–279. Subsequent references are taken from these pages and will appear within parentheses in the text.

[6] That Tennyson himself was especially impressed by the "Theodicaea" is clear from a letter he wrote to Henry Hallam concerning the latter's plan to publish his son's *Remains*: "I know not whether among the prose pieces you would include the one which he was accustomed to call his Theodicaean Essay. I am inclined to think it does great honor to his originality of thought" (Eversley *Works*, III, 258).

It was partly on the evidence of the metaphysical gymnastics in this work that a brilliant future was forecast for Hallam by his contemporaries. Typically, the Christian love Hallam finds synonymous with godhead owes much to a Neoplatonism that he imbibed through his Italian studies. His enthusiasm for Dante and to a lesser extent for Petrarch he was able to communicate to Tennyson. For what there is in Tennyson's conception of love that is consciously Neoplatonic he absorbed in large measure from Hallam's energetic espousal of Renaissance Italian Platonism.[7]

Yet Hallam, as devoted a child of the nineteenth-century religious revival as Tennyson, provides a Christian setting for the Platonic idea of love as "the Base and Pyramidal point of the entire universe and the broad and deep foundation of our moral nature." Since God is the Love toward which all men aspire, "erotic feeling is of origin peculiarly divine, and raises the soul to heights of existence, which no other passion is permitted to attain" (203). And while such an eros can be unhealthy in man, a personal God returns this "passion" toward the universe He has created without danger ("In our frail nature strong feeling is prone to error; but are we afraid for God?"). Hallam defines love as the "direct, immediate, absorbing affection for one object, on the grounds of similarity perceived, and with a view to more complete union, as it is the noblest quality of the human soul" (204). Its interchange between man and God shows both at their most magnanimous. This "similarity perceived," a respect for the principle of reciprocity, is the essential prerequisite of love between man and God as well as between human beings.

Of course man, or even the magnified Son whom the Father especially loves, cannot be quite the equal of God even in so generous a feeling as love. A personality created by God must in all senses be subordinate to Him: "How then will the requisite similarity be possible, since the nature of God is Infinite, Absolute, Perfect? And how will the Reciprocity be possible, since the attributes of God are all infinite, and that great attribute so infinite to Him,

[7] T. Herbert Warren, "Tennyson and Dante," in *Essays of Poets and Poetry, Ancient and Modern* (London, 1909), pp. 243–269.

that the Apostle asserts it to be His essence, must be altogether il-
limitable" (205). Evil and suffering flourish in the world so that
man can make up for his deficiency. Only by the testing that man's
love undergoes as it is battered by evil and pain can it emerge puri-
fied and win through to a strict conformity with God's love,
achieving a sense of absolute similarity to the object adored. The
evil of the Crucifixion was thus "the necessary and only condition
of Christ's being enabled to exert the highest act of love, that any
generated Being could perform" (206).

But man in his frailty cannot always resist evil or summon forth
the erotic intensity necessary to aspire toward a feeling of similarity to God. Woman has been brought into the world precisely to
facilitate the ascent. Thus in the seven-hundred-line "A Farewell
to the South" Hallam gives an impassioned sincerity to the conventional theme of man's ennoblement by woman: "That Woman's Love was sent/ To heal man's tainted heart, and chasten him
for Heaven" (ll. 425–426). The speaker who has met Nina for the
first time in Rome, although their fathers are old friends, has fallen
in love with her at first sight. In the course of his extended effusions
the speaker explores the connections between poetry and love.
Man's soul, he says,

> is rife
> With deep sensations of the fair and true,
> Which brood o'er silence; but one hour may wake
> Their energies — one minute — bidding new
> Worlds of undreamt existence prisoner take
> Th' enmarvailed sense, and change our being's mode.
>
> (ll. 223–228)

Asking himself how man can break through to such a spot of time,
he evokes the vision of Beatrice, Dante's "life controlling star." Her
momentary brush against the divine poet's life had refined "his visible muse, incarnate Poesy." From her, "a gracebeam from above,"
the poet learned "to thirst for truth, to long/ For all that passes not
away, to bear/ The spurns of men" (ll. 277–279).

Genius such as Dante's flourishes best in the soul that has dedicated itself to the love of woman. Such a divine Platonization

drives not only rare spirits, but it is also an instinctive urge in all men whose barren hearts may flower beneath the glance of a woman's love. In this experience the lover is helpless and relatively passive, for "tho' ungifted, may no mind contemn/ The great magician of the soul; but each/ Must yield, when on him falls the choice of bliss" (ll. 352–354). Like Dante and like lesser men Hallam has been visited by Heaven's power in the sudden, unexpected dwelling within him of a love for Nina:

> I knew
> A power, upraising thought, as winds the ocean,
> Within me, but not of me: for it grew
> Unto my spirit, striking root, as moved
> By some supernal influence, breathing through
> The medium of the being that I loved!
>
> (ll. 483–488)

The God of the "Theodicaea" whose name is Love illuminates the soul of man with His most persuasive light if He can come to man through the agency of woman. Woman alone is worthy "to awake/ Our primal thoughts of innocence, and share/ With us that wisdom" (ll. 538–540); only from her divine intervention can man learn "that inmost valour, that bright character of Godhead stamped on woman's soul." Hallam's apotheosis of Nina, a modern Beatrice, thus perfectly exemplifies his Christian Platonism, the insistence that love is the "manifestation in man of the great informing power which brought the universe out of chaos and which now maintains it in order and concord."

A confirmation both of Hallam's devotion to Plato and Dante and of his indulgence in what Trench criticized as "the unslaked thirst for female sympathies" appears in "The Influence of Italian upon English Literature." While surveying Italian strains within the English literary tradition, Hallam outlines the historical process by which Platonic eros, "the love of a worthy object," changed its earthly base from love of man to love of woman. The resurgence of European genius in the Renaissance he attributes to the happy confluence of Christian, Teutonic, Roman, and Oriental principles. These forces have combined to generate the two great ideas whose dynamism accounts for the preeminence of modern European civilization — "enthusiasm for individual prowess, and enthusiasm for the female character" (218). In the emergence of woman worship Hallam sees Catholic Christianity as the prime catalyst: "The inordinate esteem for chastity; the solemnity attached to conventual vows; the interest taken in those fair saints, on whom the Church had conferred beatitude, that after conquering the temptations of earth they might be able to succor the tempted; above all the worship of the Virgin, the Queen of Heaven, supposed more lenient to sinners for the lenity of her sex; and more powerful in their redemption by her claim of maternal authority over her Almighty Son — these articles of a most unscriptural, but very beautiful mythology, could not be established in general belief without investing the feminine character with ideal splendour and loveliness" (219). The generalized Platonic principle of love as the informing power which rescues the universe from chaos was consequently transformed by Christian Platonistic poets. Dante and Petrarch localized the universal love of Plato into a love associated with a specific woman. Hallam thus shows how a personal experience like the one dramatized in "A Farewell to the South," which has the sanction of a God of Love described in the "Theodicaea," receives an additional legitimacy from the genius of European history.

And finally, in "Remarks on Professor Rossetti's 'Disquisizioni Sullo Spirito Antipapale'" Hallam equates the emotion that Christian man lavishes upon God and upon His clearest surrogate on earth, woman. For in the veneration of the Virgin the Christian mind has come to the discovery of perfection in female form: "And what is that worship itself, but the exponent of a restless longing in man's unsatisfied soul, which must ever find a personal shape, wherein to embody his moral ideas, and will chuse for that shape, where he can, a nature not too remote from his own, but resembling in dissimilitude, and flattering at once his vanity by the likeness, and his pride by the difference" (269)? It is on the base of such a perception of woman analogous to God that Western man has erected a religion whose essence is an erotic relation to God: "What is the distinguishing character of Hebrew literature, which separates it by so broad a line of demarcation from that of every ancient people? Undoubtedly the sentiment of *erotic devotion* which pervades it. Their poets never represent the Deity, as an impassive principle, a mere organizing intellect, removed at infinite distance from human hopes and fears. He is for them a being of like passions with themselves, requiring heart for heart, and capable of inspiring affection because capable of feeling and returning it" (269). In a word, the analogous dissimilitude and similarity of woman and man on the one hand and God and man on the other transforms woman into the heavenly being she is in Hallam's mind.

It is dangerous to generalize about the influence such works as the foregoing may have had upon Tennyson's thought in the early 1830's. For that matter, we cannot know to what degree Hallam's speculations show the imprint of his conversations with Tennyson. For while Tennyson's principles were hardly worked out with the systematic rigor of a "Theodicaea Novissima," they were unalterably set in the general direction of Christian idealism. The view of love that Tennyson had been shaping in his mind as a result of the pietistic influences at Somersby and the God of Love that Hallam had been forging out of his early Dante studies were strikingly similar. This happy congruence no doubt helped to confirm their growing friendship.[8]

To be sure, the notion of a God of Love who makes His presence felt through the ennobling inspiration of a woman is far too traditional to trace to a single source. Nevertheless, one is tempted to read a good deal of Hallam's influence into Tennyson's conception of love, since from all accounts Tennyson was enormously impressed by Hallam's charisma and precocity during their acquaintance. In the four years before Hallam's death (Tennyson in *In Memoriam* dates the beginning of their intimate association from the spring of 1829), it seems clear that Hallam's romantic idealism and intellectual breadth were sources of both awe and comfort to Tennyson. Torn by almost pathological moods of depression brought on largely by domestic difficulties at Somersby, Tennyson found

[8] Charles Tennyson, *Tennyson*, p. 82.

relief from sorrow in his friendship with the brilliant Hallam. Undoubtedly, Tennyson agreed with Richard Monckton Milnes' estimate of Hallam at Cambridge: "He is the only man here of my own standing before whom I bow in conscious inferiority in everything." [9] And Tennyson's desolation at Hallam's death is of course proverbial in the biography of the poet.[10]

Literary echoes of Hallam's death reverberate through Tennyson's poetry from the 1842 volumes to that written toward the end of his life. The immediate sorrow and attempts at recovery find varied expression in "Ulysses," "Morte d'Arthur," "Break, Break, Break," "The Two Voices," and "Tithonus" (although the last of these was not published until 1860). "In the Valley of Cauteretz," a poem written thirty-one years after the visit by Hallam and Tennyson to the Pyrenees to deliver money to Spanish insurgents, conveys how deep a wound Hallam's death remained even later in life when time presumably would have had an opportunity to heal its memory.

But the work that most substantially bears the impress of Hallam's personality, especially his view of love, is *In Memoriam*. In the poem's one hundred and thirty-one sections Hallam's God of Love (as well as Elizabeth Tennyson's) asserts Himself with growing assurance until He emerges with full radiance in the Introduction (which was written last). In some such way, at any rate, Tennyson conceived of the elegy's inner movement: "The different moods of sorrow as in a drama are dramatically given, and my

[9] *Memoir*, I, 107. Some later critics, beginning with Arthur Benson, *Fasti Etonensis: A Biographical History of Eton* (Elton, 1899), pp. 344-345, have tended to view both Hallam's character and supposed future prospects with some reservation.

[10] Though see Ralph Wilson Rader, "Tennyson in the Year of Hallam's Death," *PMLA*, LXXVII (1962), 419-424, an attempt to soften the earlier account by Joyce Green, "Tennyson's Development during the 'Ten Years' Silence (1832-1842)." In lightening the traditional portrait of the sorrowing poet, Rader relies heavily on the diary of Tennyson's friend, the Reverend John Rashdall, for the years 1833-1835 to show that Tennyson was "more active, less of a recluse, less absolutely crushed than has been supposed, less buried in grief." Such an argument prepares one for Rader's *Tennyson's "Maud": The Biographical Genesis* in which he traces Tennyson's attachment to three women — Rosa Baring, Sophy Rawnsley, and Emily Sellwood — in the years immediately following Hallam's death.

conviction that fear, doubts, and suffering will find answer and re-lief only through Faith in a God of Love." [11] Tennyson's own the-odicy, his attempt to find some solace for the bitter constraint and sad occasion dear of his gifted friend's early death, is of course more than the undergraduate exercise in metaphysical speculation that Hallam's "Theodicaea" was; nevertheless, in its central motifs and its attempt to justify human suffering *In Memoriam* is, I be-lieve, indebted to the earlier work.[12]

Tennyson's God of Love owes less to a Neoplatonic and more to a purely Christian tradition than does Hallam's. When asked the meaning of the words "Immortal Love" in the poem's Introduc-tion, Tennyson said that he had in mind St. John's sense of them (I John, chap. iv).[13] However, Hallam's key notion of evil as a moral challenge to be met and overcome in order for man to clasp in an earned embrace a God of Love is also Tennyson's; it is implicit in the speaker's attempt to touch once more the "hand" [14] of a Hal-lam who by the poem's conclusion has been absorbed into and be-come a surrogate of Christ. As man evolves "from clime to clime" both as the herald of a higher race on earth and of his gradual ascent to a "higher place," he may,

> . . . crown'd with attributes of woe
> Like glories, move his course, and show
> That life is not an idle ore,
>
> But iron dug from central gloom,
> And heated hot with burning fears,
> And dipt in baths of hissing tears,
> And batter'd with the shocks of doom
>
> To shape and use.   (CXVIII)

[11] *Memoir*, I, 304–305.
[12] Eleanor Bustin Mattes, *"In Memoriam": The Way of a Soul* (New York, 1951), pp. 12–23 and 43–45, has a brief section summarizing the argu-ment of the "Theodicaea" and considering it and the character of Hallam as influences on *In Memoriam*. She does not treat any of Hallam's other works aside from one short lyric ("To one early loved, now in India"), nor does she feel that the "Theodicaea" was a very crucial influence on Tennyson ex-cept in a negative way.
[13] *Memoir*, I, 312n.
[14] Charles Sanders, "Tennyson and the Human Hand," *Victorian News-*

For Tennyson as for Hallam this absorption of "the shocks of doom" finally becomes a willed encounter, even as the problem of will remains an impenetrable mystery.

> Thou seemest human and divine,
>   The highest, holiest manhood, thou.
>   Our wills are ours, we know not how;
>   Our wills are ours, to make them thine.
>   (Introduction)

Only when Love has survived its baptism in Death can it transcend, after incorporating, the cloistered virtue of a lesser, untested faith in the merely human:

> The love that rose on stronger wings,
>   Unpalsied when he met with Death,
>   Is comrade of the lesser faith
>   That sees the course of human things.
>   (CXXVIII)

This strengthened love for a deity that one cannot see or comprehend approximates the love of God that man finally attains in the "Theodicaea." By the conclusion of *In Memoriam* the speaker has achieved the sense of "similarity perceived" and of reciprocity that for Hallam crowned both human love and man's exchange of love with God. The climactic trance-vision in which the speaker is at last physically "touched" by the "living soul" of Hallam asserts the existence of these dual conditions:

> So word by word, and line by line,
>   The dead man touch'd me from the past,
>   And all at once it seem'd at last
>   The living soul was flash'd on mine,
>
> And mine in this was wound, and whirl'd
>   About empyreal heights of thought,
>   And came on that which is, and caught
>   The deep pulsations of the world.   (XCV)

As a result of this union, the speaker, purged of despair through contact with Christ's surrogate, can address God as an equal that "with us works" and can trust

letter, No. 11 (1957), 5–13, traces the recurring motif of the attempted touching of hands with special emphasis on *In Memoriam*.

With faith that comes of self-control,
　The truths that never can be proved
　Until we close with all we loved,
And all we flow from, soul in soul.

(CXXXI)

But a description of the poem's development stressing Tennyson's debt to Hallam's ideas may exaggerate the importance of Tennyson's abstract theories. The spiritual faith of the poem is, as a matter of fact, drenched in a highly sensual imagery. Indeed the mood of amatory affection that hovers over much of the poem has been a target of "whisper, and hint, and chuckle" ("Maud," l. 130) for the less than sympathetic reader of Tennyson. Even contemporary reviewers who were awed by the poem occasionally denigrated it for what they considered a feminine eroticism. Such strictures were always a source of great irritation to Tennyson. And he certainly did feel the need to defend himself against the charge of excess "amatory tenderness" in *In Memoriam* as well as to tone down some of the more flagrant examples in later editions.

While the matter is easy to vulgarize, it is too important for a full understanding of Tennysonian love to scant. It is true that the sorrow of *In Memoriam*, constantly expressed in corporeal and floral imagery, insists upon an almost hysterical sense of physical loss. Arthur Carr has captured the reason with precision: "Because the death of Arthur Hallam is both a real and a symbolic loss that radiates from the centre of Tennyson's art, the tone of amatory affection which suffuses *In Memoriam* cannot be read as simple evidence of an erotic relationship in fact between Tennyson and his friend. It is enough that the loss of Hallam touches Tennyson at every nerve and that the demand for reunion is expressed with an energy that will not forego the connotations of physical bereavement." [15]

I would like to suggest that the erotic apostrophe of Hallam in the poem, while no doubt a true barometer of Tennyson's feelings, also may owe something to Hallam's earlier theorizing. As we

---

[15] "Tennyson as a Modern Poet," *University of Toronto Quarterly*, XIX (1950), 361–382; reprinted in John Killham, *Critical Essays on the Poetry of Tennyson*, pp. 41–64. The quotation appears on p. 55 of the latter.

have seen, in both the "Theodicaea Novissima" and the critique of Rossetti's Dante theories, Hallam insisted on the inseparability of true spiritual emotion and the language of eroticism in Western civilization. He furthermore argued that as a result the ascent toward God would be facilitated by the presence of female influence or by the male's attribution of a polar femininity to the object of his apotheosis. *In Memoriam* describes the transformation of Hallam into an analogue of Christ; to render this Hallam-Christ accessible, Tennyson eroticizes him, giving him female attributes.

Hallam is thus occasionally, if obliquely or by analogy, addressed as a woman (mother, sister, or beloved) who can serve as man's best approach to an erotic union with God. The speaker, for instance, tries to soften the pain of his "widow'd hour" by seeing a connection between the dead Hallam and a maiden who has left the home of her parents for the first time:

> Could we forget the widow'd hour
> And look on Spirits breathed away,
> As on a maiden in the day
> When first she wears her orange-flower!
>
> When crown'd with blessing she doth rise
> To take her latest leave of home,
> And hopes and light regrets that come
> Make April of her tender eyes;
>
> And doubtful joys the father move,
> And tears are on the mother's face,
> As parting with a long embrace
> She enters other realms of love;
>
> Her office there to rear, to teach,
> Becoming as is meet and fit
> A link among the days, to knit
> The generations each with each;
>
> And, doubtless, unto thee is given
> A life that bears immortal fruit
> In those great offices that suit
> The full-grown energies of heaven.   (XL)

The task of woman on earth parallels that of Hallam in heaven; both will disperse their energies to ennoble all they touch.

Man's reason also may tempt him into doubts about the existence of a beneficent, personal God who assures an eventual reconciliation between the living and the dead. It is woman's simple, uncomplicated faith in the immortality of the soul that can serve as an exemplary model to lead man from such incertitude. The story of Mary's instinctive acceptance of her brother Lazarus' return from the dead ("All subtle thought, all curious fears/Borne down by gladness so complete") introduces the speaker's praise of an imaginary, paradigmatic young girl. He warns her imaginary more intellectual brother not to undermine or confuse her orthodox faith with "shadow'd hints":

> Her faith thro' form is pure as thine,
> Her hands are quicker unto good.
> O, sacred be the flesh and blood
> To which she links a truth divine!

(XXXIII)

Hallam was aware of the special quagmires that bog down the Christian's erotic devotion to God: "Not the gross and evident passions of our nature, but the elevated and less separable desires are the dangerous enemies which misguide the poetic spirit in its attempt at self-cultivation";[16] and Tennyson was also developing serious reservations about his habitual dalliance in sense. The extravagent display of sorrow at Hallam's death, as revealed in the sensuous detail of *In Memoriam*, perhaps quickens Tennyson's turning away from the "Beautiful." Partially conscious of these excesses, Tennyson becomes inordinately aware of the dangers of passionate sorrow (the grief-laden protagonist of "Maud" is a madman). He becomes convinced that the address to Christ's analogue (Hallam and the women of the later poetry) can pass into a self-destructive passion: Lancelot's apotheosis of Guinevere makes it all too easy for her to become a bearer of carnality. *In Memoriam* therefore insists upon a "faith that comes of self-control" (CXXXI) and one that constantly flees from "the reeling Faun, the sensual feast" (CXVIII).

[16] See p. 40.

Aside from becoming the overt or barely disguised subject of many poems, Hallam's death touched Tennyson's art and view of love in other, more oblique ways. Several of Tennyson's modern readers, applying more or less openly the insights of a Freudian psychology to his biography, have seen Hallam's death as an avenue of psychic release for Tennyson from his moated grange of sorrow. An early, unspoken, all but unremembered emotional crisis which had given a definitive cast to Tennyson's melancholic temperament found its repetition in the loss of Hallam: ". . . whatever the initiating cause, Tennyson became conscious in childhood of Hamlet's problem, the religious significance of his own existence. Emotions of early childhood are hard to express except accidentally because the original events associated with them are not remembered. Hallam's death, a repetition of the abandonment experience, gave Tennyson the symbolic event which mobilized what he had already suffered and gave his fear a focus and a *raison d'être*." [17] The anguish of the "infant crying in the night;/ An infant crying for the light,/ And with no language but a cry" of *In Memoriam* (LIV) had always been just below the surface of Tennyson's work. The appeal especially of the early poetry resides in the credibility of its scarcely controlled terror at the sound behind the moldering wainscot, of a despair floating free in the middle distance without definable cause. What drives a twentieth-century reader to Kafka and De Chirico makes it possible for him to enter the ominous Tennyson landscapes ("a height, a broken grange, a grove, a flower") and to understand their desolate human extensions.

Hallam's death by itself conceivably might not have initiated radical changes in the quality of Tennyson's melancholy. But the early 1830's had brought to Tennyson's troubled spirit one formidable blow after another: in 1831 his father had died, necessitating his return to Somersby from Cambridge with substantial debts but without a degree; Christopher North's slightly hostile review of *Poems, Chiefly Lyrical* had appeared in *Blackwood's Magazine* in 1832; Alfred's favorite brother, Charles, had succumbed to the

[17] Auden, *Selected Poems*, pp. xvi–xvii.

opium habit, while another brother, Edward, was undergoing a complete mental breakdown; and in April of 1833 John Wilson Croker viciously attacked Tennyson's early poetry in the *Quarterly Review*. To this abundant structure of sorrow Hallam's death in Vienna on September 15 provided the tragic capstone.

This series of disasters culminating in the death of his friend gave to the dream-shrouded anxiety that had suffused Tennyson's previous work a point in reality on which to focus. Arthur Carr in his comment on the change cites Freud's distinction between melancholia and mourning as applicable to Tennyson's condition before and after Hallam's death. "Melancholia," Freud suggests, "is in some way related to an unconscious loss of love object, in contradistinction to mourning, in which there is nothing unconscious about the loss." [18] Tennyson's early poetic strategies — his mask of age, his passion for the past, and his preference for the "far, far away" — were indulgences of an unlocalized sense of loss as well as attempts to elude its debilitating aura. Presumably the setbacks of the 1830's in their evocation of a comprehensible mourning (and the partial mastery of such grief evidenced by "Ulysses" and *In Memoriam*) led to a greater control of the melancholia. It is probable that the relatively confident Victorian sage Tennyson became in later years has his beginnings in this capacity for governing a real grief.

Whatever the truth of such speculation about the impact of this unhappy period on Tennyson's later life, the gradual change in sex of Tennyson's deserted lovers after the 1833 volume is, I believe, one of the ways it affected his poetry. In the most convincing poems of the early volumes the "infant crying in the night" is usually an Oenone, a Mariana, an Oriana, the mourning shades of "A Dream of Fair Women," or a Lady of Shalott. It is a woman, the *anima*, "the unconscious self which is always of the opposite sex" (to return momentarily to Stevenson's Jungian categories). After

[18] *Collected Papers* (1925), IV, 155; as quoted in Carr, "Tennyson as a Modern Poet," p. 54. Supporting Paden's contention that in the "Morte d'Arthur" Tennyson conceivably merged the figures of his father and Arthur Hallam (*Tennyson in Egypt*, pp. 86–88), Carr sees Hallam as a possible surrogate for Tennyson's father, who died in March 1831.

Hallam's death the deserted lovers of Tennyson's major works — such figures as Enoch Arden, the protagonist of "Maud," or Arthur in the *Idylls* — tend more frequently to be men. The clarification of Tennyson's melancholia into a sharply focused mourning may have helped to prompt this transformation. The new assertiveness Tennyson was able to summon as a response to suffering enabled him to feel, on whatever level of consciousness, that he had been personifying the image of his melancholia, projecting it upon actual female protagonists or upon a female soul ("The Palace of Art"). Hereafter, while the central figures of Tennyson's poetry still betray signs of passivity and recessive dependence upon women, they are usually men who either have a confident male identity or try to forge one in the course of the poem.

But Tennyson had to pay an aesthetic price for this new maturity, for the "psychological completeness" Stevenson describes. By the time of the 1842 volumes he has withdrawn from a commitment to a sensuous art and projects himself into female protagonists only in a limited way. But it seems that the later Tennyson is at his best — as in the songs from *The Princess*, in "Lancelot and Elaine," "Guinevere," and "Demeter and Persephone" — primarily when he returns to this earlier vein, when he once more projects himself imaginatively through a female voice.

The creative confluence of sensuousness and sexuality that had made his work quite powerful will now in an important measure be dammed up. To the degree that he shifts to male protagonists, Tennyson in his later poetry tends, even more drastically than before, to polarize conceptions of love and women in a traditional way. Indeed women, with rare exceptions like Guinevere, come close to what Simone de Beauvoir has called the "absolute Other," complete functions of the men they serve to define.[19] Hereafter woman's role as comforter and ministering angel (a role Tennyson has prepared for her in "Isabel" and "Supposed Confessions") is the only legitimate expression of female love. Once Tennyson has turned away from a conviction that the artist lives by the five senses,

---

[19] *Le Deuxième Sexe* (Paris, 1949); published in English as *The Second Sex*, ed. and trans. H. M. Parshley (New York, 1953).

sensual woman becomes Tennyson's *bête noir*, his characteristic vessel of mid-Victorian sin, the *femme fatale*.

For as we have seen in the last chapter, there are few threatening women in Tennyson's poetry before the 1842 volumes: [20] the high-born maiden is after all a victim — she is cut off from human contact; she radiates the fear of her surrounding landscape. As the transformation of Mariana into a Lady Clara Vere de Vere progresses, as the women of Tennyson's lyrical dream world enter the narrative English idylls, they can become aggressive and haughty. In this transformation the female soul of "The Palace of Art" is a transitional figure: she is not yet a fully objectified woman, but has the arrogance and disdain of Tennyson's portrait of a thoroughly destructive woman, the Lady Clara of the 1842 *Poems*. At the same time, in "The Palace of Art" the change of the proud female soul, a vessel of sensation, into the humble and loving Victorian maid of the valley at the poem's conclusion announces the emergence of Lady Clara's polar opposite. Gradually Tennyson confirms his sense that there exists a substantial difference between the moral range of woman and of man:

> "Not mount as high!" we scarce can sink as low;
> For men at most differ as heaven and earth,
> But women, worst and best, as heaven and hell.
> ("Merlin and Vivien," ll. 811–813.)

To this differentiation of women, the recuperation from the blows of the early 1830's lent emphatic support. The gradual release from the shadow of Hallam's death facilitated Tennyson's withdrawal from female protagonists and encouraged the expression of the psyche through a male hero, uncertain of himself as he

---

[20] The four conceivable exceptions to this generalization are the Helen of "Oenone," the Helen and Cleopatra of "The Dream of Fair Women," the maiden in "Anacaona," and the seductive Eleänore of the 1830 lyrical portraits. But Helen is merely alluded to in "Oenone" — she does not partake in the poem's dramatic action — our center of interest is Oenone herself. In "The Dream of Fair Women" Cleopatra and Helen are both mourning shades: Helen's "star-like sorrows of immortal eyes" render her a pitiable figure. And as the discussion of "Anacaona" has implied, the maid is far more likely a victim of betrayal than a betrayer herself. The case of Eleänore I shall take up in Chapter VII.

might still be. The consequent division of woman into Cosmic Birth Giver and devouring Terrible Mother is a thoroughly conventional one. Archetypal in the Western mind, it is the literary sign of an assertive male vantage point.

The stream that the second-generation Romantics had creatively muddied is now fairly pure: the relative self-assurance of Tennyson's middle and later years begins with a new certainty after the psychic resolution triggered by Hallam's death as to just where soul leaves off and sense begins. And if the change in sex of Tennyson's major protagonists is a significant effect of this resolution, *The Princess* may profitably be considered as a transitional work in that transformation.

CHAPTER V

The Strange Diagonal

ENNYSON'S own assessment of his development during the 1830's is difficult to evaluate. The recorded comments concerning his response to the shocks of this period are not always helpful. His insistently spiritual interpretation of *In Memoriam*, the artfully contrived recollections in the *Memoir*, and the evasive explanations to such friends as James Knowles and Edward Fitzgerald do not intimate a sophisticated awareness of the changes that he must have undergone. Yet a remark to John Tyndall that "the power of explaining . . . concentrated expressions of the imagination [is] very different from that of writing them" [1] may indicate, in its insistence on reserve, a greater intelligence about such matters than his most severe critics have been willing to grant him. Tennyson, whose "hate of gossip parlance" finds continual expression in his work, was always infuriated by what C. S. Lewis has called the personal heresy, the reader's tendency to treat poetry as thinly disguised autobiography.[2] Tennyson would undoubtedly have seconded Eliot's contention that "the progress of an artist is a continual self-sacrifice, a continual extinction of personality" and

---

[1] *Memoir*, II, 475.

[2] C. S. Lewis's theory and E. M. W. Tillyard's critique of it in *The Personal Heresy: A Controversy* (London, 1939) are anthologized in *The Modern Critical Spectrum*, ed. Gerald and Nancy Goldberg (Englewood Cliffs, N.J., 1962), pp. 206–214.

that "honest criticism and sensitive appreciation is directed not upon the poet but upon the poetry."[3] When "indolent reviewers" tried to equate the speaker of "Maud" with the poet himself, Tennyson insisted upon distinguishing the teller from the tale: "The mistake that people make is that they think the poet's poems are a kind of 'catalogue raisonné' of his very own self, and of all the facts of his life, not seeing that they often only express a poetic instinct, or judgment on character real or imagined, and on the facts of lives real or imagined. Of course some poems, like my 'Ode to Memory,' are evidently based on the poet's own nature, and on hints from his own life."[4] At the same time he was notoriously unhappy with the personal way in which some of his readers trusted the tale, and he did not hesitate to correct "wrong" interpretations both during his life and for posterity in the *Memoir*.

In the context of such discriminations, *The Princess* becomes an interesting poem. It is one of the few works in which Tennyson (or a narrator in the frame who is almost identical with him) appears alongside characters in a tale, and these characters have transparent thematic connections with the frame's narrator. When these links are thoroughly explored, it becomes clear not only that Tennyson was a consummate craftsman but also that he reached a subtle understanding, even in terms that post-Freudian readers can appreciate, of the changes that were going on within himself during the late 1830's and the 1840's.

For in *The Princess* Tennyson is, among other things, working out in a complex, ingenious parable his psychological realignment described in the last chapter. First published in 1847, three years before *In Memoriam*, the work was composed shortly *after* the better part of *In Memoriam* was completed. Edmund Lushington recalled that during his visit to Tennyson in the summer of 1845 the poet showed him the completed version of many of *In Memoriam*'s cantos, including the marriage song of the Epilogue which cele-

---

[3] "Tradition and the Individual Talent," *Selected Essays*, p. 7.

[4] *Memoir*, I, 402. The degree to which Tennyson tried to dissociate himself from his protagonist in "Maud" is expressed with unexpected humor: "Adulterer I may be, fornicator I may be, murderer I may be, suicide I am not yet" (Charles Tennyson, *Tennyson*, p. 286).

brated the wedding of Lushington to Tennyson's sister, Cecilia. Though he was at that time working on *The Princess*, he had only finished the first section.[5]

The overt subject of the poem is a slightly misleading one. The poem is sometimes read as a partial response to the reviews of the 1842 *Poems*. While generally favorable, these reviews urged Tennyson to enter more directly into the spirit of modern poetry. To do so he was to keep in mind the following goals: "(1) modern poetry must idealize and mirror contemporary life and thought; (2) the highest type of poetry must be concerned with human existence; (3) the poet's primary duty is to teach; (4) Tennyson's poetry must display more human sympathy; and (5) Tennyson, if he is to establish his claim to greatness, must write a long poem — a sustained work on a single theme."[6] Tennyson's extended medley on women's rights teaching his generation of readers the proper relation of man and woman admirably fills each of these requirements. But though the volume achieved a mixed critical success in England and a brilliant one in America on the basis of its Victorian wisdom concerning woman's proper role,[7] it is admired today largely as a period piece or for the fragile grace of such songs as "Tears, Idle Tears," "Ask Me No More," "Now Sleeps the Crimson Petal," and "Come Down, O Maid." The first of those long narrative poems for which Tennyson had a limited gift, it seems to justify Eliot's comment, typical of a modern response, that "an idyll protracted to such lengths becomes unreadable."[8]

But the more one contemplates the poem, the more one realizes that Tennyson has used the pretext of women's rights as a jumping-off point for the exploration both of traditional comic patterns and of his own changing psyche. Relevant to this work is E. D. H. Johnson's explanation of the Victorian poet's "double awareness," that ability of Tennyson to give a Victorian audience what it

[5] *Memoir*, I, 402.

[6] Quoted from Shannon, *Tennyson and the Reviewers*, p. 92.

[7] The English reviews are summarized in Shannon, *Tennyson and the Reviewers*, pp. 171–172, and the American in John O. Edison, *Tennyson in America* (Athens, Ga., 1943), pp. 57–73.

[8] "*In Memoriam*," *Essays Ancient and Modern* (New York, 1936), p. 180.

wished while at the same time creating conditions for the free play of private insights.[9]

One of the most moving anecdotes about Tennyson's life describes his leaving of it. For several days before his death, aware of its imminence, it was his custom to ask for his copy of Shakespeare. "Where is my Shakespeare? I must have my Shakespeare," his son remembers him calling out. On the evening of his death, his last food taken, he tried reading but found it impossible. In the moon-drenched room he opened his book to Act V, scene v of *Cymbeline*, to Posthumus' beautifully understated reconciliation scene with Imogen. Shortly after, he spoke his last words before Hallam and Emily and died, his copy of *Cymbeline* to be buried with him.[10]

The page had lain open to one of the three exchanges in Shakespeare which had always especially touched Tennyson by their consummate simplicity:

One is in *King Lear* when Lear says to Cordelia, "So young and so untender," and Cordelia lovingly answers, "So young, my lord, and true." And in *The Winter's Tale*, when Florizel takes Perdita's hand to lead her to the dance, and says, "So turtles pair that never mean to part," and the little Perdita answers, giving her hand to Florizel, "I'll swear for 'em." And in *Cymbeline*, when Imogen in tender rebuke says to her husband,

> "Why did you throw your wedded lady from you?
> Think that you are upon a rock; and now
> Throw me again!"

and Posthumus does not ask forgiveness, but answers, kissing her,

> "Hang there like fruit, my soul,
> Till the tree die." [11]

As he approached middle life, in other words, Tennyson like so many before and after him, like his early model Keats just before *his* death, separated Shakespeare from the rest of the English writers and created for him a redoubt of special eminence.

---

[9] *The Alien Vision of Victorian Poetry* (Princeton, 1952), p. 42.
[10] *Memoir*, II, 425–429.
[11] *Ibid.*, p. 290.

There are several characteristics to be noticed about these passages that Tennyson especially prized. While one is from a great tragedy and two are from late problem comedies, all three typify the situation in Tennyson's early poetry that finds its clearest echo in "Mariana." They all involve lost or deserted ladies: Cordelia is banished from the heart of the father she loves; Perdita's very name signifies her exile from a rightful father and mother; and Imogen until *Cymbeline*'s conclusion must disguise herself and flee her husband's wrath. Furthermore, Tennyson seems to be attracted to Shakespearean heroines from the later comedies where genre — whether the play is comedy or tragedy — is blurred; Mariana, like Perdita and Imogen, is out of a late dark comedy.

The Princess also looks back to Shakespearean drama. I should like to consider it as Tennyson's attempt to explore the spirit if not the form of Shakespearean comedy, for Tennyson's medley has elements in common with both the late dark comedies and the earlier romantic ones.

To begin with the obvious, one of the poem's many sources is Shakespearean.[12] The plot of *The Princess* contains a sexual inversion of *Love's Labour's Lost*. In Shakespeare's early burlesque, Ferdinand, King of Navarre, and three young nobles decide to found an academy of learning exclusive of female company. Gradually and one by one, they are seduced from their resolve by the arrival at court of the Princess of France and her three ladies-in-waiting. Tennyson changes numbers and sex: the determination of his Princess Ida and her *two* companions to set up their women's academy

[12] John Killham (*Tennyson and "The Princess": Reflections of an Age* [London, 1958]) meticulously examines the sources in Tennyson's early Eastern readings and in the literature of the contemporary women's rights struggle in England and on the Continent (especially France). His final reading of the poem, founded upon the careful collation of the sources, is quite convincing, though it is different in emphasis from the present one.

Killham, while he acknowledges *Love's Labour's Lost* as a source of *The Princess*, does not consider the Shakespearean influence or analogy at any great length. He notes that the plot resembles the plot of *Love's Labour's Lost* with the sexes reversed (p. 7), shows that one of the earliest of the poem's editors had noticed this (p. 16) and that a later one had not (p. 17), and realizes that the poem turns away from the mocking spirit of Shakespeare's play as it moves toward its close (pp. 143–144).

of learning is undermined by the love of the prince and his *two* friends. But the spirit of *The Princess* is darker than that of *Love's Labour's Lost*. The resistance of Tennyson's princess is considerably harder to wear down than that of the King of Navarre; moreover, the themes of death and disease that haunt only the later Shakepearean comedies are present throughout Tennyson's poem in Ida's intention to kill all men who enter the female sanctuary, in the prince's strange seizures, and in the final bloody battle.

The poem, in other words, approaches the mood of such a play as *The Winter's Tale*. The Prologue contains hints that Tennyson set out to suffuse his medley with the spirit of Shakespeare's late comedies. In this frame the guests gathered at Sir Walter Vivian's are preparing to improvise their story. Lilia, of whom Princess Ida in the narrative is the transparent double, asks for a tale of the sort men exchange on winter nights at college. Sir Walter in reply nods at the narrator, one of the seven young men to tell the tale, a poet and clearly the mask of Tennyson himself:

> 'He began,
> The rest would follow, each in turn; and so
> We forged a sevenfold story. Kind? what kind?
> Chimeras, crochets, Christmas solecisms;
> Seven-headed monsters only made to kill
> Time by the fire in winter.'
> "Kill him now,
> The tyrant! kill him in the summer too,"
> Said Lilia; "Why not now?" the maiden aunt.
> "Why not a summer's as a winter's tale?
> A tale for summer as befits the time. . . ."
>
> (Prologue, ll. 196–205)

The Shakespearean allusion in this exchange is picked up shortly thereafter when the poet, ready to launch into the first section of the tale, comments "we should have him back/Who told the 'Winter's Tale' to do it for us" (Prologue, ll. 230–231). In a very early draft of the poem this poet had been named "Arthur Clive," the "one central star" of a college set called The Shakespeare. His physical attributes — rough soft hair, swarthy skin, prematurely wrinkled face — all suggest Tennyson himself.[13] And indeed *The Princess* does begin in the festive spirit of *Love's Labour's Lost* ("an amusing entertainment . . . a musical comedy, a revue, a trifle for the amusement of a select audience at a Christmas house party")[14] and gradually darkens toward the mood of near tragedy, as in *The Winter's Tale.*

Tennyson is thus engaging in a contest of genres, exploring the range of comedy in two directions. He makes his reader aware of this purpose both in the tale's plot and in the competition between the poem's alternating styles — narrative versus song.

Tennyson's competitive plan emerges when we examine the changes from edition to edition in this, his most heavily altered major work. The poem only reached its definitive state after having undergone four distinct revisions. The first edition in 1847 contained 3,016 lines of blank verse in a Prologue, seven cantos narrated in turn by each of the seven young college students, and an Epilogue that returns to the setting of the Prologue. Scattered throughout the framed narrative were five lyrics, also in blank verse, sung by the women at the entertainment "Between the rougher voices of the men,/ Like linnets in the pauses of the wind" (Prologue, ll. 237–238). In the second edition (1848) Tennyson made few changes in the text but added the dedication to Henry Lushington. Of the many omissions and additions in the third edition (1850) the most important was the introduction of six new songs to be sung by the ladies. But unlike the five songs of the first edition which were in the blank verse of the narrative that enclosed them, these new songs were in varied meters and were inserted between cantos. While Tennyson had considered placing songs between the cantos in the first edition, he did not actually do so until the third, and then only because "the public did not see the drift."[15]

---

[13] See unpublished Tennyson paper No. 196 now in the Houghton Library of Harvard University as cited on p. 94 of Jerome Buckley's *Tennyson: The Growth of a Poet* (Cambridge, Mass., 1960). Buckley's is the first general criticism to rely on the Houghton's unpublished notebooks and papers, which were not available until a few years ago.

[14] G. B. Harrison, *The Complete Works of Shakespeare* (New York, 1952), p. 394.

[15] *Memoir*, I, 254.

In addition he placed an Interlude between Cantos IV and V. In the fourth edition (1851) he introduced the strange, repetitive descriptions of the prince's "weird seizures." And in the fifth and essentially final text of 1851 he inserted the fifteen lines in the Prologue beginning with "O miracle of women." [16]

From this history of the text it is possible to advance two generalizations. First, each revision intensifies further the contrast between the poem's styles and between the sexes associated with the styles; thus the women's lyrics of the third edition are in varied meters rather than in the blank verse of those in the first edition which perhaps blended in too smoothly with the blank verse of the male narrative. And the lyrics are intercalated in the third edition where they were not in the first, so that no one can mistake the sharp contrast that Tennyson intends. Second, by the insertion in 1851 of the prince's seizures, the role of the prince is accentuated so that he becomes at least as important a figure as Princess Ida, if he does not become the center of focus completely. Thus Tennyson intentionally dilutes his apparent subject, the establishment of a women's academy and a concern with women's rights, in order to give submerged, highly personal interests a freer play. It would seem pertinent to explore each of these changes in turn.

If, as suggested earlier, we compare *The Princess* with Shakespeare's comedies, we see that Tennyson's male narrators, the brash young collegians who in their recourse to burlesque and satire do not take the tale very seriously, approximate the style and mood of Shakespeare's early comedies. And the lovely lyrics that the ladies, linnets in the wind, pit against the mock-heroic voices of the male narrative capture the sad farewells of Shakespeare's late period, the insubstantial pageants through which his late heroines move.

The contest of voices and genres emerges with a final resonance in the Conclusion. After the tale has been given its rambling, random narration by the seven collegians and the ladies, Sir Walter

---

[16] The changes are conveniently summarized in George O. Marshall, Jr., *A Tennyson Handbook* (New York, 1963), pp. 110–111. An abbreviated explanation appears on p. 115 of the Cambridge *Works*.

asks the poet, the first of the seven speakers, to "dress the tale up poetically" (an apt description of Tennyson's later rococo style), to give it a final form. The poet ponders the request:

> Yet how to bind the scatter'd scheme of seven
> Together in one sheaf? What style could suit?
> The men required that I should give throughout
> The sort of mock-heroic gigantesque,
> With which we banter'd little Lilia first;
> The women — and perhaps they felt their power,
> For something in the ballads which they sang,
> Or in their silent influence as they sat,
> Had ever seem'd to wrestle with burlesque,
> And drove us, last, to quite a solemn close —
> They hated banter, wish'd for something real,
> A gallant fight, a noble princess — why
> Not make her true-heroic — true sublime?
> Or all, they said, as earnest as the close?
>
> (Conclusion, ll. 8–21)

But the assembled company cannot find a compromise of styles, and the poet must become an intercessor in the "little feud" that breaks out between the "mockers" and the "realists" (Conclusion, ll. 23–28).

Which of these attitudes and styles more essentially conveys Tennyson's evaluation of his material is an open question among the poem's readers. The "Tory member's elder son" at the poem's conclusion looks across the straits to condemn the "mock-heroics" of revolutionary France: "Too comic for the solemn things they are,/ Too solemn for the comic touches in them" (Conclusion, ll. 67–68). This critique perhaps sums up the judgment of many readers who feel the attempt to combine genres an ill-fated one. Outside of Shakespeare the results of such fusion in English poetry have rarely been happy; certainly Tennyson's attempts at a like mixture in his late "Elizabethan" plays are not very successful. On the evidence of the anthologies of Victorian literature, however, the elegiac mood of the female lyrics has clearly evoked a more lasting poetry. If Tennyson's own words, again spoken during his last days, can be made to apply to a work he had written half a cen-

tury before, his own preference seems clear: "Burlesque, the true
enemy of humour, the thin bastard sister of poetical caricature,
would, I verily believe, from her utter want of human feeling, in
a revolution be the first to dabble her hands in blood." [17] Such a
late deprecation of mockery as a human attitude may shed some
light on the purpose of the Conclusion to *The Princess*, which is
otherwise difficult to explain. The Tory member's elder son (a
figure, to be sure, etched in some irony) identifies the chaos of
"Revolts, republics, revolutions" with the schoolboy immaturity of
mock-heroic raillery.

But this contest between styles, between the moods of early and
late Shakespearean comedy, between elegiac lyric and burlesque
narrative mode, is not an end in itself: it represents a sexual competition — the contest between male story and female song.

In its most blatant form this sexual competition in all its symmetry is easy to summarize. The prince who desires to marry
Princess Ida must first overcome several obstacles: his own emotional imbalance and metaphysical anxiety represented in part by
his seizures; the princess' legitimate complaints against a world in
which women can be treated as little more than chattel; and her
pride and apparent cold-heartedness related to the passivity of her
father. Through her instinctive love of a child the princess escapes
from her murderous isolation and enters into true womanhood, as
the prince is cured of his seizures. In the course of the narrative
several alternate positions on the proper role of women in the
world emerge: the male chauvinism of the prince's father (V, 147–
164); the strict egalitarianism of the princess as defined by her
handmaiden, Lady Psyche (II, 154–164); and finally the prince's
long epithalamic rhapsody which presumably represents the "wisdom" of Tennyson, the Victorian teacher, celebrating "true marriage" in which

> "Each fulfils
> Defect in each, and always thought in thought,
> Purpose in purpose, will in will, they grow,
> The single pure and perfect animal,

[17] *Memoir*, II, 423.

The two cell'd heart beating, with one full stroke,
Life."   (VII, 285–290)

The marriage of the prince and the princess in the harmony they now share presages a future golden age founded in the right relationship of man and woman.

But such a plot summary — or even one that would take peripheral details into account — does scant justice to Tennyson's subtle and original exploration of traditional comic patterns to resolve a topical Victorian dilemma. Once more, I suspect, he is following Shakespeare as a model with a good deal of consciousness.

Northrop Frye has summarized the mythos of New Comedy, the comedy whose leading early exponents were Menander, Plautus, and Terence, as contrasted to the Old Comedy of Aristophanes. It is the Menandrine tradition that Shakespeare and, for that matter, most Western writers of comedy work in:

What normally happens is that a young man wants a young woman, that his desire is resisted by some opposition, usually paternal, and that near the end of the play some twist in the plot enables the hero to have his will. In this simple pattern there are several complex elements. In the first place, the movement of comedy is usually a movement from one kind of society to another. At the beginning of the play the obstructing characters are in charge of the play's society, and the audience recognizes that they are usurpers. At the end of the play the device in the plot that brings hero and heroine together causes a new society to crystallize around the hero, and the moment when this crystallization occurs is the point of resolution in the action, the comic discovery, *anagnorisis* or *cognitio*.[18]

The *cognitio* is sometimes frustrated through several acts by the insistence of the characters upon disguising themselves. This convention is just one more indication of the unnatural, fallen world that the comic spirit seeks to redeem. There are two kinds of maskers in Shakespearean comedy — those who wear masks to fool others or just to stay alive in the dangerous world of comedy until the moment of *cognitio*, of unmasking (Imogen in *Cymbeline*), and those who are masked from themselves but do not realize it until

[18] Northrop Frye, *Anatomy of Criticism* (Princeton, 1957), p. 163.

approximately the moment of *cognitio* (Posthumus). The former sometimes wear a physical mask (disguise themselves as young boys or shepherds, for example), while the mask of the latter is psychological and moral, a self-deception about their own true natures.[19] The audience laughs with the first kind of masker; it laughs at the second. Sometimes the masking suggests an important sexual involution in the society — girls disguise themselves as boys and men endow themselves with female traits. The classical Shakespearean instance of this pattern, especially of the brilliant sexual confusion engendered by comedy's fallen world, is *Twelfth Night*.

This formula encompasses the plot of *The Princess* except for one important variation. And it might be profitable to explore what is conventional about Tennyson's "festive comedy" as a preparation for the discussion of what is apparently not.

The Princess does concern the successful maneuvering of a young prince to possess the girl of his choice with marriage as a tonic resolution. The device in the plot that brings the hero and heroine together is Melissa, Blanche's daughter. Tennyson insists upon the importance of the child to both plot and theme: "The child is the link thro' the parts as shown in the songs which are the best interpreters of the poem." [20] And the pattern of masking also seems to apply, for the prince represents the first variety of masker. In order to win his princess from her resolve and in order to stay alive in the confines of her sanctuary which it is death for man to enter, he and his two companions must disguise themselves in women's clothing, and they do so in the specific context and language of theatrical performance — of "masque" and court "pageant" (I, 192–195). The danger of such deception is obvious: the masker can easily be discovered. The prince becomes "half oblivious of my mask" while awed by the princess' vision that

> . . . was, and is, and will be, are but is,
> And all creation is one act at once,
> The birth of light; but we that are not all,
> As parts, can see but parts, now this, now that,

[19] See Joseph Summers, "The Masks of *Twelfth Night*," *University of Kansas City Review*, XXII (1955), 25–32.

[20] *Memoir*, I, 254.

And live, perforce, from thought to thought, and make
One act a phantom of succession.   (III, 307–312)

Insofar as the princess can deliver to the prince a vision of future psychic coherence which can replace his shattered self, to that extent is he tempted to drop his disguise.

But the princess must entirely strip her own mask of self-deception before the prince can feel it safe to discard his assumed role. The princess is the second kind of masker, one who wears a mask and does not know it. Trapped within a narcissism that makes her "see . . . herself in every woman else" (III, 94), especially in Lady Blanche and Lady Psyche, she "blinds the truth" from herself and from all who follow her. The barrier she has set up against men is the frigid cry of the self-contemplating soul, a *noli me tangere* that in its turn causes and excuses the unhealthy, immature masking of the prince.

This egoism finds its appropriate trope in the frustrating sexual circularity of the three ladies (again Tennyson's "three sisters"), especially in the princess' attachment to Lady Psyche. Psyche and Blanche are extensions of Ida, two contending sides of herself who are jealous of each other and bicker throughout the narrative. Melissa reports one such quarrel between the "two arms," Psyche and Blanche, and the "head," Ida (III, 16–23). In the fragmented personalities of both the prince and the princess one is reminded of the dissociation of the faculties that Hallam had described as characteristic of the age in his review of Tennyson's *Poems, Chiefly Lyrical.*

Ida's narcissism resolves itself when she is finally able to release Lady Psyche, her image in the pool of death, from her fixed stare. The scene turns on Cyril's (one of the prince's companions) wooing of Lady Psyche:

> When Cyril pleaded, Ida came behind
> Seen but of Psyche; on her foot she hung
> A moment, and she heard, at which her face
> A little flush'd, and she past on; but each
> Assumed from thence a half-consent involved
> In stillness, plighted troth, and were at peace.
>   (VII, 63–68)

(One is, by so deft a touch, reminded ironically of the more confident modern expressions of superiority to Tennyson, "the stupidest" of English poets.) [21] It is only after she has released Lady Psyche that Ida can enter fully into a love for the prince. Once the *cognitio* has taken place at the narrative's conclusion, the prince can place into true perspective her masking which has necessitated his own "pranks of saucy boyhood" (VII, 319–323).

From such an analysis it is possible to appreciate how successfully Tennyson has reworked the traditional formulas of comedy. But in one important way *The Princess* does not seem to fit the mythos of comedy that modern theorists have described. If we return to Frye's discussion of New Comedy, we see that frequently the obstacle to the union of the hero and the heroine is paternal:

New Comedy unfolds from what may be described as a comic Oedipus situation. Its main theme is the successful effort of a young man to outwit an opponent and possess the girl of his choice. The opponent is usually the father (*senex*), and the psychological descent of the heroine from the mother is also sometimes hinted at. The father frequently wants the same girl, and is cheated out of her by the son, the mother thus becoming the son's ally. The girl is usually a slave or courtesan, and the plot turns on a *cognitio* or discovery of birth which makes her marriageable. Thus it turns out that she is not under an insuperable taboo after all but is an accessible object of desire, so that the plot follows the regular wish-fulfillment pattern. . . . Whether this analysis is sound or not, New Comedy is certainly concerned with the maneuvering of a young man toward a young woman, and marriage is the tonic chord on which it ends. The normal comic resolution is the surrender of the *senex* to the hero, never the reverse.[22]

Now it must be admitted that this outline with its emphasis upon *senex* does not sound very much like the plot of *The Princess*. But the difficulty is only a superficial one. The fathers in *The Princess* can be seen as crucial obstacles to the marriage of the lovers, even if not in a conventional sense, for it is they who are responsible for the sickness of the state at the opening of the narrative. The rela-

---

[21] Auden, *Selected Poems of Tennyson*, p. x. "There was little about melancholia that he didn't know; there was little else he did."

[22] Northrop Frye, "The Argument of Comedy," *English Institute Essays* (New York, 1948), pp. 58–59.

tionship of the sexes within society is an unbalanced one, and Tennyson takes pains to emphasize the legitimate grievance of Ida and her vassals (V, 364–379). The absurdity of this relationship is in part symbolized by a childhood marriage compact between the prince and Ida arranged by the two families: the fact that the marriage bond was sealed in "the year in which our olives failed" would seem to indicate the hostility of nature to arranged marriages. In addition, the opposed fathers are partly to blame for the psychological flaws in their respective offspring. The prince's seizures and his fluttery search for Thanatos, especially during the final battle, are tied by implication to the overbearing bluster of his father, while the aggressive pride of the princess clearly stems from the weakness of her father, a "garrulous," "oily," "little dry old man, without a star" (I, 116). Indeed the perfect symmetry of the opposing principles throughout the poem, especially the polarity of the prince and his father on the one hand and princess and her father on the other, suggests to the reader that he is observing not only a confrontation of character, but once again a barely disguised psychomachy. For the playful contest between male and female adumbrated in the "frame" moves into the romantic comedy in the body of the poem to mirror the psychic struggle within Tennyson himself.

Both the princess and the prince express different sides of Tennyson. Many of his readers have noticed his habitual practice of having a character who is a version of himself besieged by "Two Voices." In such early works as "The Two Voices" and "The Palace of Art" or the even earlier "Sense and Conscience" Tennyson's divided self is heard through the debate of disembodied voices. In the later narrative works these voices are transformed into "parabolic" characters in dramatic conflict. In *The Princess*, Tennyson's trial attempt at the long narrative poem, the poet appears *both* as a voice in the frame (the earlier practice) and in the divided disguise of the tale's heroine and hero (the first instance of his later practice). (The distinction becomes clear if we parallel the early and late uses of these devices in the Arthurian material. The Prologue to the 1842 "Morte d'Arthur" ["The Epic"] has within it the same

autobiographical voice of the poet as does *The Princess*. As a result
Tennyson establishes a counterpoint between the Prologue and enclosed narrative of Arthur's death. In the 1859 "The Passing of Arthur" the same tale without any Prologue is strictly parabolic, part
of the larger "parabolic drift" of what Tennyson conceived to be
the dramatic war between soul [Arthur] and sense [Guinevere].)

The first "voice" of *The Princess*, the princess herself, has pre-
viously been mentioned as a late version of the *anima*, the female
projection of the poet's soul. Her egoism approaches the haughti-
ness of the soul ensconced in her mountainous Palace of Art and of
Lady Clara Vere de Vere among her halls and towers. In her song
at the conclusion of *The Princess* she beautifully recapitulates that
by now familiar descent of the proud artist's psyche from the
heights in Tennyson's early poetry into the valley of Victorian
love in his later work:

> "Come down, O maid, from yonder mountain height.
> What pleasure lives in height (the shepherd sang),
> In height and cold, the splendor of the hills?
> But cease to move so near the heavens, and cease
> To glide a sunbeam by the blasted pine,
> To sit a star upon the sparkling spire;
> And come, for Love is of the valley, come,
> For Love is of the valley, come thou down
> And find him. . . ."   (VII, 177–185)

Her intimation of the future as she announces it to the prince in a
passage already quoted (III, 307–312) is a noble vision of "The
Poet" of 1830 ("The poet in a golden clime was born, with golden
stars above"), for she is indeed an artist, "that strange poet-princess
with her grand/ Imaginations" (III, 256–257) whom the prince almost despairs of winning. She is renowned for her awful odes,

> odes
> About this losing of the child; and rhymes
> And dismal lyrics, prophesying change
> Beyond all reason.   (I, 139–142)

But she most interestingly embodies a Tennysonian voice in her
response to the song "Tears, Idle Tears." The princess and her
company have just descended from the mountain precipice, the

topological equivalent of her magnificent vision of the human race's future which she has announced from the Promethean height. Now the company has come once more into the valley; the peace of twilight settles over the weary climbers as they settle down in relaxation before the evening meal. And then a maid steps forth upon request, stroking her harp, and fashions "Tears, Idle Tears," one of the loveliest gems of the language. The princess' response to the song, spoken "with some disdain," follows:

> "If indeed there haunt
> About the moulder'd lodges of the past
> So sweet a voice and vague, fatal to men,
> Well needs it we should cram our ears with wool
> And so pace by. But thine are fancies hatch'd
> In silken-folded idleness; nor is it
> Wiser to weep a true occasion lost,
> But trim our sails, and let old bygones be,
> While down the streams that float us each and all
> To the issue, goes, like glittering bergs of ice,
> Throne after throne, and molten on the waste
> Becomes a cloud; for all things serve their time
> Toward that great year of equal mights and rights.
> Nor would I fight with iron laws, in the end
> Found golden. Let the past be past, let be
> Their cancell'd Babels; tho' the rough kex break
> The starr'd mosaic, and the beard-blown goat
> Hang on the shaft, and the wild fig-tree split
> Their monstrous idols, care not while we hear
> A trumpet in the distance pealing news
> Of better, and Hope, a poising eagle, burns
> Above the unrisen morrow."   (IV, 44–65)

The maiden's song and the princess' response to it convey the dialectic of sorrow and hope within Tennyson during the 1840's. And the passage also suggests that Tennyson may have been as aware as any modern critic of the distinction between his "melancholia" before Hallam's death and his "mourning" after it. The distinction that the princess makes between "fancies hatch'd/ In silken-folded idleness" and "a true occasion lost" certainly argues for such an understanding on Tennyson's part. Furthermore the passage sheds light on Tennyson's attempt to turn away at this time from the "moulder'd lodges" of his poetic past. The "idle tears" that he has wept for the Marianas, the Oenones, the Ladies of Shalott in the past are "fatal to men," and perhaps to manhood. They are like the "sweet . . . and vague" voices of the sea fairies, of the Sisters of the Hesperides, and of the inhabitants of Lotosland. And like Ulysses who has acted before as the mythic antiphonal voice to Tennyson's lotos-eaters, the princess too feels the need to "cram our ears with wool/ And so pace by." Her insistence that we "trim our sails, and let old bygones be" even more explicitly picks up the nautical imagery of "Ulysses," Tennyson's other poem of this period that attempts to deal positively with the "true occasion lost" of Hallam's death. Once more, as in the *In Memoriam* we have already examined, Tennyson relies on the argument of Hallam's "Theodicaea" to shore up his own ruins. The refusal of the princess to "fight with iron laws in the end/ Found golden" recalls both the "iron dug from central gloom" that man can "shape and use" (*In Memoriam*, CXVIII) and Hallam's theodicy of compensation from which they both in part may stem.

Thus far the argument has concentrated on the princess, who I feel represents one side of Tennyson's personality, one of the two contesting, oxymoronic "voices" in the poem. The prince just as clearly represents the other. Like Ida, he possesses the soul of a poet, if of a less terrible sort. His seizures parallel similar trances Tennyson experienced throughout his life. Such doubts about the solidity of his own existence had sent him as a boy racing through the countryside calling out his own name, and he had treated them as the subject of several poems since the early play, *The Devil and the Lady*. The prince is unable to distinguish shadow from substance. At times of crisis he is suddenly visited by the feeling that everything he sees is but the "shadow of a dream," for all things are and are not. These seizures express the relative impotence of his finely tuned sensibility in a world requiring heroic action. As Tennyson described him in the *Memoir*, "his too emotional temperament was intended from an artistic point of view to emphasize his comparative want of power." [23]

[23] *Memoir*, I, 251.

This "emotional temperament" that Tennyson is in the late 1840's trying to devalue was the source of his own early power. And the prince in the poem is visited by the "gleam" that in one form or another had always led the young Tennyson into his mystical communions with the nature of things. Thus when the prince hears the whispers and the shrieks of the wild woods together with a voice that cries, "Follow, follow, thou shalt win" (I, 99), the reader is reminded of the young Tennyson "spreading my arms to the wind, and crying out 'I hear a voice that's speaking in the wind,' and the words 'far, far away.' . . ." [24] And the shadowy unreality of the self that the prince feels recalls the description of the young Tennyson's same obstinate questionings of sense and outward things, alluded to in "The Ancient Sage":

> for more than once when I
> Sat all alone, revolving in myself
> The word that is the symbol of myself,
> The mortal limit of the Self was loosed,
> And past into the Nameless, as a cloud
> Melts into heaven. I touch'd my limbs, the limbs
> Were strange, not mine — and yet no shade of doubt,
> But utter clearness, and thro' loss of self
> The gain of such large life as match'd with ours
> Were sun to spark — unshadowable in words
> Themselves but shadows of a shadow-world.
>
> (ll. 229–239)

But in *The Princess* the mystical loss of self is not wholly admirable, as it tends to be in Tennyson's later "gleam" poems; the prince's inability to tell shadow from substance here points to a deficiency in manliness, a "comparative want of power." The defect of the princess' Faustian intellectuality is thus complemented by that of the prince's Werther-like hypertrophy of feeling.

It is primarily the "weird seizures" that make the prince relevant to Tennyson's biography, for with their addition in 1851 the prince becomes both as important a figure as the princess in the dramatic conflict and a firm expression of one side of Tennyson's personality. In this character Tennyson for the first time presents his read-

[24] *Ibid.,* p. 11.

ers with a male lover who convincingly dramatizes his own search for psychic integration and stability.

This emergence becomes clear if we compare the prince to figures whom he resembles out of the earlier poetry. The Lady of Shalott suffers from a like confusion of substance and shadow; "half sick of shadows," she attempts to enter the world of conventional reality and thereby dies. The prince represents Tennyson's attempt to come to terms with this same problem in a male protagonist. When we do find a male narrator in an early love poem, as in "The Day Dream" whose situation and characters foreshadow those of *The Princess*, the poem's protagonist, an unrealized, nondescript figure who enters the dangerous thicket of sense, contrasts sharply with the concretely individualized prince.

This comparison of the princess and the prince, then, supports the claim introduced at the end of the last chapter: *The Princess* is a key poem because it dramatizes Tennyson's shift from female to male autobiographical protagonists. But it is a transitional work, for the princess is still a "voice" of Tennyson, even though balanced very clearly by the voice of a male lover who is recognizably autobiographical.

The balance is reinforced by three interpenetrating sets of image patterns: the familiar contrast between East and West; a new geographical opposition of North and South; and a floral contrast of lily and rose that makes its first attenuated appearance in *The Princess* and will turn up more prominently in "Maud" and the *Idylls of the King*. Each of these patterns is embedded in the male narrative before it receives recapitulation in one of the female songs.

The earlier discussion of "The Hesperides" has indicated that Tennyson typically sets up an East-West dualism to signify the conflict between strenuous, forward-looking activity and his fascination with states of quiescence and erotic self-indulgence: the movement from West to East captures the spirit of the former, from East to West the eros of the latter. This polarity is hinted at in *The Princess* too. Princess Ida, when describing an ideal future in which woman will be free and prearranged marriage contracts will be outlawed, makes her vigorous movement from West to

East by seeking a model for her own independence in that of an Eastern queen:

> "And as to precontracts, we move, my friend,
> At no man's beck, but know ourself and thee,
> O Vashti, noble Vashti! Summon'd out
> She kept her state, and left the drunken king
> To brawl at Shushan underneath the palms."
> (III, 210–214)

The prince's reply confirms the intention of symbolic import: " 'Alas, your Highness breathes full East,' I said" (III, 215). Thus also in the lullaby "Sweet and Low" the mother lulls her child to sleep by singing of the father who will be blown to him by the "Wind of the western sea," who will come in "Silver sails all out of the west."

In addition to this East-West opposition Tennyson establishes a pattern of North-South movement which is more pronounced. The prince is a child of the North, for the Northern star shone upon his cradle and the country he comes from, while not identified, is quite explicitly a Northern one. Traditionally and in this poem, the North is associated with a masculine wildness and barbarous aggressiveness; accordingly the princess addresses the prince in his disguise as "you young savage of the Northern wild" (III, 230), and the prince's father is the exaggerated embodiment of this Northern hardness. The princess on the other hand is from the South, a place of wantonness and passion from which "came murmurs of her beauty" (I, 35) to the prince. One of the signs of sexual dislocation in the poem is the fact that the prince and the princess do not really express the nature of their respective origins at the poem's opening. The princess' mannish arrogance is out of keeping with the soft clime from which she comes; the prince on the other hand, hardly the representative of Northern virility, is "blue-eyed, and fair in face,/ Of temper amorous as the first of May,/ With lengths of yellow ringlets, like a girl" (I, 1–3).

The song that summarizes the implications of the North-South division is the prince's "O Swallow, Swallow, flying, flying south."

After the princess has thrown her angry, disdainful rebuke at the maiden who has sung "Tears, Idle Tears," she asks the prince, still in female disguise, for a melody to counteract the mournful languor of the maiden's lyric:

> "Know you no song of your own land," she said,
> "Not such as moans about the retrospect,
> But deals with the other distance and the hues
> Of promise; not a death's-head at the wine?"
>
> (IV, 66–69)

When he replies with a lyric (the songs in the poem are usually sung by women), his female disguise once more accentuates the sexual dislocation the North-South opposition represents as he tries to "ape" the "treble" of the female voice. The song itself is a plea for the integration and interpenetration of the Northern and Southern principles. North and South are first placed side by side; the prince, remembering the swallow who flies South, tells it to take a message to his love in the South. The bird, an ideal messenger, is acquainted with each region and knows "That bright and fierce and fickle is the South,/ And dark and true and tender is the North" (IV, 79–80). The Northern prince then asks to be enfolded within the Southern princess:

> "O, were I thou that she might take me in,
> And lay me on her bosom, and her heart
> Would rock the snowy cradle till I died!"
>
> (IV, 84–86)

And then the prince gives the true reason he wishes to journey South, the immersion in a love, in a wantonness that will make his resurrection in his true Northern home possible:

> "O, tell her, Swallow, that thy brood is flown;
> Say to her, I do but wanton in the South,
> But in the North long since my nest is made."
>
> (IV, 90–92)

Finally he announces the major theme of the poem, that only love can harmonize the seemingly opposed principles of North and South:

"O, tell her, brief is life but love is long,
And brief the sun of summer in the North,
And brief the moon of beauty in the South."

(IV, 93–95)

Only through such a union can the "two-cell'd heart beating, with one full stroke" be effected.

One is tempted to speculate about Tennyson's motives for choosing a new North-South polarity to complement the East-West opposition of his earlier work and for creating, consequently, the symbolic diagonal movement that characterizes *The Princess*. One reason may be that while the East-West confrontation does not carry with it a pronounced sexual emphasis, the North-South one does. The North of the "sun of summer" is associated with a male aggressiveness and the South of the "moon of beauty" with a feminine passion. As the North-South opposition suggests, the prince's and the princess' deviation from the natural tendencies of their respective sexes defines the weakness of each.

A final pattern of imagery, the floral contrast of rose and lily which is thoroughly developed in "Maud," makes a tentative appearance in *The Princess*. Both Lilia and Ida are associated with the rose of aggressive passion. Lilia, the modern woman, is "a rosebud set with little wilful thorns" (Prologue, l. 153); as Ida in the narrative she is occasionally decked in crimson. The lily of innocence and passiveness is associated with Melissa, Blanche's "lily-shining child." The opposition of rose and lily thus signifies Ida's early belief in the discontinuity between womanhood and childhood, her immature desire to "lose the child, assume the woman" (I, 36). Through her natural love of a child she eventually learns that "distinctive womanhood" means the absorption of "the child-like in the larger mind" (VII, 268), the intertwining of the lily and the rose. The floral imagery achieves its final effects in the song "Now Sleeps the Crimson Petal, Now the White." This catalogue of interpenetrating natural forces at evening that parallel and encourage human love suggests that, though the symbolic values of the narrative are muted, the princess is now prepared to embrace the lily and to accept love:

> Now folds the lily all her sweetness up,
> And slips into the bosom of the lake.
> So fold thyself, my dearest, thou, and slip
> Into my bosom and be lost in me.

(ll. 171–174)

The polarity of East-West, North-South, lily-rose thus all point to a sexual dislocation or a character imbalance that must somehow be set in order. Only when this has been accomplished within each can the prince and princess set themselves to each other, "like perfect music unto noble words." Only then can they prepare for that "statelier Eden" to come, the "crowning race of humankind," that "higher race" *In Memoriam* also prophesies (CXVIII). But in this process it is clearly the woman whose will is crucial, the princess who by exorcising her own immaturity establishes the psychic equanimity of the prince. At the conclusion of the tale, in the prince's description of his mother's wisdom, Ida merges into the mother herself, Tennyson's wife-mother upon whose resolve all happiness depends. The prince though cleansed is still ultimately dependent for his manhood upon the princess, as he realizes when he says in the penultimate line of the narrative, "Accomplish thou my manhood and thyself" (VII, 344). To return to the foil of Shakespearean comedy discussed earlier in this chapter, in accomplishing the prince's manhood, the princess has been transformed from the heroine of an early festive comedy (Katherina in *The Taming of the Shrew* or Beatrice in *Much Ado about Nothing*) into a "true heroic — true sublime" figure resembling the Imogens, Hermiones, and Marinas of Shakespeare's winter's tales.

The Princess with its conclusion in reconciliation and marriage stands in contrast to the earlier Tennyson poems that end with the frustration of love ("Oenone," "Locksley Hall," or "The Lady of Shalott"). But it can be even more interestingly compared to earlier poems that do end with marriages of sorts, "The Two Voices" and *In Memoriam*. The married couple linked by a child that the speaker of "The Two Voices" sees from the window saves him from the voice of despair within, but he is still a spectator of the joy he contemplates, an exile like the later Enoch Arden. The Conclusion of *In Memoriam* brings us closer to that of *The Princess*, though an important distinction remains. The speaker's climactic trance-vision of Hallam, a death and transfiguration, is similar in both conception and language to the prince's serious illness, contracted during the final battle, from which the princess nurses him back to physical and psychic health. After touching the spirit of Hallam, the reborn speaker of *In Memoriam* can disperse his grief with an epithalamium; the poem becomes in Tennyson's own words "a sort of Divine Comedy, cheerful at the close." [25] But the wedding the speaker celebrates is someone else's, that of Edmund Lushington and Tennyson's sister, Cecilia. The speaker is still outside of the magic circle of happiness; the integration of the single personality while associated with marriage does not yet take place within it. Marriage, this time of real people, merely stands as an appropriate symbol for such psychic rebirth. The progression reaches its close in *The Princess* where the defect in each human being is corrected by the marriage of that person: the Lady of Shalott and the speaker of "The Two Voices" have, as it were, joined themselves to a mate with whom they can become "the single pure and perfect animal."

The connection of this progression to Tennyson's biography is obvious. After a parting in 1839, Tennyson apparently renewed his correspondence with Emily Sellwood in November 1849. Their formal engagement was resumed in April 1850, and they were married on June 13. With the publication of *In Memoriam* and Tennyson's acceptance of the laureateship in that same year, 1850 did indeed become the *annus mirabilis* of his life.

A final point to be made about *The Princess* concerns the correlative movement it describes in the lover and artist, represented respectively by the prince and the poet who narrates the tale. If the prince's seizures and his inability to tell shadow from substance are symptoms only of a sexual dislocation, the poet in the Prologue has a parallel aesthetic difficulty. The story is to be told by the seven

<hr>

[25] Quoted from a conversation with James Knowles in A. C. Bradley, *A Commentary on Tennyson's "In Memoriam"* (London, 1915), pp. 237–238.

collegiate youths, "seven and yet one, like shadows in a dream" (Prologue, l. 222). In the *Memoir* Tennyson specifically connects this line with the prince's seizures, especially with the following description of them:

> And like a flash the weird affection came,
>
>   *   *   *
>
> I seem'd to move in old memorial tilts,
> And doing battle with forgotten ghosts,
> To dream myself the shadow of a dream.
>   (V, 466–470)[26]

The reason for this association becomes clear in the Conclusion. After the seven young men and ladies have spun out their narrative and sung their lyrics in a "random scheme," it is up to the poet "to bind the scatter'd scheme of seven/ Together in one sheaf" (Conclusion, ll. 8–9). At this point the quarrel among the young men and ladies concerning the proper style for the tale breaks out. The poet's task of mediation, of binding the random sheaves into a coherent work of art, becomes the frame's aesthetic correlative to the princely lover's quest to bind together the fragments of his shattered psyche through love. Poet and lover, of imagination all compact, are exemplars of a single creative principle.

The poet's task, like the lover's, is to mediate between sense and soul, a movement that has a crucial sexual component. Both must entwine lily and rose, constantly reverse their directions between Eastward and Westward motion, integrate within themselves the masculine North and the feminine South like the swallow of the prince's song. The poet who describes this complex vacillation must move as on a "strange diagonal" between the mockers and the realists, between the narrative and the lyric mode, making "the man be more of woman, she of man." This bisexual zigzag movement of the artist is as dangerous a journey psychically as any prince in romance may undertake, and it is a dialectic that invites constant frustration and misunderstanding by one's audience:

> And I, betwixt them both, to please them both,
> And yet to give the story as it rose,

[26] *Memoir*, I, 251.

I moved as in a strange diagonal,
And maybe neither pleased myself nor them.
                    (Conclusion, ll. 25–28)

But the poet's diagonal is an enlightened and an enlightening one: it imitates and heightens the swallow flight of Western love, the male and female principles between which all lovers move in the complex interplay of sense and soul.

CHAPTER VI

The Holy Power of Love

W HEN Tennyson published *Maud, and Other Poems* in
1855, the public and most professional critics were taken
aback by the laureate's strange new volume. The title poem's seem-
ing endorsement of the unpopular Crimean War and war in general, the metrical experiments, the apparent backsliding into mor-
bidity were all something of a disappointment to an audience prepared to meet a new work by the author of *In Memoriam* with a
grateful sympathy.[1] But whatever the surface appearance of retro-
gression or radical change, "Maud" completes the sexual metamorphosis of the Tennysonian protagonist that has been traced in the
last three chapters. The movement from the female autobiographical *anima* to the male deserted lover who, despite Tennyson's pro-
testations, resembles the poet reaches its uneasy, tentative close.
The narrator of "Maud" is more exclusively at the center of his
poem than was the prince who shared the center of *The Princess*
(uncertainly and belatedly, as a result of the 1851 additions) with
Princess Ida; Maud is a shadowy wisp compared to the substantial,
concretely realized princess.

"Maud" also resolves the generic duel of *The Princess*, which

[1] For a description of the way "Maud" was received see Charles Tennyson, *Tennyson*, pp. 286–290, and for Tennyson's strenuous defense of this, his
favorite among his works, *Memoir*, I, 393–406.

Tennyson had subtitled *A Medley* precisely because of its clash of lyric and narrative sections. In "Maud" the lyric is subsumed into the more objective form of a "Monodrama," "where successive phases of passion in one person take the place of successive persons." [2] For the poem provides a literary instance of the biological principle that ontogeny recapitulates phylogeny: the evolution of "Maud" into its final form captures in microcosm the larger history of Tennyson's attempted progress from subjective lyricism to more objective forms.

The poem grew out of the lyric "O that 'twere possible," two versions of which, dated 1833, are in the J. M. Heath *Commonplace Book*. Similarities between the second version in the Heath manuscript and sections of *In Memoriam* suggest that this lyric could have been Tennyson's immediate poetic response to Arthur Hallam's death.[3] It was originally printed as Tennyson's contribution to *The Tribute*, an isolated volume published for the benefit of a partially deaf and blind minister. Thereafter it went generally unnoticed because Tennyson did not include it in his 1842 *Poems*. It had long been believed, largely on the basis of Aubrey de Vere's detailed account in Hallam Tennyson's *Memoir* (I, 378–379), that Sir John Simeon, Tennyson's friend and neighbor on the Isle of Wight, was the prime mover behind "Maud." Impressed by the lyric while looking through a copy of *The Tribute* in 1854, Simeon

[2] Cambridge *Works*, p. 198, from a conversation between Tennyson and James Knowles.

[3] George O. Marshall, Jr., "Tennyson's 'Oh! That 'Twere Possible': A Link between *In Memoriam* and *Maud*," *PMLA*, LXXVIII (1963), 225–229. Marshall demonstrates that Tennyson uses similar language to describe the grief of a lover over a dead woman and to convey his grief at the loss of Hallam in *In Memoriam*. In such a shift, "Tennyson sought an emotional release by objectifying his emotions." Thus in the monodrama, Tennyson develops the motif of the ghost of the departed (Hallam and later Maud) as both consoling good spirit and haunting evil spirit.

The important Heath *Commonplace Book* contains copies of Tennyson's poetry collected by an Apostle friend, John Moore Heath. A flyleaf inscription indicates that Heath began copying the poetry on September 24, 1832; he probably stopped doing so by 1835. Charles Tennyson describes both the Heath-Tennyson friendship and the contents of the *Commonplace Book* in "Tennyson Papers: II. J. M. Heath's 'Commonplace Book,'" *Cornhill Magazine*, CLIII (1936), 426–449.

was supposed to have urged upon Tennyson the idea of composing a longer poem about it and another fragment (the "shell lyric" of "Maud," II, ii). But Ralph Wilson Rader has recently shown that Simeon could not have played the seminal role traditionally assigned to him, because "Maud" existed in some form before Tennyson ever met him. It is nevertheless true that Simeon's suggestion to build a longer poem around "O that 'twere possible" was "the final act of midwifery" that brought "Maud" to birth in 1855.[4] Whatever Simeon's role, the elegiac sorrow brought on by the death of Hallam, as it moved through "O that 'twere possible" and *In Memoriam*, gradually became in "Maud" a man's dramatized passion for a woman.

The shift in sex of Tennyson's deserted lover and the attempted movement from a lyrical mode to objective drama reflect and reinforce each other. Tennyson's projection of himself into a male rather than female lover indicates the maturity of one who has partially mastered his sorrows; the new detachment from the passion of his earlier despair has made for a self-identification that is unambiguously, if not very aggressively, male. And this control facilitates the complex, sustained combination of poetic elements that we usually associate with longer objective forms, with narrative or drama. On the whole, Tennyson's gift is at its most powerful a lyrical one; as a narrative poet and as a dramatist he stands far below Shakespeare. Yet in "Maud" the broad and melodramatic plot structure, the characterization that is psychologically more interesting than usually supposed, the several subtly interwoven image patterns — these elements and their interplay make for a richness of effect that has sometimes been underestimated.

The essential model for "Maud," as Tennyson himself stated, is *Hamlet*:

[4] *Tennyson's "Maud": The Biographical Genesis*, pp. 2–10. Christopher Ricks has confirmed Rader's reevaluation of Simeon's role with proof, based on an examination of the earliest drafts of Hallam Tennyson's *Memoir* at the Tennyson Research Center in Lincoln, that the reference to Simeon's role in the composition of "Maud" was an interpolation of Hallam Tennyson into the account of Aubrey de Vere rather than the statement of de Vere him-

This poem of "Maud, or the Madness" is a little Hamlet, the history of a morbid, poetic soul, under the blighting influence of a reckless-ly speculative age. He is the heir of madness, the egoist with the makings of a cynic, raised to a pure and holy love which elevates the whole nature, passing from the height of triumph to the lowest depth of misery, driven to madness by the loss of her whom he has loved, and when he has at last passed through the fiery furnace, and has recovered his reason, giving himself up to work for the good of mankind through the unselfishness born of a great passion.[5]

But "Maud" also has a structural kinship with Tennyson's subjective comedy, *The Princess*. My discussion of *The Princess* has stressed the importance of the two fathers as obstacles to the marriage of the prince and princess. While the fathers do not intentionally stand in the way of the union, their complementary vices become internalized in their offspring; and *The Princess* charts the gradual healing of these interior flaws in the prince and princess. In treat-ing the mythos of Tennyson's tragedy, we might begin by con-centrating on the tragic equivalent of the comic obstacle. Instead of the *senex* that poses a threat in *The Princess*, tragedy offers the hostility of *nemesis* to the protagonist. According to Northrop Frye once more, tragedy like comedy imitates an *agon*, a struggle between two contesting forces. The source of the *nemesis* that sets out to destroy the protagonist through the agency of an antagonist varies from tragedy to tragedy: it may be a god who decrees the tragic action (Athene in *Ajax*, Aphrodite in *Hippolytus*, or God the Father in *Paradise Lost*); it may be an invisible force discover-able only by its effects (*Tamburlaine*); it may be a ghost (*Ham-let*); or it may be an event that has taken place before the opening of the play's action (*Oedipus Rex*).[6]

The *nemesis* of "Maud" working through an antagonist resem-bles the comic obstacle in *The Princess*. Once more the antagonist is "split," as it were, into two fathers, and the protagonist (this time not split as in *The Princess*) must fight to overcome both an

self ("Tennyson's 'Maud,'" letter to the *London Times Literary Supplement*, Dec. 31, 1964).
[5] Quoted in Eversley *Works*, IV, 270–271.
[6] *Anatomy of Criticism*, pp. 206–223.

external opponent and the internalized vice of the father. Once again a brother (though much more crucially than in *The Princess*) stands in the way of the lover and his beloved, a fact which necessitates a climactic battle. Once more the lover is driven into a kind of death as a result of this duel and is nursed back to health by the spirit, if not as in *The Princess* the actual person, of the beloved. Because the fable of "Maud" details the narrator's reaction to three distinct personalities (or "sets" of personalities) — two fathers, the beloved's brother as a father surrogate, and the beloved herself — we can take them up in turn, suggesting the ways in which their treatment at times echoes Tennyson's treatment of their counterparts in his comic medley, *The Princess*.

The Princess has already demonstrated Tennyson's inclination to split the function of the father as obstacle in comedy, but there is an apparent difference between the split in *The Princess* and the division in "Maud." [7] While in *The Princess* the fathers are equally guilty for what is wrong with their offspring, in "Maud" Tennyson insists on a more overt moral distinction between the fathers. Maud's father is not quite a murderer of the protagonist's father, but there is a link in the narrator's mind between his father's death

[7] The "splitting" of *nemesis* as it occurs in "Maud" receives a relevant elaboration in modern applications of psychoanalytical insights to literature. The Oedipal pattern of tragedy that Ernest Jones (*Hamlet and Oedipus* [New York, 1958]) describes in *Hamlet* is even more obvious in "Maud." The primary difference between *Hamlet* and "Maud" in this context is that while both works "split" the image of the father and/or father surrogate despised as murderous usurper, only *Hamlet* splits the mother into female counterparts. In the related characters of Gertrude and Ophelia, Shakespeare effects "the splitting of the mother image which the infantile unconscious effects into two opposite pictures; one of a virginal Madonna, an inaccessible saint towards whom all sensual approaches are unthinkable, and the other of a sensual creature accessible to everyone" (*Hamlet and Oedipus*, p. 97).

Maud, like many of Tennyson's women, combines attributes of wife and mother. What is remarkable about *The Princess* and "Maud," in both of which maternal love is constantly applauded, is the complete absence of living mothers for the pairs of protagonists in both poems; only the fathers are alive or important in the action. But both Ida and Maud are associated with the mother of the male protagonist and as the poems move toward their close merge into practical identity with the mother. Thus the "splitting" of the mother image that Freud and Jung felt to be a characteristic, though not absolutely necessary, motif in the Oedipal pattern is absent in "Maud" (as, for instance, it is in *Oedipus Rex* itself).

by suicide after "a vast speculation had fail'd" and the parasitic success of "that old man, now lord of the broad estate and the Hall,/ Dropt off gorged from a scheme that had left us flaccid and drain'd" (I, 19–20). The "gorging" of Maud's father connects him to the whole series of vile and disgusting animals (rats, "little breed," "long neck'd geese," serpents, the fly, "the lean and hungry wolf") scattered through the first section of the poem as examples of the murderous commercial spirit of the age and of man's ageless Yahoo nature. As the protagonist is drawn into a love for Maud, the animal imagery gradually becomes less repulsive. As animals are associated with Maud herself, they become the attractive and the gentle "milk-white fawn," the peacock, the "bird with a shining head," and the "dove with the tender eye" of the poem's middle and final sections.[8]

Such an association with animal voraciousness certainly separates Maud's father from the victim that the protagonist's father is. Yet the speaker feels equivocal about his own father because of his madness, which was partially responsible for the early death of the speaker's mother, and whose taint the speaker fears may have been passed down to him.

The two fathers represent both the external and the internal evil that the protagonist must overcome, although ultimately the hero's own father is more dangerous to him as an agent of *nemesis* than Maud's father. For while the latter's dishonest speculations represent the evils of a corrupt society, the madness that the "morbid, poetic" speaker falls into is his heritage from his own father. The sick-souled inner man and the "recklessly speculative age" are thus as much different sides of a comprehensive rottenness in the state of England as are the "honest" but weak father of the speaker and the predatory strong one of Maud.

In *The Princess* the malign influence of the two fathers was critical, but strangely enough they had no role to play as actively hostile barriers. One of the ways they prevented a mature balance be-

[8] John Killham, "Tennyson's *Maud* — The Function of the Imagery," in *Critical Essays on the Poetry of Tennyson*, pp. 219–235, examines the imagery of stones, animals, and flowers in the poem.

tween prince and princess was through the marriage compact they had arranged which the princess had found anathema. In "Maud" a similar bond has been sealed between Maud's father and the speaker's on the day of Maud's birth, but this bond is presented attractively. Only the death of the speaker's father has broken this compact which, blessed by Maud's dying mother, was meant to unite the two families in lasting harmony:

> But the true blood spilt had in it a heat
> To dissolve the precious seal on a bond,
> That, if left uncancell'd, had been so sweet;
> And none of us thought of a something beyond,
> A desire that awoke in the heart of the child,
> As it were a duty done to the tomb,
> To be friends for her sake, to be reconciled.

$$(I, 727-733)$$

Tennyson, we see, is completely ambivalent about such compacts: arranged marriages, especially for commercial purposes, are the objects of his almost obsessive scorn;[9] yet marriages settled at birth, even if for commercial purposes, prepare the couple for eventual happiness because their love can flower in the innocence of childhood and thus be exempt from the lubricity of sexual encounter. Tennyson's divided feelings receive their classic expression in *The Princess* where a serious criticism is leveled at the "baby troth" of the prince and the princess concluded by their fathers for reasons of state; at the same time the conclusion of the poem proves that this arranged marriage at any rate was a wise one. And in "Maud" a love between the narrator and Maud that had grown during their childhood had been prepared for by a marriage bond contracted by their fathers at Maud's birth. The language of the fathers ("Well, if it prove a girl, the boy/ Will have plenty") sug-

---

[9] See the two "Locksley Hall" poems, "Edwin Morris," "Aylmer's Field," and the later plays. Ralph Wilson Rader in *Tennyson's "Maud": The Biographical Genesis* ties this lifelong hatred to Rosa Baring's rejection of Tennyson's suit during the late 1830's. In 1838 she married instead Robert Shafto, a wealthy Lincolnshire landowner, presumably at the behest of "trustees" who urged the marriage upon her after having discouraged her attachment to the relatively poor poet. Tennyson thereafter frequently returned to the evil of arranged marriages and marriages of convenience as a theme in his poetry.

gests the commercial emphasis of the arrangement, and yet the reader is clearly meant to approve of it:

> Maud's dark father and mine
> Had bound us one to the other,
> Betrothed us over their wine,
> On the day when Maud was born;
> Seal'd her mine from her first sweet breath!
> Mine, mine by a right, from birth till death!
> Mine, mine — our fathers have sworn!
>
> (I, 720–726)

In *The Princess* the only final physical hindrance to the prince is not either father but Ida's brother, Arac, who leads the forces against the prince in a climactic battle. So too in "Maud," the speaker's father is dead and Maud's father never actually appears in the action (though he is "now lord of the broad estate and Hall"). His role as external *nemesis* is actively taken over by his son,

> that dandy-despot, he,
> That jewell'd mass of millinery,
> That oil'd and curl'd Assyrian bull
> Smelling of musk and of insolence.
>
> (I, 231–234)

And certainly in the narrator's eyes, Maud's father who has driven his own father to suicide and the brother who stands between himself and Maud are one in their malignity:

> Why sits he here in his father's chair?
> That old man never comes to his place;
> Shall I believe him ashamed to be seen?
> For only once, in the village street,
> Last year, I caught a glimpse of his face,
> A gray old wolf and a lean.
>
> (I, 466–471)

The "gray old wolf and a lean" presents no immediate threat; it is the brother who must be dealt with in the narrator's generation, especially since Maud "cannot but love" this "rough but kind" brother.

Similarly in *The Princess* Arac's words mean "thrice" more to Ida than do those of her father. The prince does not wish to fight for the princess. But as soon as he comes into the presence of Arac and hears the martial song by which Arac walks forth, the prince is roused by the "wild beast of force" that he feels stirring within. While the trance that the prince falls into when wounded in the tournament results in the happy resolution of *The Princess*, the duel in "Maud" has a doubly tragic outcome. It leads to the death of Maud's brother and it necessitates the narrator's flight to France, in effect his final separation from Maud who dies during his exile and period of madness.

The duel illustrates the manner in which a crime of sense quite readily degenerates into a crime of malice, a progress that Tennyson had already defined in the 1842 "The Vision of Sin." In that vehement repudiation of the sensuous and sensual which extends the attack initiated by "The Palace of Art," an old "gray and gap-tooth'd man as lean as death" appears in the mind of a narrator and fills a ruined inn with a macabre drinking song shot through with the same self-hatred and cynicism that embitters the narrator of "Maud." After the song a new image enters the narrator's head of men and horses pierced with worms among whom a voice cries:

> "Behold! it was a crime
> Of sense avenged by sense that wore with time."
> Another said: "The crime of sense became
> The crime of malice, and is equal blame."
>
> (ll. 213–216)

"Maud" repeats this movement from a crime of sense into a crime of malice (a transformation that in the mythic poems will become the alliance of Venus and Mars) through a variation of the floral opposition that Tennyson has explored in *The Princess*. In "Maud" the lily represents the shrinking reticence of the lover and the rose his potential for aggressive passion, the two sides of his personality that he projects onto Maud. When he is quiet and reserved she is described as a lily, and when he is torn by his passion she is identified with the rose; for Maud has both "a garden of roses" and "lilies fair on the lawn." [10] And the rose is associated with both the

[10] E. D. H. Johnson, "The Lily and the Rose: Symbolic Meaning in Tennyson's *Maud*," *PMLA*, LXIV (1949), 1222–1227. Rader associates the imagery of the rose with Rosa Baring, the lily with Sophy Rawnsley, and the

West and the South of luxuriant quiescence and wanton sexual abandon in earlier poems:

> Rosy is the West,
>   Rosy is the South,
> Rosy are her cheeks,
>   And a rose her mouth.
>
> (I, 575–578)

The climax of the poem occurs during the "Come into the garden, Maud" section when "the soul of the rose went into my blood," when the rose of passion becomes, under the pressure of the narrator's frustration, the rose of malice and blood. It is as a result of this transformation that the fatal duel takes place and the brother is killed, just as in "The Vision of Sin" God makes his terrifying presence felt as "an awful rose of dawn." In the passion that the lover feels for Maud, Tennyson dramatizes his now confirmed division between sense and love, between what the "awful rose" alone comes to represent and what the balanced "lily and rose in one" can mean as a salvation for man.

Maud thus encompasses the alternate possibilities of her sex. She can suggest woman both at her most destructive and at her most creative for the man she infuses with her spirit. When the narrator first thinks about her, he remembers only her almost "dead perfection." The only thing that saves Maud from being "faultily faultless, icily regular, splendidly null" is

> . . . a chance of travel, a paleness, an hour's
>   defect of the rose,
> Or an underlip, you may call it a little too
>   ripe, too full,
> Or the least little delicate aquiline curve in a
>   sensitive nose,
> From which I escaped heart-free, with the least
>   little touch of spleen.
>
> (I, 84–87)

"Queen Lily and Rose in one" with Emily Sellwood. For Rader, Tennyson's less purely physical love for Emily Sellwood represents his recovery from the excessively physical passion that he lavished upon Rosa Baring, and the poem is, among other things, a disguised description of this transformation (*Tennyson's "Maud,"* pp. 81–121).

The narrator initially imagines her as a temptress, the Tennysonian female serpent who wishes to reduce him to a slave:

> What if with her sunny hair,
> And smile as sunny as cold,
> She meant to weave me a snare
> Of some coquettish deceit,
> Cleopatra-like as of old
> To entangle me when we met
> To have her lion roll in a silken net
> And fawn at a victor's feet.
>
> (I, 212–219)

This same image of the lion entrapped by passion appears in the description of Maud's garden gate whereon "A lion ramps at the top,/ He is claspt by a passion-flower" (I, 495–496). But the verb "claspt" is already ambiguous, for the embrace may just as well supply a fierce emotional sustenance as a venomous entanglement. And as the poem develops, the grasp is seen to offer the former. For the spirit of the lion is in the martial song that the speaker overhears Maud singing in her garden, "A passionate ballad gallant and gay,/ A martial song like a trumpet's call" (I, 165–166). When the speaker begins to recover from his madness through the realization of "a hope for the world in the coming wars," the lion manifests his final affirmative connotation. Maud appears to the speaker

> in a dream from a band of the blest,
> And spoke of a hope for the world in the coming wars –
> "And in that hope, dear soul, let trouble have rest,
> Knowing I tarry for thee," and pointed to Mars
> As he glow'd like a ruddy shield on the Lion's breast.
>
> (III, 10–14)

Once more as in *In Memoriam* and *The Princess* the communion with the beloved achieved during a trance-vision is a prelude to recovery.

Maud's exemplification of woman's indispensable generative role achieves its full traditional resonance when the speaker at the height of his sensual ecstasy identifies Maud with Eve in her garden. He wonders whether he is

> haunted by the starry head
> Of her whose gentle will has changed my fate,
> And made my life a perfumed altar-flame;
> And over whom thy darkness must have spread
> With such delight as theirs of old, thy great
> Forefathers of the thornless garden, there
> Shadowing the snow-limb'd Eve from whom she came?
>
> (I, 620–626)

Maud's "thornless garden" with its suggestion of Edenic self-control and order is pitted throughout the poem against the "dark wood" of prolix, wild imaginings in which the speaker lives. (One is reminded again of Tennyson's lifelong hatred of "the lavish profusion . . . in the natural world . . . from the growths of the tropical forest to the capacity of man to multiply.") While Maud's garden holds out to the disturbed narrator the stability and the love he has been denied in his life, the murderous duel between lover and brother occurs in "the red-ribb'd hollow behind the wood." And when Maud's brother is dead, the narrator understands the archetypal meaning of Maud's garden as the Eden from which he has now been forever expelled:

> What is it, that has been done?
> O dawn of Eden bright over earth and sky,
> The fires of hell brake out of thy rising sun,
> The fires of hell and of hate.   (II, 7–10)

The earlier Tennysonian garden of sensuous delight has given way to the garden of spiritualized love, blasted though it be by the fires of hate.

For the central idea of "Maud," as Tennyson emphasized in his notes to the poem, is the "holy power of Love."[11] Henry Van Dyke, who best captures the violent energy with which Tennyson threw himself into his famous readings of "Maud," was

amazed at the intensity with which the poet felt, and the tenacity with which he pursued, the moral meaning of the poem. It was love, but not love in itself alone, as an emotion, an inward experience, a selfish possession, that he was revealing. It was love as a vital force, love as a part of life, love as an influence — nay, *the* influence

---

[11] *Memoir*, I, 404.

which rescues the soul from the prison, or the madhouse, of self, and leads it into the larger saner existence. This was the theme of "Maud." And the poet's voice brought it out, and rang the changes on it, so that it was unmistakable and unforgettable.[12]

But the "love" of "Maud" has a strange bedfellow, the war in which the lover fights. One of the difficulties with "Maud" ever since its initial hostile reception by a Victorian audience has been "the cause . . . pure and true" which the spirit of Maud urges upon the narrator and which rescues him from his madness. Not only our own recognition of the horrors of modern war but even the contemporary knowledge that the Crimean War was an incredible international "blunder" undercuts the historical and moral effectiveness of Tennyson's conclusion. Tennyson's own rationale for this ending in which he invokes the reasoning of the hero in "Maud" does not really alleviate the reservations one might feel: ". . . the sins of the nation . . . are deadlier in their effect than what is commonly called war, and . . . they may be in a measure subdued by the war between nations which is an evil more easily recognized." [13]

Critics attempting a defense of Tennyson's conclusion have had to rely on various psychological or formalist explanations to counter the poem's embarrassing historical connotations.[14] But considerations of technique are ultimately escapes from an important truth about Tennyson's life and poetry — war did serve as a public release for some of the unresolved conflicts of his inner life. Paden has shown that characters in Tennyson's early poetry rarely allow

[12] "The Voice of Tennyson," *Century Magazine*, XLV (Feb. 1893), 540–541.
[13] *Memoir*, I, 401.
[14] Roy P. Basler, "Tennyson the Psychologist," in *Sex, Symbolism and Psychology in Literature* (New Brunswick, N.J., 1948), pp. 84ff, argues unconvincingly that the narrator's mind is still unbalanced at the poem's conclusion, so that his espousal of the public cause of the Crimean War does not represent a Tennysonian impulse. John Killham, "Tennyson's *Maud* — The Function of the Imagery," pp. 220–221, rejects both ideological and psychological conjectures about the inadmissibility of war as a solution to the speaker's problem. Killham insists rather that the critic's concern is with the dramatic life, with the effectiveness of characterization and the consistency of action, which he proceeds to illustrate in the poem.

themselves aggressive actions without immediate remorse; but heroes committed to larger causes seem exempt from feelings of guilt. Arthur's battles in the "Morte d'Arthur" are fought "for the ordinance of God," the equivalent of a "just" Crimean War.[15] This flight from private aggressions into the safe anonymity of national ones would seem to be an important impulse behind Tennyson's poetry. Of course, one is struck by the fact that the best of the military poems are accounts of or reactions to the death of the hero — an Arthur or a Duke of Wellington; and military disasters rather than victories are usually the occasion of poems that deal with actual battles. The most famous, "The Charge of the Light Brigade" describing how six hundred died because "Some one had blunder'd," appears, appropriately enough, in *Maud, and Other Poems.* It is perhaps misguided to link a short work based upon an important public event with the longer one spun entirely out of the poet's imagination. Still, one is tempted to believe that Tennyson's choice of the doomed charge as a natural subject for poetic treatment indicates that he dimly appreciated the kind of experience the dead Maud is sending her lover to in the Crimean War. (The prince of *The Princess* had been an earlier hero who courted a public death inspired by his love: "Yet she sees me fight,/ Yea, let her see me fall" [V, 505–506].) On the evidence of later poems Tennyson well understood the degree to which love and war are dangerous companions. In "Lucretius," as we shall see, the union between Venus and Mars is obscene and unholy.

But in "Maud" the partnership is creative in that the "holy power" of Maud's love which takes the form of her martial song and call to war rescues the narrator from his madness. While the early sections of the poem hint at her destructive potential, Maud is, finally, unambiguously virtuous; the inability of the narrator to recognize this fact all along is a sign of his incipient madness. For the sexual metamorphosis of the Tennysonian protagonist, reinforced by the shift in genre, mutes the possibility of moral com-

---

[15] *Tennyson in Egypt*, pp. 75–94. Paden once more associates both Tennyson's fear of and attraction to violence with his equivocal feelings for his father.

plexity in Tennyson's women. His projection of himself into a male hero and his attempted curbing of his "female" lyric impulse has made for a strict polarization. Maud is Tennyson's most programmatic evocation of one of these polar types — the saintly, restorative figures who dominate the English idylls. She looks forward to the faithful wife of "Romney's Remorse," the wifely comforter of "Sea Dreams," the nurse of the poor in "Aylmer's Field," and the Annie of "Enoch Arden." But such avatars of Victorian virtue, witnesses to Tennyson's belief in a spiritualized love, have a dark, sensuous sister who remains to be examined.

CHAPTER VII

The Fatal Woman

WHILE cataloguing the "fatal women" of nineteenth-century literature in order to assert their emergence as a pervasive literary type during the second half of the century, Mario Praz does not once mention Tennyson.[1] Such an absence is noteworthy since even Tennyson's contemporaries recognized in his early work a leaning toward dangerous sensuality. Even later, when Tennyson had wrapped himself in the mantle of the Victorian sage, readers would occasionally notice vestigial "fleshly" tendencies in his female portraits. Robert Buchanan in his attack on Morris, Swinburne, and Rossetti saw the whole Aesthetic movement as little more than an offshoot of Tennyson:

. . . it is scarcely possible to discuss with any seriousness the pretensions with which foolish friends and small critics have surrounded the fleshly school, which, in spite of its spasmodic ramifications in the erotic direction, is merely one of the many sub-Tennysonian schools expanded to supernatural dimensions, and endeavouring by affectations all its own to overshadow its connection with the great original. In the sweep of one single poem, the weird and doubtful "Vivien," Mr. Tennyson has concentrated all the epicene force which, wearisomely expanded, constitutes the characteristic of the writers at present under consideration; and if in

[1] "La Belle Dame sans Merci," *The Romantic Agony* (New York, 1956), pp. 187–286.

"Vivien" he has indicated for them the bounds of sensualism in art, he has in *Maud*, in the dramatic person of the hero, afforded distinct precedent for the hysteric tone and overloaded style which is now so familiar to readers of Mr. Swinburne. The fleshliness of "Vivien" may indeed be described as the distinct quality held in common by all members of the last sub-Tennysonian school, and it is a quality which becomes unwholesome when there is no moral or intellectual quality to temper and control it.[2]

But it is also understandable that a modern reader like Praz would not think of Tennyson in connection with the Aesthetic movement or with its dominant female type. It is his sugary Annies and Ediths whom we usually associate with "Tennysonism." One of the ways that the Pre-Raphaelites and the likes of Swinburne and Pater reacted against the poetic hegemony of Tennyson, which was becoming increasingly suspect in advanced literary circles during the 1860's, was to put forth a radically different conception of woman. The Victorian "angel in the house" naturally evoked her polar opposite — the Delores and Faustine of Swinburne, the Lady Lilith and Sister Helen of Rossetti, the Gioconda of Pater's famous description, the Salome of Wilde, to name obvious English examples. Still, as the Buchanan quotation suggests, Tennyson himself forged audacious versions of the Victorian *femme fatale*.

There are many possible reasons for the literary emergence of woman as vampire, as succubus, at this juncture in European intellectual history (her dominance was a European rather than a peculiarly English phenomenon, and in fact the English type was often a sensational imitation of the more genuine figure in Continental, especially French, literature). Fashion is surely one of the explanations. In creating her the artist could indulge in that favorite of *fin de siècle* pastimes, a desire *pour épater le bourgeois*. And the tendency toward radical bifurcation in nineteenth-century thought might well have facilitated the polarization of women into hard and fast categories: Rossetti's Beata Beatrix makes almost obligatory the crystallization of her moral opposite, Lady Lilith; Pater's

[2] "The Fleshly School of Poetry: Mr. D. G. Rossetti," *Contemporary Review*, XVIII (Oct. 18, 1871), 334–350.

androgynous Gioconda, "the head upon which all 'the ends of the world are come,' " has her unfathomable origins both in Leda, Helen of Troy's mother, and in Saint Anne, the mother of Mary.[3] Romanticism in its celebration of infinite energy and the passionate moment would naturally extend its exploration of both man and woman to angelic heights and satanic depths. Finally, the nineteenth century is clearly a time of growing sexual dislocation. While Tennyson's "maiden passion for a maid" and his paeans to Victorian marriage seem comfortably distant from the self-confident decadence of Swinburne, it is possible to read into the sexual confusions of a poem like *The Princess* a forecast of the epicene heroes and heroines of the Aesthetic movement.

John Keats is especially seminal to the nineteenth-century evolution of the *femme fatale*. It is his work that gives play to a penchant for a self-destructive voluptuousness embodied in woman which the Pre-Raphaelites and *Symbolistes* found congenial later in the century;[4] it is his Lamia and La Belle Dame sans Merci that become the prototypes of subsequent maidens who enthrall their palely loitering knights. Clyde de L. Ryals, in an essay to which this chapter is indebted, argues that Tennyson relied primarily on Keats for his fatal women, especially on La Belle Dame sans Merci. After considering the type in the late poetry of Keats, Ryals traces the figure through Tennyson's poetry of the 1830's and suggests that, after vestigial appearances as Princess Ida and Maud as seen by the narrator early in the poem, she never "appear[s] again with the same intensity."[5] I should, however, like to argue that Tenny-

[3] Walter Pater, "Leonardo da Vinci," in *The Renaissance* (London, 1910), pp. 124–125.
[4] Praz, *The Romantic Agony*, pp. 201–203, traces the type from Keats to the aesthetes, from Gautier downward into her general dispersion among the *Symbolistes*.
[5] "The 'Fatal Woman' Symbol in Tennyson," *PMLA*, LXXIV (1959), 438–443. Ryals conceives of his essay as a companion piece to Lionel Stevenson's earlier article, and of the "Fatal Woman" as an inversion of Stevenson's "High-Born Maiden." Enlarging upon Stevenson's Jungian vocabulary, he sees both figures as symbolic of the conflict within Tennyson between a "Romantic" taste for sensuous indulgence and the "Victorian" drive to forge a high moral purpose. The high-born maiden is the "regressive symbol" of this struggle while the fatal woman is the "aggressive" one. Both figures are "soul images" of the poet.

son adapted the type from other sources besides Keats and, more important, that she appears in Tennyson's later poetry with increasing rather than diminishing frequency and intensity, either as fatal woman or as fatal classical goddess.

If Charles Tennyson is correct in his assertion that Tennyson first read Keats after going to Cambridge, Tennyson's source for the fatal woman must have been various. For she makes her first full-blown appearance in Tennyson's adolescent play, *The Devil and the Lady*, and comes forth occasionally in *Poems by Two Brothers* (as Thais in "Persia," Cleopatra in "Antony to Cleopatra," and the serpentine maiden of "Did Not Thy Roseate Lips Outvie"). This is not to deny that Tennyson's female portraits are indebted to the Keatsian lamias once he actually read Keats. It is just that Tennyson's childhood reading in the Elizabethan dramatists, in Milton (he especially liked *Samson Agonistes*), in the Eastern works of his father's library, and in Byron would have been sufficient to influence the type that appears in his adolescent works. If Tennyson's fatal woman owes anything to his predecessors, we are as likely to find a key to her in Elizabethan satanism, filtered through Byron, as in Keatsian sensuousness.

It therefore seems useful to distinguish poems dominated by a Keatsian fatal woman from ones in which we find what may be called her "Byronic" or "Faustian" equivalent. The distinction arises as much from a difference in the quality of the men destroyed as from the fatality of the women's power. Keats' lovers, wanderers in the dreams of their desires, are attracted to maidens whose unearthly charms entrap them. But the doom that the fairy's child and lamia bring to their lovers is not intentional; the inability to achieve union with a mortal is a source of tears and pain for the divine intruders into human affairs.

The Byronic or Faustian hero, a more aggressive and energetic quester than Keats' languishing knight, is frequently driven by a pride of intellect that renders him vulnerable to the wiles of a woman or goddess who actively tries to frustrate his aspiration toward godhead. Mario Praz describes the historical discreteness of the Byronic hero and the fatal woman in a way that implies their complementary movement through nineteenth-century literature. "The function of the flame which attracts and burns," he suggests, "is exercised, in the first half of the century, by the Fatal Man (the Byronic hero), in the second half by the Fatal Woman; the moth destined for sacrifice is in the first case the woman, in the second the man." [6] Whatever the truth of this characterization for the century as a whole, in Tennyson's poetry the two figures at times appear side by side. When Tennyson creates a male protagonist confident of his intellectual or magical powers, he is accompanied and undermined by a destructive female, either human or divine. It is this pattern rather than the Keatsian one that Tennyson explores in his later poetry.

The earliest example of this combination is also its serio-comic apogee. *The Devil and the Lady*, an unfinished blank verse drama that Tennyson wrote when he was fourteen, was excluded from the 1827 *Poems by Two Brothers* because it was "too much out of the common for the public taste." [7] The play dramatizes an aged magician's attempt to avoid cuckolding by his beautiful young wife. Because he must go on a journey Magus, the sorcerer, summons up the Devil to protect his wife's virtue from the suitors he expects may try to seduce her. But the Devil knows all about the treachery of women and attempts to evade the task:

> A very decent, tolerable task —
> Outwit a woman — that were difficult;
> Place in one scale my graceless Devilship —
> Her ladyship in t'other — weigh us both,
> I do much fear me lest her ladyship
> Untwist my meshes, foil my purposes
> And by her subtile intricacy of wit
> Mislead my choicest, noblest, nicest guile.
> The very fuscous and embrownéd cheek
> Of his Satanick Majesty might blanch
> Before a woman's art.   (p. 5)

Before leaving on this first Tennysonian sea journey, Magus, al-

---

[6] *The Romantic Agony*, p. 206.
[7] *Memoir*, I, 23. All references to *The Devil and the Lady* will be to the Charles Tennyson edition.

though suspicious of his wife, vows to Amoret that his belief in her faithfulness is the compass that keeps him to the pole of optimism:

> For in life's passage would I always look
> Upon that side of things which shewest fairest,
> Else were our days but one continued gloom,
> A weary scene of surmise and mistrust.
>
> (p. 11)

As soon as he has gone Amoret rages against the "shrunken, sapless, wizen Grasshopper" that consumes the green promise of her youth. The Devil now has his hands full, sending Amoret to bed and in disguise receiving her various lovers in her place. When Magus returns unexpectedly, his journey halted by bad weather, the would-be lovers hide, the Devil mocks his victims, and Magus meditates on the meaning of life.

The Devil and Magus are clearly "two voices" of the same personality. Once he is fully aroused to the treachery of Amoret for which his cynicism has already prepared him, the Devil is himself thrown into a familiar metaphysical quandary. He does not know whether Amoret is shadow or substance, a question that we have seen to be a *Leitmotiv* in Tennyson's poetry:

> Oh! Amoret! there is no honour in thee;
> Thou art the painted vision of a dream,
> Whose colours fade to nothing, a fair rainbow
> Mocking the tantalized sight, an airy bubble,
> O'er whose bright surface fly the hues of light,
> As if to hide the nothingness within.   (p. 19)

The confusion of Amoret's surface beauty and inner hollowness soon after widens into doubt about the reality of the universe:

> O suns and spheres and stars and belts and systems,
> Are ye or are ye not?
> Are ye realities or semblances
> Of that which men call real?
> Are ye true substances? are ye anything
> Except delusive shows and physical points
> Endow'd with some repulsive potency?
> Could the Omnipotent fill all space, if ye
> Or the least atom in ye or the least

> Division of that atom (if least can dwell
> In infinite divisibility) should be impenetrable?
>
> (p. 24)

The epistemological breakdown that Amoret generates turns into a Jonsonian comedy of humors as the various suitors, who do not know Amoret's true nature, are gulled by the Devil disguised as Amoret.

Before the manuscript ends abruptly, Magus returns to describe the "Black shapes" that had cut short his sea journey:

> The seas divide and dim Phantasies
> Came thronging thickly round me, with hot eyes
> Unutterable things came flitting by me;
> Semblance of palpability was in them,
> Albeit the wavering lightnings glitter'd thro'
> Their shadow'd immaterialities.   (p. 62)

The combat that Magus wages against the black shapes clinging about his boat ends in his triumph. This victory contrasts sharply with the moral defeat that the Devil has suffered in his cynical despair at the "shadow'd immaterialities" of Amoret and the universe. After the Devil reveals the assault by the suitors on Amoret's virtue to his Prospero-like master (the generous Devil does not mention Amoret's willingness to betray Magus), the aged necromancer associates the assault of the wooers with the dark spirits he has had to overcome during the ocean voyage:

> And they would pluck from th' casket the sole gem
> Of mine affections, taint its innocent lustre,
> And give it back dishonour'd, they would canker
> My brightest flower, would muddy the clear source
> Whence flows my only stream of earthly bliss;
> Would let the foul consuming worm into
> The garner of my love.   (pp. 64–65)

He then distinguishes between "Boyhood's passionless tranquillity" in which it is possible for a human being to keep a natural mind "warm and yielding,/ Fit to receive the best impressions" and the "rude breath of dissipation" that blights the atmosphere of manhood. Through the magic power of his art Magus has been able to keep the disillusionment of the Devil at bay — indeed, the Devil acts as a sacrificial victim for the willed innocence of Magus. But the reader, like the Devil, knows the truth that Magus will not admit — his "brightest flower" is already cankered. The foul consuming worm is within Amoret herself; she is both flower and worm.

We do not know what Magus' response would have been to his recognition of this first and in some ways most interesting of Tennyson's destructive ladies. For it is only in the youthful *The Devil and the Lady* that we hear under the dramatic mask of age the two voices of Tennyson, the Devil's voice of despair and Magus' voice of hope, contesting the nature of the universe conceived of as a woman. And the treachery of Amoret, the play would imply, is the key to which of the voices is closer to the truth. To see what Magus' informed reaction to the reality of Amoret would have been, we may examine the awakening of later Faustian necromancers to other Amorets.

When Tennyson did enter Cambridge and did, on the evidence of the 1830 and 1833 volumes, absorb the influence of Keats, Magus and the Devil combine into a single vulnerable lover in the presence of inaccessible women. As we have seen above (pp. 41–42) there is a wide psychological range to the Lilians, Madelines, and Margarets as they are lyrically wooed, but they are all unattainable. And at least one of them, the Keatsian Eleänore, is actually dangerous to the mind that contemplates her mysterious reserve:

She cannot partake of man's feelings: she is impervious not only to love's arrows but also to life. By seeking her out and gazing on her, the poet feels that he can become somewhat like her — sterile, and lost in contemplation. For Tennyson, Eleänore is *the* fatal woman: she is that powerful figure who traps the minds of all men who gaze on her; but she gives nothing. She merely accepts their votive offerings and receives their admiration only with a slight smile which cannot be comprehended. She is neither human nor divine, but an inhabitant of the dream world of the poet's mind:

> Far off from human neighborhood,
>   Thou wert born, on a summer morn,
> A mile beneath the cedar-wood.[8]

[8] This description by Ryals does full justice to Eleänore. See "The 'Fatal Woman' Symbol in Tennyson," p. 439.

In the 1833 volume the avenging sister of "The Sisters" and the disdainful maiden of "The May Queen" are attempts to transform the lyric portraits into narrative tales of destructive maidens.

It is to be noticed, however, that Tennyson's women do not begin to get monstrously vicious until he tries to turn away from a poetry of sense. The women in the volumes of the 1830's with the few exceptions noted are harmless enough even if they are inaccessible. The "Lady Clara Vere de Vere" of 1842, though a weak poem, marks a turning toward extremes of cruelty. The lady, a "great enchantress" who enjoys shattering "a country heart/ For pastime" is more arbitrarily tyrannical than any woman we have encountered before this. And for the first time the "I" of a Tennyson love poem is actively hostile toward such a woman. Realizing that Lady Clara is "sickening of a vague disease," the speaker feels only disdain for such a female enigma; he does not find it fascinatingly attractive as did the worshipper of Eleänore.

After the 1842 volumes when the fatal woman appears she does so with increasing virulence. While Princess Ida and Maud skirt close to the abyss of the type before being rescued into maternal saintliness at the conclusion of the poems in which they appear, it is in the evolving *Idylls of the King* that Tennyson confirms his polarization of woman into saint and *femme fatale*. The Enid of the 1857 *Enid and Nimuë: The True and the False* is a paragon of redemptive womanhood, just as the Nimuë (the "Vivien" to come) of the second idyll is Tennyson's most deliberate experiment in the "fleshly" mode. With the addition of Elaine and Guinevere to either side of the balance in the 1859 *Idylls of the King* the extreme division receives its most systematic and coherent expression. While this careful precision is blurred in the subsequent growth of the *Idylls* toward the twelve of traditional epic projected in the 1842 Prologue to "Morte d'Arthur," the severe contrast of sacred and profane love, of woman as ministering angel and destructive fury, is one of the key structural elements even in the completed work. We might therefore attempt at this point to trace the naturalistic passion of an Isolt who joins herself in adulterous union with Tristram in "The Last Tournament"; or to describe the ugliness of soul beneath the glittering exterior of an Ettarre who cynically betrays her youthful devotee in "Pelleas and Ettarre." But perhaps it would be best to concentrate upon *the* Tennysonian paradigm of an all-corrupting sensuality and slander disguised by the beautiful body of a woman, the character of Vivien.

As the Buchanan quotation above might suggest, "Merlin and Vivien" (the later version of "Nimuë") has been read as Tennyson's attempt to go Swinburne one better (although *Poems and Ballads* did not appear until 1866), as what Benjamin Jowett called Tennyson's "naughty" idyll. In the scene during which Vivien first attempts to wind herself around Merlin, one does have a prefiguration of the serpentine *femme fatale* and of other Aesthetic tendencies becoming apparent in the 1860's:

> And lissome Vivien, holding by his heel,
> Writhed toward him, slided up his knee and sat,
> Behind his ankle twined her hollow feet
> Together, curved an arm about his neck,
> Clung like a snake.   (ll. 236–240)

Because of Vivien's blatant lubricity the idyll has sometimes been taken as an allegory that depicts the undermining of intellect (Merlin) by sense (Vivien). In such a reading "Merlin is the type of the skeptical intellect which can discern the true spiritual king and enlist in his service, and therein perform the mighty works, but which is not spiritual itself, and is thus exposed to the snares of Sense." [9] This would explain the declension whereby Vivien makes her successful assault on Merlin only after Arthur, the "true spiritual king" has repulsed her "flutter'd adoration." But Paull Baum has convincingly shown the many inconsistencies that arise when this idyll is read even "parabolically" as shadowing the war between intellect and sense.[10] Both Vivien and Merlin are many things: Merlin, for one, is not primarily the victim of Vivien's sensual allurements but rather of her flattery. Vivien's corruption of the word is the important intellectual thrust that has as debasing an effect upon Mer-

---

[9] Frederick S. Boas, "Tennyson and the Arthurian Legend," in *From Richardson to Pinero* (New York, 1937), p. 218.

[10] *Tennyson Sixty Years After* (Chapel Hill, 1948), pp. 179–181.

lin's already shaken confidence in the solidity of this world as the
appeal of her body which by itself he might have resisted.

Merlin is, indeed, a later Magus, a Faustian old man whose magical control of the world around him depends upon his confidence
in its substance. Magic has in Merlin's age become a way to hold
on to a love that in youth came to him as a matter of course:

> "Full many a love in loving youth was mine;
> I needed then no charm to keep them mine
> But youth and love."   (ll. 544–546)

But he is less fortunate in his illusions than Magus: when Vivien
first approaches Merlin after having been repulsed by Arthur, he,
unlike Magus, is already convinced of the hollowness of the universe about him and of the canker within *his* Amoret. It is this cynicism that renders him "tolerant of what he half disdain'd" and
which makes him accept the venomous flattery he does not really
believe. The great melancholy he then falls into drives him, like
the mad speaker of "Maud," to exile in Brittany where Vivien begins in earnest to wean from him a secret charm. With it, as he has
told her in a moment of indiscretion, she may enclose whom she
pleases within the four walls of a hollow tower. Finally, "over-
talk'd and overworn," he yields the charm to her only to have her
use it on him. Like other Tennysonian figures immured within a
twilight state, he is imprisoned within a hollow oak, lying as dead,
"lost to life and use and name and fame."

Vivien, the ultimate Faustian fatal woman, thus gradually assumes the dimensions of a metaphysical terror. In the poetry of the
1830's after he had absorbed the influence of Keats, Tennyson's
commitment to a personal lyricism tended to stress the sensuous
particularity of a Keatsian Eleänore and to mute the cosmic symbolic significance that Amoret had embodied in his youthful drama.
It was only when he moved away from the lyric mode to Arthurian legend with its archetypal resonances that the notion of woman
as cosmic destructive principle became pronounced once more. As
a blighted Amoret had stood for a hollow cosmos, Vivien carries
within her the germs of universal corruption. Bearer of profound
disillusionment and psychic death, Tennyson's fatal woman gives

voice to his recurring fear that decay and death may be the essential, unredeemable law of all existence. In such a widening significance she gradually moves toward the condition of myth to become the dark antiphonal divinity to Tennyson's God of Love, the fatal goddess of the classical poems.

CHAPTER VIII

From Fatal Goddess to a God of Love

Two poems of Tennyson's 1830 volume, "Nothing Will Die" and "All Things Will Die," open in their very titles the dialogue of contrary voices that was to express one of his obsessive themes — the tragic inevitability of change and of human mortality. The "passion of the past," the desire to fix in art moments of departed joy, arose from a need both to deny and to pay grudging heed to ineluctable change. Such moving lyrics as "Tears, Idle Tears" and "Break, Break, Break" capture the sorrow which remembered days that are no more could make rise in the heart and gather to the eyes of the poet. But it was the crushing personal instances of mutability — the death of a father, a friend, or a son — that could transform a free-floating lyrical melancholy into the intense and all-inclusive mourning of works like *In Memoriam* and "Demeter and Persephone." A running down of "all things" was the resonant message that Tennyson's priestess Sorrow could hear echoing out from the death of Arthur Hallam; that meaningless snuffing out of a single life, she felt, looked forward to the extinction of the human race and to the apocalyptic destruction of the earth itself:

"The stars," she whispers, "blindly run;
A web is woven across the sky;
From out waste places comes a cry,
And murmurs from the dying sun."
(*In Memoriam*, III)

Tennyson's major poetry tries to come to terms with this "dying sun," to reconcile the fact of decay and death with the beneficent God in whom he yearned to believe; his work may thus be read as a lifelong struggle to justify the ways of a God of Love to himself and to his fellow Victorians. While the intellectual design of his theodicy was not startlingly new, Tennyson did convey his vision in the powerful imaginative structures that we associate with a major poet. I should like in this chapter and the next to sketch that deepening vision as it formed itself in the elegiac dignity, the allusiveness, and the dramatic concreteness of myth. For Tennyson's classical and Arthurian poems, taken as a body, pit against one another goddesses who through the instrumentality of change and human mortality frustrate man's eros toward them and a God of Love who has devised these very instruments to draw man's immortal soul toward Him.

Tennyson's earliest confrontation of eternal deities and a mortal hero appears in "The Hesperides," the fascinating work that has been treated briefly in Chapter III. In their song that the Carthaginian commander Hanno hears while sailing along the western coast of Africa, the three Hesperidean Sisters ask their father Hesperus, the evening star, to help them keep awake the dragon who guards the sacred tree of the Hesperides lest Heracles, "one from the East," successfully steal an apple from it as his eleventh labor. G. Robert Stange in the standard critical explication sees the work as Tennyson's early parable of the artist's secret life which must be actively defended against the destructive prying of the world. The Hesperidean song defines "the spiritual conditions under which the poetic experience comes to life," and pays tribute to the rare genius of the poetic imagination that can flourish only in a Western garden of art cut off from the sophistries of ordinary humanity.

The daughters of Hesperus, Hesperus himself, and the dragon who guards the tree represent the artist who both nourishes the tree of imagination through song and at the same time draws his vitality from it.[1]

While such a reading is in large part convincing, there are several important lines that it does not seem to explain. What, for instance, is "the old wound of the world" that would "be healéd" (l. 69) were the golden apple stolen by Heracles? Or why would "the world . . . be overwise" (ll. 63–64) should the fruit be taken? The symbolic resonance of Tennyson's mythological poems is unrestrictive enough for us to see that while the "ancient secret" that Heracles intends to seize may indeed be the vatic key to poetic creativity, it may at the same time be the formula of immortality that would explain such otherwise puzzling lines.

The eternal life that man has attempted to wrest from the gods since the beginning of time has frequently been represented by the symbol of a holy fruit tree in the mythological systems of the East.[2] Because the apples are magic devices for gaining immortality, the minor Hesperidean goddesses, in their intermediate position between earth and heaven, must

> watch, watch, night and day,
> Lest the old wound of the world be healéd,
> The glory unsealéd,
> The golden apple stolén away,
> And the ancient secret revealéd.
>
> (ll. 68–72)

[1] "Tennyson's Garden of Art: A Study of *The Hesperides*," pp. 732–743. "The Hesperides" was first singled out as an interesting early work by T. S. Eliot who read it as an illustration of Tennyson's classical learning and mastery of meter (*Essays Ancient and Modern*, pp. 176–178). Douglas Bush seconded Eliot's high valuation of the "remarkable *Hesperides*," calling it "the purest piece of magic and mystery" (*Mythology and the Romantic Tradition in English Poetry* [Cambridge, Mass., 1937], pp. 200–201).

[2] See George Stanley Faber, *The Origins of Pagan Idolatry* (London, 1816), III, 231. W. D. Paden, *Tennyson in Egypt*, pp. 154–155, believes "The Hesperides" to be a thoroughgoing adaptation of Faber, a famous mythologist of the early nineteenth century whose work, Paden argues, supplied Tennyson with a continuing source of myth, symbol, and imagery. According to Faber's interpretation of all gentile mythologies as versions of a Mosaic archetype, the Garden of the Hesperides was a type of Eden and Ararat; the Hes-

That the "old wound of the world" may refer to the fact of nature's mutability and man's death is suggested by the Miltonic context that the poet supplies. Tennyson's Epigraph to the poem, "Hesperus and his daughters three,/ That sing about the golden tree," is taken from the Epilogue of *Comus* in which the Attendant Spirit describes his Edenic home (ll. 976–1023). That same passage alludes to the myth of Adonis whose archetypal "deep wound" (ll. 999–1000) did indeed have its correlative in the old wound of the world, as a late Victorian like Sir James Frazer has described in detail and as such sophisticated mythologists as Milton and even the early Tennyson would have known. Furthermore, given such a Miltonic key as the Epigraph, we cannot avoid an association between the "old wound" of "The Hesperides" and the "wound" that earth feels when Eve first tastes of the apple in *Paradise Lost* (IX, 780–784), one that brings death and mutability into the world.[3]

The old wound of the world that assures the inevitable death of man differentiates him from the gods. It must be kept from healing so that the Olympian gods will remain unchallenged, for "If the golden apple be taken,/ The world will be overwise." Should Heracles, the hero in quest of the ancient secret, manage to steal the apple and take it back to the East, the world of activity and everyday life in Tennyson's lifelong symbolic geography, such "wisdom" in the possession of humanity would presumably heal the wound and thereby threaten the serenity and the very rule of the gods. It is absolutely imperative to their "eternal pleasure" (l. 24) that "Kingdoms lapse, and climates change, and races die" (l. 46), for they are secure only in the certitude of nature's constant mutability. Their immortality raises them to a supreme height above dying man, and their assurance of uniqueness directly assuages their pride.

Heracles is thus the first in a line of Tennysonian protagonists who try to wrest a "wisdom" from the gods. To the extent that

peridean tree an adaptation of the fatal tree in Eden; and the Hesperidean Sisters themselves a triplicated Eve.

[3] The extent of Milton's profound influence on Tennyson is treated in "Milton and Tennyson," a chapter in James G. Nelson's *The Sublime Puritan: Milton and the Victorians* (Madison, Wisc., 1963), pp. 106–125.

Tennyson's classical poems are veiled parables concerning poetic aspiration, such wisdom certainly alludes to the poet's "vatic nature, the qualities of the poetic charism." [4] Yet this "wisdom" achieves a wider reach — the ancient secret that man seeks can take such various forms as the heavenly beauty that Paris takes as a gift in "Oenone," the knowledge that Ulysses insists upon following beyond the utmost bound of human thought, the "Passionless bride, divine Tranquillity" of "Lucretius," the divine knowledge associated with Pallas Athene in "Tiresias," and the immortality that Tithonus asks of the goddess Eos in "Tithonus."

Each of the heroes is doomed to frustration whether he gains the object of his quest or not, because the gods are able to fend him off or betray him with the weapon of mystery. The Sisters know that "Honor comes with mystery;/ Hoarded wisdom brings delight" (ll. 47–48). Elsewhere in his poetry Tennyson claims for his own uses the "quiet gods" of Lucretius' *De Rerum Natura*, deities who, "careless of mankind,"

> lie beside their nectar, and the bolts are hurl'd
> Far below them in the valleys, and the clouds are
>   lightly curl'd
> Round their golden houses, girdled with the
>   gleaming world;
> Where they smile in secret, looking over wasted lands,
> Blight and famine, plague and earthquake, roaring
>   deeps and fiery sands,
> Clanging fights, and flaming towns, and sinking ships,
>   and praying hands.
>   ("The Lotos-Eaters," ll. 110–116)

While the Hesperidean Sisters lack the serenity of the quiet gods and their bemused "secret smiles" at the universal chaos far below them, the guardians of the sacred tree do understand that it is the fact of universal change — of kingdoms lapsing, of wave clashing against wave, of mountains weakening — counterposed against the enigma of divine immobility and repose that makes for the "bliss of secret smiles" among the gods:

[4] Stange, "Tennyson's Garden of Art," p. 102.

> Wandering waters unto wandering waters call;
> Let them clash together, foam and fall.
> Out of watchings, out of wiles,
> Comes the bliss of secret smiles.
> All things are not told to all.   (ll. 75–79)

The "honor" of the Hesperidean Sisters thus depends upon their ability to veil their formula in mystery in order to preserve their monopoly on immortality; the "delight" and "eternal pleasure" that accompany the honor of the gods flourish at the expense of a suffering humanity. The particular form of the Hesperidean "wiles" is suggested by the blank verse prologue to their song in which the Carthaginian commander Hanno, passing between the southern and western Horn, hears the Sisters' melody, a siren song that can lure him to his death.

The gods do tantalize man with an intimation of the mystery's meaning through the riddle of number. "The Hesperides" abounds in references to five and three. The incantatory lines

> Five links, a golden chain, are we,
> Hesper, the dragon, and sisters three,
> Bound about the golden tree
>   (ll. 65–67, 106–108)

appear twice, and the arcane portentousness of such magic numerals is evident from the message that wisdom whispers "in a corner": "Five and three/ (Let it not be preached abroad) makes an awful mystery" (ll. 28–29). The Sisters repeat these numbers over and over to keep the sleepy dragon awake:

> Number, tell them over and number
> How many the mystic fruit-tree holds
> Lest the red-combed dragon slumber
> Rolled together in purple folds.
>   (ll. 49–52)

Both the history of numerology and Tennyson's symbology in this and other works have tempted commentators upon the poem to assign meanings to the numbers: perhaps the association of the three with the root, the bole, and the fruit of the sacred tree "suggests the ancient distinction among body, soul, and spirit, as well as the organic principle of multiplicity in unity," and the five refers to the five senses upon which Tennyson's early poetic imagination depends (Stange); perhaps "the five and three make up an awful mystery because they add up to *eight*, the sacred ogdoad of the mysteries" according to the speculations of George Stanley Faber which Tennyson may have been following in "The Hesperides" (Paden); perhaps there was a book in the Reverend George Clayton Tennyson's extensive and widely ranging Somersby library, an obscure work gnomic or hermetic in nature, that would supply the key to Tennyson's numerology.

My own feeling is that all such attempts to render explicit the magic of number violate the "awful mystery" that wisdom, whispering in her corner, wishes to keep secret; such efforts represent the critical equivalent of Heracles' invasion of the Western garden. Tennyson's poetry is full of numbers whose numinosity and power defy wholly persuasive explication. The number symbolism of four, as a case in point, is a significant motif in "The Palace of Art": the speaker builds four courts for his proud soul within the great mansion, while four currents of water flow down from it through four jets. And the *Idylls of the King*, as we shall see, frequently resorts to mysterious number. But while the ingenuity of mankind can certainly discover plausible ways to pierce its mystery, number is merely another of the silent forms that Tennyson's goddesses use to tease us out of thought.

Although "The Hesperides" is one of Tennyson's most interesting early works, it is a poem whose complexity and importance have not been generally acknowledged. If we move on to the dramatic monologues on classical subjects which are recognized as being among his most mature and lasting productions, it is in "Tithonus" that Tennyson mounts the most direct and representative classical variation of the mortality theme he broached in "The Hesperides."

The Hesperidean song is chanted entirely by the divine Sisters who wish to protect their ancient secret; Heracles, the intruder from the East, is alluded to in a single line. If "The Hesperides" dramatizes in their own voices the frenzied attempts of semi-god-desses to ward off the challenges of man, "Tithonus" inverts that perspective and provides the lament of a mortal who has managed to wrest eternal life from the gods, only to find that he has been cursed with a "cruel immortality" that does not include eternal youth.

Eos, who had fallen in love with Tithonus, seems as despondent at the effects of her careless generosity as Tithonus himself. She genuinely regrets what her gift has done to her human lover: her tears flow down the cheeks of the wizened old man (l. 45). And yet the changes that took place between Tennyson's first version of the Tithonus story, the "Tithon" that appeared in the J. M. Heath *Commonplace Book*, and the final poem suggest that the goddess' tears do not mitigate her role in a divine plan whereby human pride must be severely chastised, even if she herself does not desire such revenge. In the 1833 "Tithon" the possibility that Tithonus is be-ing punished for agreeing to unite himself with a heavenly beauty is missing. The lines that open the second verse paragraph outlining his dilemma stress only his pain:

> Ay me! What everlasting pain,
> Being immortal with a mortal heart,
> To live confronted with eternal youth:
> To look on what is beautiful nor know
> Enjoyment save thro' memory.
>
> (ll. 11–15)

In the "Tithonus" published in the *Cornhill Magazine* of February 1860 and reprinted in the *Enoch Arden and Other Poems* of 1864,[5] these relatively neutral lines give way to ones which emphasize the narcissism of Tithonus and the *hubris* of believing himself a god:

> Alas, for this gray shadow, once a man —
> So glorious in his beauty and thy choice,

[5] The history of the poem's composition and an indispensable, detailed comparison of the versions in the Heath *Commonplace Book*, *Cornhill Magazine*, and the *Enoch Arden* volume appear in Mary Joan Donahue's "Tennyson's *Hail Briton!* and *Tithon* in the Heath Manuscript," *PMLA*, LXIV (1949), 385–416. The quotation from "Tithon" is taken from Miss Donahue's article which reprints the poem.

> Who madest him thy chosen, that he seem'd
> To his great heart none other than a God!
> I ask'd thee, "Give me immortality."
>
> (ll. 11–15)

The Homeric *Hymn to Aphrodite* on which Tennyson based his poem does not accentuate the vengeance of the gods. There Eos' failure to ask Zeus for eternal youth as well as eternal life is just a mistake. "Tithonus" does not allude to Zeus at all. That the terrible gift seems to come directly from Eos makes her responsibility for Tithonus' plight even more direct than it was in Tennyson's source. Tithonus himself indicts the agency not of Zeus but of the goddess in the description of his aging:

> . . . thy strong Hours indignant work'd their wills,
> And beat me down and marr'd and wasted me,
> And tho' they could not end me, left me maim'd
> To dwell in presence of immortal youth,
> Immortal age beside immortal youth,
> And all I was in ashes.   (ll. 18–23)

Tithonus' decline is underscored by a basic light-heat/dark-cold contrast. Tithonus, now a "gray shadow," was born in a "dark world" for which he once more yearns. In his description of Eos rising in the East, Tithonus emphasizes the light that she sheds over his darkness, and the sexual union of Tithonus and Eos is rendered primarily through this sensual mingling of his cold darkness and her light and heat:

> I used to watch — if I be he that watch'd —
> The lucid outline forming round thee; saw
> The dim curls kindle into sunny rings;
> Changed with thy mystic change, and felt my blood
> Glow with the glow that slowly crimson'd all
> The presence and thy portals.   (ll. 52–57)

But the sexual energy of their meeting has long since dissipated and the memory of former warmth is indeed part of his punishment. He must greet the goddess anew daily, although now "Coldly thy rosy shadows bathe me, cold/ Are all thy lights" (ll. 66–67). He is trapped within the "ever silent spaces" of the Tennysonian East, within the awful rose of Eos' dawn. Though Eos can weep for the mortal she once loved, his request to be lapped "deep within the lonely West" ("Tithon," l. 27) of death goes unheeded by the goddess at the poem's conclusion, whatever the case in other versions of the myth.

While "Tithonus" has treated the ravages of soul attendant upon the indulgence of self-love, the dramatic monologue of 1868, "Lucretius," concerns itself with intellectual pride. Relying on Roman rather than Greek material, the poem describes the revenge of the senses upon the soaring intellect through the combined agency of a woman and a vengeful goddess. The Roman artist-philosopher who had given poetic shape to the *De Rerum Natura* moves away from love of the merely human, his intelligence ranging in rarefied isolation far beyond earthly bounds. In his quest for the "Passionless bride, divine Tranquillity" he has tried through ascetic self-discipline to live as securely as the gods themselves about whose existence he, paradoxically, has serious doubts. But his wife, Lucilia, "wrathful, petulant" because her husband spends all his time poring over the three hundred scrolls left him by his master Epicurus, tries to win Lucretius back from his speculative heights. She finds a witch who brews for her a magic philter with the power to "lead an errant passion home again." It is this potion "tickling the brute brain within the man's" which undermines Lucretius' "power to shape" and drives him to suicide. His despair generates the final thrust that takes him over into virtual atheism; he leaps beyond his master Epicurus, who believed in the gods because all men believe in them, to the doubt to which his own belief in an atomistic cosmos has brought him.

The collapse of personality takes the form of three related nightmares brought on by the magic potion, as the naturalistic cosmos of Lucretius erupts into a night of naturalistic passion. The first dream confronts him, a philosopher who has prized serenity above all things, with a vision of his atomistic universe whirling about in eternal, chaotic change. This attack on his intellectual system precipitates the next two dreams which demonstrate that the explosion of the universe has its human correlative in an uncontrollable carnality. The "mulberry-faced" dictator Sylla now appears to the horrified Lucretius murdering Roman citizens with indiscriminate abandon, the political expression of the universal chaos in the first dream. The blood he sheds becomes an obscene distortion of the myth of Cadmus. From the blood spring no dragon warriors associated with the founding of a city,

> But girls, Hetairai, curious in their art,
> Hired animalisms, vile as those that made
> The mulberry-faced Dictator's orgies worse
> Than aught they fable of the quiet Gods.
> And hands they mixt, and yell'd and round me drove
> In narrowing circles till I yell'd again
> Half-suffocated, and sprang up, and saw —
> Was it the first beam of my latest day?
>
> (ll. 52–59)

The *Walpurgisnacht* of passion, prefiguring nothing so much as the diseased nightmare that undermines the last vestiges of control in Gustave von Aschenbach of *Death in Venice*, leads directly into Lucretius' third dream, a vision of Helen, for whom the Hetairai have prepared:

> Then, then, from utter gloom stood out the breasts,
> The breasts of Helen, and hoveringly a sword
> Now over and now under, now direct,
> Pointed itself to pierce, but sank down shamed
> At all that beauty; and as I stared, a fire,
> The fire that left a roofless Ilion,
> Shot out of them, and scorch'd me that I woke.
>
> (ll. 60–66)

The significance of the sword as an instrument both of destruction and of masculine penetration is masterfully recapitulated a few lines later in the appearance to Lucretius of a satyr chasing an oread. His tortured reaction to the oread as she threatens to fling herself upon him recaptures in dramatic terms the "twy-natured" force of the sword:

> such a precipitate heel,
> Fledged as it were with Mercury's ankle-wing,
> Whirls her to me — but will she fling herself

> Shameless upon me? Catch her, goat-foot! nay,
> Hide, hide them, million-myrtled wilderness,
> And cavern-shadowing laurels, hide! do I wish —
> What? — that the bush were leafless? or to whelm
> All of them in one massacre?   (ll. 200–207)

The sword that hovers about Helen implies the same double movement.[6] But the impulses of sexual fulfillment and destruction are both frustrated as the sword sinks down, "shamed at all that beauty." The counter-thrust of Helen's fire that leaves a roofless Ilion relates the third dream back to the second: both Sylla and Helen, personifications of a murderous carnality, destroy entire civilizations. And the razings of Rome and Troy are pitted ironically against Cadmus' founding of Thebes.

The alliance of the Greek Helen and the Roman Sylla has its divine equivalent in the sexual union of Venus and Mars. For the three nightmares lead Lucretius to believe that they represent the vengeance of Venus upon him. And he asks Venus

> To kiss thy Mavors, roll thy tender arms
> Round him, and keep him from the lust of blood
> That makes a steaming slaughter-house of Rome.
>   (ll. 82–84)

But as the dreams have shown us, the request is a futile one, for the Mars of Sylla and the Venus of Helen are united in their assault on human sensibilities. The invocation of Venus as buffer against Mars is a direct paraphrase of lines 34–52 of the *De Rerum Natura* proem.[7] Tennyson thus suggests that Venus has explicitly rejected the invocation of the *De Natura* in her alliance as Helen with Sylla.

Venus, the relentless goddess who oversees the gradual disintegration of Lucretius, is a complicated figure who avenges herself

---

[6] Paden, *Tennyson in Egypt*, pp. 73–74, describes "Mungo the American," a tale Tennyson wrote when he was thirteen or fourteen. According to the only published account of the tale, it shows how Mungo "found a sword, and afterwards how it came to the possession of the right owner, after the space of two years." Paden feels that this tale, the earliest of Tennyson's writing of which there is any record, is "the only one in which the result of aggression is a joyous and lasting triumph; and that even there the hero is temporarily deprived of the symbol of his masculine integrity."

[7] *On the Nature of Things*, trans. W. E. Leonard (London, 1921), p. 4.

for several reasons. In her human form of Lucilia, the spurned wife of Lucretius, she is incensed by a man who has turned away from erotic passion. Lucilia dreams that there is a female rival that has torn the affection of Lucretius away from her and she is right, for Lucretius prefers the "Passionless bride, divine Tranquillity." But Venus has another motive for hating Lucretius. In the proem to the *De Rerum Natura* he has rejected her mythological status as goddess of erotic love (and Lucretius mentions three specific tales about her that he does not believe), although he has embraced her larger significance as Venus genetrix, the principle of aesthetic and philosophic creation and the life force.[8] A poet, he took

> That popular name of thine to shadow forth
> The all-generating power and genial heat
> Of Nature, when she strikes thro' the thick blood
> Of cattle, and light is large, and lambs are glad
> Nosing the mother's udder, and the bird
> Makes his heart voice amid the blaze of flowers;
> Which things appear the work of mighty Gods.
>
> (ll. 96–102)

He has transformed the passionate goddess who intercedes in the life of man into one of those "quiet Gods" who, far removed

> From envy, hate and pity, and spite and scorn,
> Live the great life which all our greatest fain
> Would follow, centred in eternal calm.
>
> (ll. 77–79)

In other words Venus is for Lucretius an analogue for the "Passionless bride, divine Tranquillity" for whom he yearns. Such Epicurean gods, suggested to Tennyson by the third book of the *De Re-*

---

[8] For the complicated history of the Uranian and Pandemic Aphrodite of whom the Venus genetrix, the creative and vivifying force of nature, and Venus, the goddess of erotic passion, are Roman versions, see "Aphrodite" and "Venus" in *Harper's Dictionary of Classical Literature and Antiquities*, ed. Harry Thurston Peck (New York, 1963), pp. 95–97, 1642–1643. For a critical discussion of the opposition between the "heavenly" and "common" Aphrodite in the nineteenth century relevant to Tennyson, see Allen Tate, "A Reading of Keats," *The Man of Letters in the Modern World* (New York, 1953), pp. 207–210. Tate sees the attempt to reconcile the claims of the Uranian and Pandemic Aphrodite as the lifelong concern of Keats.

rum Natura,[9] had been alluded to in the "secret smiles" of the Hesperidean Sisters and had received a full description in the 1842 revision of "The Lotos-Eaters." Now in "Lucretius" we see how terrible these quiet gods, spiritualized by a questing poet-philosopher into an "immortal bride," can really be.

For Venus refuses to be one of the quiet gods that the apostrophe of Lucretius has evoked as an escape from passion. He has been an artist as well as a philosopher, "shutting up reasons in rhythm,/ Or Heliconian honey in living words,/ To make the truth less harsh" (ll. 223–225). As such, as a lord of the five senses despite his ascetic intentions, he needs the *sensuous* Venus to inspire his work. The way of the poet as of the lover is to the spirit, but to the spirit through the senses. And this is the trap that a fatal goddess sets for him (the same trap that Eros in *Death in Venice* sets for a later proud artist). At the conclusion of the poem Lucretius does find "divine Tranquillity" in the partner of Venus. Fleeing one fatal goddess he falls into the embrace of another. The peace he seeks is the oblivion of death, as he addresses his new passionless bride whom he woos as his "soul flies out and dies in the air."

"Tiresias" confirms the hostility between mortals and gods that Tennyson had dramatized in earlier monologues on classical subjects. Like Lucretius, Tiresias undertakes an intellectual journey toward godhead, though his are not the quiet gods who recline unconcernedly above the affairs of men — he firmly believes in gods who love and hate "with mortal hates and loves." As he tells Menoeceus to whom he addresses his complaint,

> My son, the Gods, despite of human prayer,
> Are slower to forgive than human kings.
> The great God Arês burns in anger still
> Against the guiltless heirs of him from Tyre,
> Our Cadmus, out of whom thou art, who found
> Beside the springs of Dircê, smote, and still'd
> Thro' all its folds the multitudinous beast,
> The dragon, which our trembling fathers call'd
> The God's own son. (ll. 9–17)

[9] See Malcolm MacLaren, "Tennyson's Epicurean Lotos-Eaters," *Classical Journal* (March 1961), pp. 259–267.

In fact it is for a *hubris* analogous to Cadmus' that Tiresias is punished in his life. Like the Heracles of "The Hesperides," like Ulysses, and like Lucretius, Tiresias is on a voyage [10] through the wilderness of thought searching for some ultimate wisdom, "to get larger glimpses of that more than man/ Which rolls the heavens, and lifts and lays the deep" (ll. 20–21). In the mythological fable of the poem this pilgrimage takes the form of his scaling "the highest of the heights/ With some strange hope to see the nearer God" (ll. 27–28). The quest reaches its close when one day in a secret olive glade Tiresias sees Pallas Athene, the goddess of knowledge, climbing naked from her bath. Athene's revenge on Tiresias is immediate, rather than the gradual wasting that Tithonus comes to undertsand only as he grows older. The light of knowledge reflected from her golden hair, her golden helm, her golden armor, her virgin breast and eyes blinds Tiresias. Like Heracles he has sought a "golden" wisdom; like Tithonus he is given a tauntingly ambiguous gift by a goddess. His sight of Athene's "ineffable beauty" has endowed him with the knowledge he has been searching for, but the virginal goddess exacts a terrible price. Once again, as in "Lucretius," a terrible goddess joins forces with the god of war to ravage Thebes, whose history since its founding by Cadmus has been one of continual bloodletting and revolution. The unforgiving Arês that Cadmus had insulted is reinforced by an avenging Pallas Athene to frustrate in the generation of Tiresias a human desire for peace and social stability. The truths that Tiresias tells are meant as "a voice to curb/ The madness of our cities and their kings." But no man will believe the truth that Tiresias speaks.

To summarize the comprehensive implications of man's relationship to Tennyson's classical goddesses, their effect, whatever the appearance may be, is never anything but disastrous. The Hesperidean Sisters, the Eos of "Tithonus," the Venus of "Lucretius," and the Pallas Athene of "Tiresias" guard their prerogatives, their "wis-

---

[10] C. F. G. Masterman describes in *The Condition of England* (London, 1909), p. 243, the "two voyages" of Victorian literature, "a voyage without in the actual encounter with primitive and hostile forces and in a universe of salt and bracing challenges; and a voyage within and across distant horizons and to stranger countries than any visible to the actual senses."

dom," from men with a degree of aggressiveness that varies from poem to poem. If we compare Tennyson's fastidious quiet gods who take their ease far above a struggling humanity, the Sisters who jealously protect their Hesperidean garden at the edge of the world from human intrusion, Eos who destroys her human lover despite her best intentions, and such relentlessly vengeful furies as Venus and Pallas Athene, we see that the differences among them are not as important as their similarity. All of Tennyson's classical deities, even when they are not actively hostile, are ruinous to mankind. His fatal goddesses, when they enter the world of men, do so like the Zeus of William Butler Yeats' "Leda and the Swan": their ravaging gifts are too terrible for man to bear; the price they exact for the power they offer or are forced to relinquish is catastrophic. Man is damned if he unites with (Tithonus), tries to escape from (Lucretius), or moves toward (Tiresias) the fatal goddess.

The pessimistic irony that emerges from the four poems considered side by side also throws a new light on the fatal choice in "Oenone." One can now more readily sense the inexorable quality of Paris' doom. The awarding of the apple to Aphrodite was, as the fall of Troy it precipitates testifies, a grievous mistake. (The "subtle smile in her mild eyes" as she promises Helen to Paris [l. 180] recalls the "secret smiles" both of the Hesperidean Sisters and of the quiet gods in "The Lotos-Eaters.") But the gift that Hera offers, power, "which in all action is the end of all" might have been just as devastating. For this is the kind of power that Lucretius mistakenly cherishes, the doom of godlike quiescence that the Lotos-eaters offer the mariners of Ulysses. Hera would have made Paris like the Epicurean quiet gods:

> men, in power
> Only, are likest Gods, who have attain'd
> Rest in a happy place and quiet seats
> Above the thunder, with undying bliss
> In knowledge of their own supremacy.
>
> ("Oenone," ll. 127–131)

Athene's offer of "self-reverence, self-knowledge, self-control" seems to be a more attractive gift than that proffered by either

Aphrodite or Hera. It is the one that Oenone advises Paris to accept, and the three terms are frequently intoned by commentators looking for an apt, short phrase to capture the nub of Tennyson's moralism. But the description of Pallas that precedes the introduction of the phrase does not suggest a very pleasant context for the gift:

> but Pallas where she stood
> Somewhat apart, her clear and bared limbs
> O'erthwarted with the brazen-headed spear
> Upon her pearly shoulder leaning cold,
> The while, above, her full and earnest eye
> Over her snow-cold breast and angry cheek
> Kept watch, waiting decision. . . .
>
> (ll. 135–141)

Athene here suspiciously resembles the icy divinity that Tiresias surprises in her olive glade, to his lasting regret.

There is, in other words, little guarantee that Paris' choice would have been any less ruinous had he preferred the gift of Hera or Pallas Athene to that of Aphrodite. Paris gives voice to this sense of man's total entrapment in the 1892 "The Death of Oenone." Dying of a wound inflicted by a poisoned arrow, he appeals to Oenone, justifying his earlier betrayal: "Man is but a slave to Fate," he cries. The fates put us into a position where we have to make a choice among the goddesses and then destroy us for a choice which can only be wrong. As Freud has suggested, the third goddess of classical myth that the hero chooses, no matter which of the three she may be, is usually "the third of the fates alone, the silent Goddess of Death." [11]

The work which treats the Christian equivalent of the "awful mystery" that Tennyson's classical goddesses in one way or another keep away from man is the *Idylls of the King*. Whereas the goddesses do all they can to keep their "ancient secret" from man, a God of Love sends Arthur, "the King/ In whom high God hath

[11] "The Theme of the Three Caskets," *Complete Psychological Works*, XII (London, 1961); included in *On Creativity and the Unconscious: Papers on the Psychology of Art, Literature, Love, and Religion*, ed. Benjamin Nelson (New York, 1958), pp. 63–75. The quotation appears on p. 75 of the latter.

breathed a secret thing" ("The Coming of Arthur," ll. 499–500),
to cleanse the wasteland of the world. "The Coming of Arthur"
offers three natural explanations of Arthur's birth and a supernatural one, but we are clearly meant to believe the last, Bellicent's
tale of Arthur's miraculous arrival on the crest of a flaming ninth
wave. The presence at his coronation of the Lady of the Lake and
of the three queens who support him through life testifies readily
enough to his supernatural origin, as does Camelot itself, his "city
built to music" that "moved so weirdly in the mist" ("Gareth and
Lynette," ll. 238–274).

But the burden of man's relation to Arthurian mystery is intimated in the story of Arthur's passing and in the attempt of Bedivere, the first and last of his knights, to frustrate its inevitability by
prolonging Arthur's honor and fame. That the death of Arthur
constituted the key to the king's entire life for Tennyson is indicated by the fact that the trial run for the *Idylls of the King*, the
"Morte d'Arthur" of 1842, concerns itself entirely with Arthur's
end. Bedivere's twice-repeated refusal in "The Passing of Arthur"
to relinquish Excalibur, a relic proving Arthur's supernatural origin, as his dying king has commanded may be read as an Arthurian echo of other attempts by Tennysonian heroes to claim for
mankind a divine power.

In his first effort Bedivere keeps Excalibur from the mere for
reasons that are clearly selfish. He is dazzled by its rare beauty, by
its haft that "twinkled with diamond sparks,/ Myriads of topaz-
lights, and jacinth-work/ Of subtlest jewellery" (ll. 224–226). But
as Bedivere tries unsuccessfully a second time to fulfill his king's
command, Tennyson complicates the motive of simple greed. It
is, to be sure, a grievous fault to disobey one's king, "Seeing obedi-
ence is the bond of rule." But what if the mortally wounded king
is making a mistake? If Excalibur disappears from the earth, Bedivere speculates,

> "What record or what relic of my lord
> Should be to aftertime, but empty breath
> And rumors of a doubt? But were this kept,
> Stored in some treasure-house of mighty kings,

> Some one might show it at a joust of arms,
> Saying: 'King Arthur's sword, Excalibur,
> Wrought by the lonely Maiden of the Lake.
> Nine years she wrought it, sitting in the deeps
> Upon the hidden bases of the hills.' "

(ll. 266–274)

Though the narrator assures us that this rationalization is made by a Bedivere "clouded with his own conceit," the reader cannot but treat it with a measure of respect. If Bedivere can show Excalibur to doubters, Arthur's legend is more apt to sound credible when "some old man," like himself, "speak in the aftertime/ To all the people, winning reverence" for Arthur (as well, perhaps, as for himself). There is after all a difference between the voice of an old, broken Bedivere and the voice of a living Arthur which has received at least part of its authority from his skillful wielding of Excalibur. "The Passing of Arthur" is, as a matter of fact, related by a Bedivere who in the "white winter of his age" is "no more than a voice." One can well imagine the "rumors of a doubt" that must have dogged the ancient knight's retelling of his fabulous tale. It is therefore understandable that Bedivere should have tried to do all in his power to keep a cloud of mystery from Arthur's name and deed. Bedivere had not actively sought out the "ancient secret" that Arthur brought to redeem the wasteland of the world. But once that wisdom has made its power felt through Arthur's work, Bedivere does insist upon trying to retain its talisman. Bedivere's initial reluctance to return the magical brand to the Lady of the Lake may thus be read as a defensive version of Heracles' attempt to take the golden apple from the Hesperidean Sisters.

"Much honor and much fame were lost" (l. 277), Bedivere believes, if Excalibur disappeared from the earth. In answer, Arthur's insistence that Excalibur be thrown into the mere restates the theme of "The Hesperides" that "Honor comes with mystery." But whereas the Hesperidean Sisters, like the other classical goddesses, were concerned with the protection of their own honor, Arthur cares primarily for the welfare of his realm — his good name is bound to the former perfection of Camelot. Arthur knows that his honor and that of the world through which he moved will be kept alive not through vain quests after palpable fact and material evidence of his existence but by the ability of his legend to inspire noble belief and virtuous deed as his mystery moves through time. ("The Holy Grail" makes a related point about the Christian mystery: the Holy Quest after visions of the chalice used at the Last Supper is for most of human society a vain, destructive pursuit of wandering fires. Visions come "as they will" to those who do not strive to penetrate the mystery, to those who do not stray from their allotted tasks in the fields of the world.)

A similar distinction can be made between the Hesperidean garden and Avilion. The Avilion, "deep-meadow'd, happy, fair with orchard lawns/ And bowery hollows crown'd with summer sea" ("The Passing of Arthur," ll. 430–431), to which Arthur travels to heal his wounds, is the Celtic equivalent of the Garden of the Hesperides. Both evince Tennyson's lifelong fascination with places of fecundity and freedom from worldly care, Miltonic places of rest, of "bowery loneliness/ The brooks of Eden mazily murmuring,/ And bloom profuse and cedar arches" ("Milton," ll. 9–11), though in his more ascetic moods he can summon forth a gnostic horror of such profusion. But while the Hesperidean grove is a refuge of divine repose and generation jealously guarded against human intrusion and utterly hostile to man, Avilion will send Arthur back into the world after his recovery to will his will and work his work anew for the good of mankind. The ultimate character of Avilion's ancient secret may remain clothed in mystery, but the effective agent of that mystery will move with a "power on this dark land to lighten it,/ And power on this dead world to make it live" ("The Coming of Arthur," ll. 92–93) after periodic regeneration in the island-valley of the West.

The difference in the relation of Hesperides and Avilion to the world is best illustrated by the ways that the works in which they appear use the same image. The guardians of the Hesperidean sacred tree form a "golden chain" about it:

> Five links, a golden chain are we,
> Hesper, the dragon, and sisters three,

> Daughters three,
> Bound about
> The gnarléd bole of the charméd tree.
>
> (ll. 106–110)

In contrast, Arthur in his final speech of consolation assures Bedivere that the "earth is every way/ Bound by gold chains about the feet of God" ("The Passing of Arthur," ll. 422–423), a notion that recalls the golden chain linking Heaven and the world in *Paradise Lost*. The chain of "The Hesperides" serves to exclude mankind, to hem in the tree from the depredations of the world; the chains of the *Idylls* fasten the world to a beneficent God.

That God asserts himself through the mystery of number. When Bedivere finally throws Excalibur into the mere, an arm "clothed in white samite, mystic, wonderful . . . caught him by the hilt, and brandish'd him/ Three times, and drew him under in the mere" (ll. 312–314). The *Idylls of the King* is filled with threes. What, we ask, is the significance of the "vast charm" in the stars that Merlin contemplates, that "single misty star/ Which is the second in a line of stars/ That seem a sword beneath a belt of three" ("Merlin and Vivien," 506–508)? Why do three queens follow Arthur through life and accompany him to Avilion? To such questions we can again supply the numerologist's answer that three is the primary odd number, the emblem of multiplicity in unity, or the mythologist's answer that, like the three Sisters of "The Hesperides" and the three goddesses of "Oenone," the queens are a type of the triplicated great mother, a cosmic female presence that broods over the life of Camelot in several forms, both natural and supernatural. Tennyson himself insisted on the inviolability of his symbols. When the Bishop of Ripon, Boyd Carpenter, asked him whether those who had interpreted the three queens as Faith, Hope, and Charity were correct, Tennyson characteristically tried both to embrace and to disavow an allegorical intention; "They are right, and they are not right. They mean that and they do not. They are three of the noblest of women. They are also those three Graces, but they are much more. I hate to be tied down to say, '*This* means *that*,' because the thought within the image is much more than any one interpretation." [12] Such equivocation may suggest that in his treatment of classical and Arthurian myth Tennyson meant to evoke the sacred mystery of numerical as well as verbal symbol. But while the incantation of number in "The Hesperides" was intended to keep a misanthropic dragon awake, the numbers of the *Idylls* are signs of a universe through which man can walk in self-assurance because of Arthur's benign, if intermittent, presence.

The benignity of this universe and its God must somehow encompass the fact of mutability and mortality, of Arthur's death and the disappearance of Excalibur that Bedivere finds so hard to accept. The conclusion to "The Passing of Arthur" answers Bedivere's doubt with a Christian variation of the Hesperidean "wisdom" and of the understanding that Tithonus had come to by the time of his monologue:

> "The old order changeth, yielding place to new,
> And God fulfils himself in many ways,
> Lest one good custom should corrupt the world."
>
> (ll. 408–410)

This climactic message seems to echo a Hesperidean notion: it is necessary that "Kingdoms lapse, and climates change, and races die," that Arthur die and that Camelot come to blight. But the Hesperidean Sisters had celebrated natural mutability because it assured their "bliss of secret smiles" and the smug knowledge of divine uniqueness. The "High God" of the *Idylls* who perceives the world from beyond and enters it to make it beautiful ("The Passing of Arthur," ll. 16–17) withholds immortality from the world for man's good as well as His own, lest man come to know the stagnation of a Tithonus. While the Hesperidean Sisters oversee a random clashing of "wandering waters," while Tennyson's fatal goddess is indifferent to man's discomfiture, the high God of the *Idylls* fulfills Himself in a teleology. He oversees a controlled progress wherein man moves toward Him as He increasingly adapts the world to express Himself in changing forms and as He evolves to man's apprehension of Him. To retain a single good custom too long would frustrate this process.

[12] *Memoir*, II, 127.

CHAPTER IX

From Lyrical Death in Life to Mythic Kindlier Gods

A T THE end of his life Tennyson drew together his classical deities and the high God of the *Idylls* in a climactic work, the "Demeter and Persephone" of his 1889 volume. But long before writing that poem, Tennyson had discovered a name, "Death in Life," which may serve as an apt designation for the deity under whom his classical protagonists suffer. Because this name for the hypertrophied, twilight state of a Tithonus or Tiresias emerges at the conclusion of "Tears, Idle Tears" before finding its clearest mythic elaboration in "Demeter and Persephone," we can at this point trace an instance of the Tennysonian lyric impulse flowing all but imperceptibly toward the condition of myth. For the 1847 song from *The Princess* may be considered a lyric forerunner of the later dramatic monologue on a classical subject. In these pendants Tennyson indulged his sorrow for lost love, a version of his "passion of the past," in the two genres which gave form to his best poetry.

Tennyson said of the song that "The passion of the past, the abiding in the transient, was expressed in 'Tears, idle Tears,' which was written in the yellowing autumn-tide at Tintern Abbey, full for

me of its bygone memories." But like so many of the pieces written
during the 1830's the work was probably a veiled response to Arthur Hallam's death.[1] Thus Tennyson was able to achieve a creative distance between a sorrow whose genesis he must have understood and the "idle tears" whose meaning the speaker of the poem
questions with increasing urgency.

> "Tears, idle tears, I know not what they mean,
> Tears from the depth of some divine despair
> Rise in the heart, and gather to the eyes,
> In looking on the happy autumn-fields,
> And thinking of the days that are no more.
>
> "Fresh as the first beam glittering on a sail,
> That brings our friends up from the underworld,
> Sad as the last which reddens over one
> That sinks with all we love below the verge;
> So sad, so fresh, the days that are no more.
>
> "Ah, sad and strange as in dark summer dawns
> The earliest pipe of half-awaken'd birds
> To dying ears, when unto dying eyes
> The casement slowly grows a glimmering square;
> So sad, so strange, the days that are no more.
>
> "Dear as remember'd kisses after death,
> And sweet as those by hopeless fancy feign'd
> On lips that are for others; deep as love,
> Deep as first love, and wild with all regret;
> O Death in Life, the days that are no more!"
>
> (IV, 21–40)

The lyric, which has been given a close, sympathetic reading in
recent years even by critics who have otherwise been hostile to
Tennyson, is one of his perfectly wrought works. Its structure
arises from the speaker's repeated attempts to explain to himself
what the idle tears of the first line "mean." Each stanza surrounds

---

[1] Tennyson's description of the poem's background appears in *Memoir*, I,
253. A. C. Bradley shows that Section XIX of *In Memoriam* was written at
Tintern Abbey in his *Commentary on "In Memoriam,"* p. 100; and Graham
Hough, "Tears, Idle Tears," *Hopkins Review*, IV (1951), 31–36, make the
connection between the two poems to argue that "Tears, Idle Tears" was
linked to Hallam's death.

the tears with fresh adjectives which, in substituting for the epithet "idle," gradually elucidate the meaning that the speaker seeks. The complexity of that meaning becomes clear as the epithets are opposed, and as the similes attached to these adjectives carry forward the force of this oxymoron. Each pairing mingles the joy of remembered life and the sorrow at its passing to capture the Janus-like posture of the speaker, frozen as he is between present and past. The concrete images of the happy "days that are no more," a generalizing refrain with which each stanza ends, intensify the sorrow and indicate the speaker's growing abandon. In the last stanza as he approaches the subject of lost and unrealized love, the adjectives achieve a climactic desperation. The last two phrases, "Deep as first love, and wild with all regret" — especially the final, long-voweled "wild" — open the speaker to the shock of recognition:

O Death in Life, the days that are no more!

This culminating paradox summarizes all the earlier concrete oppositions. Tonally, the "idle tears" of the speaker's initial musings have reached the emotional heights of epiphanic invocation by the time of the poem's closing line.

Several readers who suggest that Death in Life is a deified abstraction have speculated about the theological status of the emergent "god." Both Graham Hough and Leo Spitzer recognize the pagan context of the speaker's despair and feel that the language of the poem prepares for the final address to a specifically classical, pagan deity. The friends of the second stanza come from the "underworld," from the geographical antipodes in a primary sense. But surely the secondary meaning of the underworld as the classical land of shades is so strong, given the poem's additional references to the gods, that it all but smothers the primary denotation. Furthermore, the tears rise up from "the depth of some divine despair." For Hough, the fact of this despair, reinforced as it is by the allusion to the Greek underworld, confirms the pagan identity of the poem's tears and of the god who is addressed. Because despair is a sin according to Christian moral theology, the "divine despair" must exist within a non-Christian context: the despair is "not divine in the Christian sense, but only in the sense of being somewhat daemonic, some more than personal force, with some other than private cause." [2]

Leo Spitzer, as he charts the gradual appearance of the god in the poem, defines his nature even more precisely:

The particular god (or *Sondergott*, to use the classical scholar Usener's term) of Tennyson's making is neither Life nor Death, but Death-in-Life; surely not the Christian deity, as Hough has felt; no more is he Thanatos or Pluto, the God of the underworld before whom man is doomed to appear after death, or even one of the aloof, serene Gods of Epicurus who dwell in the *intermundia*, unconcerned with man. The God Death-in-Life, who, like Christ, has his dwelling-place among the mortals as his name indicates, while sharing the aloofness of the Epicurean Gods, is an impressive and sterile dark God wrapped in his own "despair" (his *intermundium* is life itself), "idle" as are the tears of the poet. [3]

Death in Life, the cry that "names" Tennysonian deliquescence, may indeed evoke and invoke the dark god that Hough and Spitzer describe. My own feeling is that they have deified the abstraction too confidently by calling excessive attention to isolated phrases within the poem. Cleanth Brooks, a less relentless mythologizer, merely reads the exclamation as either a "tortured cry like 'O God! the days that are no more,'" or "a loose appositive: 'the days that are no more are a kind of death in life.'" [4] Perhaps the truth lies in a nuance between the two positions: the intensity of the speaker's apostrophe personifies — even deifies — the abstraction more surely than Brooks would allow, although the reference to the underworld and the phrase "depth of some divine despair" supply too slight a context for the elaborately identified god that Spitzer sees crystallizing in the poem's last line. The abstraction Death in Life, that is, verges, in its contingent state, upon apotheosis. As the idle tears of the speaker and the psychic probing they stimulate lead to the naming of Death in Life, the speaker's act of remembering his losses approaches the deification of memory. "Tears, Idle Tears" de-

[2] "Tears, Idle Tears," *Hopkins Review*, p. 33.
[3] "'Tears, Idle Tears' Again," *Hopkins Review*, V (1952), 71–72.
[4] "The Motivation of Tennyson's Weeper," *The Well Wrought Urn* (New York, 1947), pp. 167–177.

scribes the evolution of one literary mode out of another: a sorrow that begins in lyric contemplation, having been widened by the speaker into an abstract universal principle, touches — however faintly — the shores of myth.

As he was coming to the end of his poetic career, Tennyson once more indulged his yearning for the days that are no more in "Demeter and Persephone," a work that modulates the possible classical overtones of "Tears, Idle Tears" into the details of one of his favorite Greek myths. Demeter is Tennyson's valedictory portrayal of the deity Death in Life. (Strictly speaking, Demeter and Persephone together, the springing blade of corn *and* the buried grain of the Eleusinian tradition that Tennyson, like Frazer, knew, are the mythical embodiment of Death in Life. But the *feeling* of Death in Life is dramatized only through the mother's voice. We may safely assume that Persephone, the poem's interlocuter, shares her mother's divine despair.)

The tears of Tennyson's 1847 lyric, we have seen, flow in part from the speaker's knowledge that seasonal change within the individual life is final. The "divine despair" arises initially in eyes that look on autumn fields, happy fields but also ones filled with the pathos of a dying summer and of the winter to come. The sounds of summer dawn that reach the dying ears anticipate the winter of life that cannot be far behind. When at the end of his life (on the evidence of such poems as "Romney's Remorse," "Rizpah," and "In the Children's Hospital") Tennyson's conception of love was becoming both more intensely maternal than it had already been and triumphantly androgynous, he chose to treat his recurring motif of lost love in the Greek goddess whom nineteenth-century tradition saw as the all-embracing Earth Mother. The figure that Tennyson had always considered "one of the most beautiful types of motherhood," [5] Demeter, in the sorrow at the loss of her daughter that stirs even the hard eternities of the gods, is able to transform the gloom of autumn into the redemptive freshness of spring.

Tennyson's dramatic monologue, occasioned no doubt by his

[5] *Memoir*, II, 364.

son Lionel's death in 1886, is spoken by Demeter to Persephone who, after having been spirited away by the god Aïdoneus to his underworld kingdom, has just been reunited with her mother in the vale of Enna. Through her lamentations and her subsequent neglect of the fruits of the earth, Demeter has forced Zeus to make his brother Aïdoneus return Persephone for nine months of every year, although Persephone must still spend the remaining three months with the god of the underworld. The fable of "Demeter and Persephone" thus repeats the circular simile of "Tears, Idle Tears" wherein the tears from the "despair of *some* God" (Spitzer) are associated both with the sail that "brings our friends up from the underworld" and with that "which sinks with all we love below the verge" as they presumably return. Persephone's ascent from the underworld is also conceived of as an arduous journey, though that of a bird rather than of a ship:

> Faint as a climate-changing bird that flies
> All night across the darkness, and at dawn
> Falls on the threshold of her native land,
> And can no more, thou camest, O my child.

(ll. 1–4)

There are significant differences between the "divine despair" of the lyric's speaker and of Demeter. For one, the tears of Demeter are never "idle" or mysterious; she understands perfectly their source and their "meaning." One can perhaps distinguish between the sorrow of the two poems by recalling an earlier distinction between the tears of free-floating, ubiquitous melancholia and the tears of mourning in which there is nothing unconscious or unlocalized about the sense of loss. While the speaker of "Tears" only discovers gradually the meaning of the tears as he piles up his relevant similes in the present tense of lyric outburst, Demeter remembers her sorrow for the most part in retrospect — she addresses Persephone after her return.

Still, the generalized melancholia of "Tears" and the mourning of "Demeter" approach each other as both poems evolve dramatically. As "Tears" moves through its four stanzas, the incomprehension of the speaker about his reason for weeping disperses while he specifies some of the causes. And conversely, as her monologue develops, the mourning of Demeter moves toward a universality and a cosmic amorphousness that transfigure the specific loss of Persephone. In Demeter's pathetic description of her search for Persephone after she had been changed into the Queen of the Dead, we find the mythic equivalent of the uncomprehended "idle tears" in the answer Demeter receives from Nature, whose moaning she both imitates and questions:

> Child, when thou wert gone,
> I envied human wives, and nested birds,
> Yea, the cubb'd lioness; went in search of thee
> Thro' many a palace, many a cot, and gave
> Thy breast to ailing infants in the night,
> And set the mother waking in amaze
> To find her sick one whole; and forth again
> Among the wail of midnight winds, and cried,
> "Where is my loved one? Wherefore do ye wail?"
> And out from all the night an answer shrill'd,
> "We know not, and we know not why we wail."
> I climb'd on all the cliffs of all the seas,
> And ask'd the waves that moan about the world,
> "Where? do ye make your moaning for my child?"
> And round from all the world the voices came,
> "We know not, and we know not why we moan."
>
> (ll. 51–66)

Demeter's movement through the universe and her discovery that all of nature is given to her own tears thus suggests that the "idle tears" of the 1847 lyric are not limited to a single human speaker. They are rather a cosmic principle, the Virgilian *lacrimae rerum* of which any specific loss is an instance but never a meaningful explanation. When one loses a friend like Arthur Hallam or a son such as Lionel, "We know not, and we know not why we moan." The mystery of human suffering is deepened, as well as exemplified, by individual losses.

As Demeter moves through the universe searching for her daughter she undergoes a crucial change:

> I thridded the black heart of all the woods,
> I peer'd thro' tomb and cave, and in the storms

> Of autumn swept across the city, and heard
> The murmur of their temples chanting me,
> Me, me, the desolate mother! "Where?" — and turn'd,
> And fled by many a waste, forlorn of man,
> And grieved for man thro' all my grief for thee. (ll. 68–74)

Her suffering has softened Demeter into one who grieves for humanity, because she has come to understand what human suffering is through its analogy to her divine despair. The climax of this new empathy occurs when she learns from the ghost of Persephone in a dream that

> "The Bright one in the highest
> Is brother of the Dark one in the lowest,
> And Bright and Dark have sworn that I, the child
> Of thee, the great Earth-Mother, thee, the Power
> That lifts her buried life from gloom to bloom,
> Should be for ever and for evermore
> The Bride of Darkness."   (ll. 93–99)

Here Tennyson provides a mythical extension to his symbolism of extreme height and extreme depth, the height of Princess Ida's mountain pride and the marine depth of the Kraken's "abysmal sea," both of which are antithetical to the human love which, Ida learns, "is of the valley." The "pleasant vale" of Enna with its pre-figuring of a Judeo-Christian Eden [6] also looks toward a new meta-spatial dispensation, what Tennyson had in "The Voice and the Peak" of 1874 characterized as

> A deep below the deep,
>   And a height beyond the height!
> Our hearing is not hearing,
>   And our seeing is not sight.
>
> The voice and the Peak
>   Far into heaven withdrawn,
> The lone glow and the long roar
>   Green-rushing from the rosy thrones of dawn!
>   (IX, X)

---

[6] G. Robert Stange, "Tennyson's Mythology: A Study of *Demeter and Persephone*," *Journal of English Literary History*, XXI (1954), 75, shows that Tennyson's description of Enna intentionally imitates Milton's picture of Eden in *Paradise Lost* (Bk. IV, ll. 268ff).

The knowledge that *both* Zeus, the "Bright one in the highest," and Aïdoneus, the "Dark one in the lowest," are brothers in their cool, fastidious contemplation of suffering makes Demeter curse the gods, refuse to partake in their feasts, and intensify her commitment to a suffering humanity: "The man, that only lives and loves an hour,/ Seem'd nobler than their hard eternities" (ll. 104–105). It is only when her tears that follow render the earth barren that Zeus, in his vanity at no longer receiving the sacrifices, prayers, and praises of men, grudgingly makes Aïdoneus surrender Persephone. She may spend nine months of the year with her mother before returning for "Three dark ones in the shadow with thy king."

In "Tears, Idle Tears," the human sorrow of the speaker is of such intensity that it is apotheothized into a "divine despair," into Death in Life. Human and divine sorrow are one. The tears of the speaker and of the "god" Death in Life flow together, for the speaker's act of remembering his losses becomes the deification of the act of memory (Death in Life is a later version of the various "Memories" in the early allegories). In his final invocation the intensity of the speaker's sorrow, his mounting of a "Pain Thermometer," makes it possible for him to unite with his sorrowing god. While "Demeter and Persephone" reverses the dramatic movement, the Janus-like point of view between the divine and the human that Demeter achieves is the same as that of the lyric. She descends to take on the identity of suffering man and rejects the "hard eternities" of the gods.

We have seen in the last chapter that Tennyson's classical deities are either hard goddesses who drive Paris, Tithonus, and Tiresias to their dooms, or the Epicurean quiet gods of "The Lotos-Eaters" who are above concern for insignificant mortals ("Lucretius" considers the alternate possibilities that the Venus who oversees the disintegration of the poet-philosopher is one or the other). Conceivably Demeter had been one of the indifferent, serene Olympian goddesses before her loss of Persephone, but she has changed. She is now man's defender, the Earth Mother.

As such she is still the Death in Life that "Tears, Idle Tears" has evoked, for Persephone must spend her gloomy winters in the underworld before the first beam glitters on the sail that brings her to the threshold of her native spring. Although partially mollified, Demeter remains "but ill-content/ With them who still are highest." She yearns for the overthrow of the Olympian system. When will they appear, she asks, that the Fates had predicted, those

> younger kindlier Gods to bear us down,
> As we bore down the Gods before us? Gods,
> To quench, not hurl the thunderbolt, to stay,
> Not spread the plague, the famine; Gods indeed,
> To send the noon into the night and break
> The sunless halls of Hades into Heaven?
> Till thy dark lord accept and love the Sun,
> And all the Shadow die into the Light,
> When thou shalt dwell the whole bright year with me.
>
> (ll. 129–137)

In the coming triumph of a gentle Christianity over the harsh Olympian gods, Demeter envisions the replacement of the quiet or avenging classical gods by the high God of the *Idylls*. Death in Life, the Tennysonian deity of fear and sorrow, will give way to a God of Life, and the Queen of Death shall be no more. "Thou," Demeter assures her daughter,

> that hast from men,
> As Queen of Death, that worship which is Fear,
> Henceforth, as having risen from out the dead,
> Shalt ever send thy life along with mine
> From buried grain thro' springing blade, and bless
> Their garner'd autumn also, reap with me,
> Earth-mother, in the harvest hymns of Earth
> The worship which is Love, and see no more
> The Stone, the Wheel, the dimly-glimmering lawns
> Of that Elysium, all the hateful fires
> Of torment, and the shadowy warrior glide
> Along the silent field of Asphodel.   (ll. 140–151)

To be sure, the "springing blade" will still have to arise out of the "buried grain": burial in the earth must still precede birth in the springtime; natural process — mutability and corporeal mortality — will still be inescapable. But when the kindlier gods come Demeter and Persephone will act in loving harmony throughout the year. The daughter shall ever send her life "along with" her mother's through the whole of organic process – the sowing, the reaping, and the harvesting. And the harvest will both be a sign of God's eternal love of man and represent a reciprocal sign on man's part, a hymn, a "worship which is Love."

The Hesperidean Sisters, we have seen, do their utmost to keep the secret of immortality from man; and Tithonus is punished because "he seem'd/ To his great heart none other than a God," an illusion that makes him ask for the terrible gift of eternal life. But the "kindlier Gods" of "Demeter and Persephone" will nourish within man an impression of godhead, will enlighten the

> souls of men, who grew beyond their race,
> And made themselves as Gods against the fear
> Of Death and Hell   (ll. 138–140)

Man will thus come to apprehend a God of Love who, neither indifferent nor the torturer of Elysium, allows man's soul a share in His bright immortality.

While Tennyson's conception of classical myth and its relation to the Christian dispensation did not receive a full poetic statement until the "Demeter and Persephone" of his 1889 volume, it was implicit in his earliest treatment of classical materials. It has thus been possible to move allusively in Chapters VIII and IX from "The Hesperides" of the 1833 volume to the late "Demeter and Persephone," connecting various classical and Arthurian poems as if they were all parts of a single consistent and coherent pattern.

Briefly, Tennyson believed in – and sometimes asserted in a poetry of philosophical reflection – the gradual evolution of a "crowning race" (*In Memoriam*, Epilogue), the consummate utopian society of "men with growing wings" whose image Merlin has sculpted on the hall he builds for Arthur ("The Holy Grail," l. 237), the "men, who grew beyond their race" of "Demeter and Persephone." For such a credo – however faint the trust in a larger hope may at times have been – Tennyson found an appropriate mythos in the displacement of the severe Olympian system by the "kindlier Gods" of Christianity. One sign for him of the human race's burgeoning spiritual maturity was its ability to metamorphose classical gods who keep their ancient secret from man into a God of Love who sends into the world surrogates like Arthur to bring man intimations of the soul's immortality.

CHAPTER X

The Myth of Western Love

ALTHOUGH in "Tithonus" the meeting of man and deity results from a goddess' love of a mortal, most of Tennyson's classical poems imply that the eros which leads to such meetings begins within the aspiring hero's will toward godhead. The love of the *Idylls of the King* embodies a counter-ideal, the Christian agape initiated by a high God who sends Arthur into the world in order to draw toward Him the mortals that He loves. The distinction that a contemporary theologian, Anders Nygren, has made between a pagan eros and a Christian agape seems applicable to Tennyson's work: the eros of the Platonic soul toward the supersensible world to which it wishes to return is wholly dependent upon the self-sustaining, if not self-generative, energy of its own will. In contrast, agape is the love of the Johannine gospel: "herein is love, not that we love God, but that He loved us." At theological issue throughout the Christian centuries has been the question of whether man can in any sense "earn" this divine love through good works or whether, as the Lutheran Bishop Nygren would have it, agape is "spontaneous and uncaused," a pure gift for which man cannot bargain with his virtue. Catholic and Protestant traditions agree, however, on the essential distinction which has usually been couched in a Platonic language of vertical direction. While eros describes the "upward" thrust of man's will, agape begins in God and flows "down" to man in order to inspire a reciprocal quest back "up" toward the spiritual city.[1]

But ultimately the difference between the eros of Tennyson's classical poems and the agape of the Arthurian is not as important as their similarity. In both cases the ascent of the soul must be made through the agency of sense, which is as potentially destructive in a pre-Christian as in a Christian setting. And the two traditions of Western love are alternate ways which Western man has devised to cope with the phenomenon of sense in his quest toward godhead.

Idylls of the King illustrates in a climactic way the maddening contradictions implicit in the dialectic of Western love and Tennyson's consequent vacillation between the two traditions. When he talks about the "parabolic drift"[2] of the *Idylls* as shadowing forth a war between sense and soul ("To the Queen," l. 37), Tennyson epitomizes his idea of love as a pilgrimage of man's soul, alternately free from and accompanied by sense, toward divine perfection. The marriage of Arthur and Guinevere, the primary representatives of soul (or conscience) and sense when the "allegory in the distance"[3] advances into the foreground of the narrative, suggests a Dantesque love wherein the embodied soul wishes to carry sense aloft with it as together they search for the beatific vision. Yet, insofar as the union of Arthur and Guinevere becomes preeminently a "war," Tennyson illuminates a second tradition in which sense and soul are at bitter enmity when soul, coming to a full

---

[1] This distinction, developed throughout *Agape and Eros*, is summarized on pp. 722–741. Martin C. D'Arcy, S.J., *The Mind and Heart of Love* (New York, 1947), pp. 15–16 and *passim*, counters Nygren's Protestant statement with a modern Catholic differentiation of agape and eros.

Clyde de L. Ryals' recent book, *From the Great Deep: Essays on "Idylls of the King"* (Athens, Ohio, 1967), has a chapter on love in the *Idylls* entitled "Eros and Agape," but his discriminations and emphases are different from my own.

[2] *Memoir*, II, 127.

[3] Benjamin Jowett's description of Tennyson's genre. See S. C. Burchell, "Tennyson's 'Allegory in the Distance,' " *PMLA*, LXVIII (1953), 418–424; and Paull F. Baum, *Tennyson Sixty Years After* (Chapel Hill, 1948), pp. 176–213, for a complete discussion of the inconsistencies of genre in the *Idylls*.

understanding of sense's corrosive powers, struggles to disengage itself as it labors to return to a discrete realm of spirit. The simultaneous principles of attraction and repulsion that inform the union of Arthur and Guinevere thus capture the interplay of sense and soul in an archetypal Western love.

This "war-marriage" is only one of several plots that coalesce into Tennyson's most comprehensive statement on love. The Arthur-Guinevere / soul-sense equation — parabolically implied in "The Coming of Arthur," reinforced by the confrontation scene of "Guinevere," and advanced discursively in the Epilogue — provides a structural frame for the quest of Lancelot and for other spiritual journeys in Camelot. Because woman is frequently the prime intoxicant or depressor of these desires for heavenly perfection, it seems appropriate to organize a discussion of the *Idylls* about the four relationships that, taken together, indicate most profoundly the dimensions of Tennysonian love: those of Arthur and Guinevere, Lancelot and Guinevere, Tristram and Isolt, and Galahad and his nun.

While Tennyson's abstract plan is rarely far "in the distance" of his central narrative, he goes to some lengths to humanize Arthur, to accentuate his significance as "Ideal manhood closed in real man" ("To the Queen," l. 38). But it is a truism of Tennyson criticism that Arthur is least credible as a "real" man. Despite the inconsistencies of the conceptual scheme that readers have noticed, Arthur is still most convincing when he assumes his parabolic role as the Ideal that has been sent to redeem the wilderness of the Real, as the soul that both wars with sense and tries to lift it above itself. What is ultimately interesting about the marriage of Arthur and Guinevere is hardly the psychological complexity of mismatched husband or wife but rather the paradox that underlies their psychomachy: soul's need of sense for incarnation is as urgent as sense's dependence upon soul for release from carnal limitation. The resulting conflict of centripetal and centrifugal impulses that can resolve itself only in the transiency of Camelot's momentary perfection suggests the intractability of such love.

Guinevere, "the fairest of all flesh on earth," is to be rescued by her marriage from the wasteland of beasts that Arthur has come to cleanse. While flesh is to be redeemed through the agency of spirit, the process is to be reciprocal. The soul, Arthur realizes, can only operate effectually on this earth as it is enclosed within flesh:

> "O ye stars that shudder over me,
> O earth that soundest hollow under me,
> Vext with waste and dreams? for saving I be join'd
> To her that is the fairest under heaven,
> I seem as nothing in the mighty world,
> And cannot will my will nor work my work
> Wholly, nor make myself in mine own realm
> Victor and lord. But were I join'd with her,
> Then might we live together as one life,
> And reigning with one will in everything
> Have power on this dead world to make it live."
>
> ("The Coming of Arthur," ll. 82–93)

But Guinevere is more than an allegorical representative of flesh — she is the most vivid expression of the female presence that hovers about the life of Arthur in both human and supernatural forms. The mystery of Arthur's divine origin is associated with the Lady of the Lake from whom Arthur receives Excalibur to rid the land of heathen, and with the three queens who escort him to Avilion in "The Passing of Arthur." In the Helio-Arkite mythology derived from Faber which Paden suggests colored Tennyson's reading of Sir Thomas Malory's *Le Morte d'Arthur*, the major source of the *Idylls*, the legend of Arthur's coming and passing is an unmistakable account of the birth and death of the Great Father: "When Adam died, he was buried in the earth, and reappeared as Noah, just as Noah entered the Ark and reappeared to people the earth; so every deity in whose form the Great Father appeared was said symbolically to die (while the earth was reduced to chaos), to be united with the Great Mother (thus forming the hermaphroditic unity that was the Great Universal Parent), and then to be reborn." [4] While the Faberian symbolism is most apparent in the 1842 "Morte d'Arthur," it also plays its role in the *Idylls of the*

[4] *Tennyson in Egypt*, p. 80.

King. The Lady of the Lake, the embodiment of woman as Great Mother, gives life to Arthur by bestowing on him the talisman of his nature as male hero, Excalibur. But even in her first appearance she foreshadows her later significance as an emblem of mortality, for the Lady of the Lake will take the sword from Arthur at his death. Engraved on one side of Excalibur are the words

> "Take me," but turn the blade and ye shall see,
> And written in the speech ye speak yourself,
> "Cast me away!"
> ("The Coming of Arthur," ll. 302–304)

The three spectral queens who, bathed in rays of flaming light, first surround Arthur's throne during his coronation are the fonts of his energy throughout his life, "friends" who by their continuing silent presence extend the generative magic of the Lady of the Lake. Their exact import has always been a matter of critical speculation,[5] but their close link to the Lady of the Lake is suggested by their development in Tennyson's mind before they first accompany Arthur on his last voyage in the 1842 "Morte d'Arthur." In Tennyson's probable Welsh sources Arthur is married to three queens rather than to the one that Malory allows him, and each one of them is named "Gwenhwyfar." The Gwenhwyfar tradition in the Welsh gives special attention to Arthur's second and third queens; the third is said to have betrayed Arthur, while the second was especially loved by him and was consequently buried by his side in Glastonbury.[6]

That Tennyson was aware of this tradition and meant to make use of it is evident from an early sketch of his over-all plan. The poet presented James Knowles with a memorandum at Aldsworth on October 1, 1869, that Tennyson said was between thirty and forty years old. This would make it, along with another early fragment that Hallam Tennyson found among his father's manuscripts,

---

[5] See *Memoir*, II, 127.

[6] Tom Peete Cross, "Alfred Tennyson as a Celticist," *Modern Philology*, XVIII (1921), 485–492. Cross also cites William Owens' *Cambrian Biography* and Edward Davies' *Mythology and Rites of British Druids* as English works in which Tennyson might have run across references to Arthur's three queens.

the earliest expression of Tennyson's allegorical intentions. In his outline Tennyson included the following notes:

K. A. Religious Faith.
King Arthur's three Guineveres.
The Lady of the Lake.
Two Guineveres. ye first prim. Christianity. 2^d Roman Catholicism. ye first is put away and dwells apart. 2^d Guinevere flies. Arthur takes to the first again but finds her changed by lapse of Time.

Modred, the skeptical understanding. He pulls Guinevere, Arthur's latest wife, from the throne.[7]

The next step in the composition, recorded in one of the 1833–1840 manuscript books, blurs the allegorical strictness somewhat and indicates that Tennyson was wavering between casting his Arthurian material into the form of an epic and turning it into a musical masque. In his outline of a five-act structure the three queens have given way to one Guinevere but now there are several "Ladies of the Lake." [8] The association of Guinevere(s) and the Lady(ies) of the Lake may have to do with the fact that the Welsh etymology of "Gwenhwyfar" is "the Lady on the summit of the water" (or so Faber felt it to be).[9]

While Tennyson eventually compressed the three Guineveres of the Welsh tradition and the several Ladies of the Lake into single figures, the existence of interlocking female witnesses to Ar-

[7] *Memoir*, II, 123.
[8] *Ibid.*, p. 124.
[9] Paden, *Tennyson in Egypt*, p. 156. According to Faber's theory there is a general merger of all the women in the Arthur story into one Great Mother. Thus Faber also fuses the figures of Vivien, Morgan le Fay, and the Lady of the Lake: this figure is "clearly the same being as the Persic Mergian Peri and the Sicilian Fata Morgana. . . . Boiardo represents her as gliding beneath the waters of an inchanted [*sic*] lake, while she caresses a vast serpent into which she had metamorphosed one of her lovers: and other romance writers describe her as the perfidious paramour of Merlin, who was wont to denominate her *the white serpent*." Paden connects the Faberian reptile woman not only with the 1859 Vivien but also with the Mermaid of the 1830 volume who was loved by a huge sea-snake.

M. W. McCallum, *Tennyson's Idylls of the King and Arthurian Story from the Sixteenth Century* (Glasgow, 1894), p. 7, however, suggests that "Guinevere" in derivation was one of the many goddesses of the dusk or dawn who, like Helen, were considered on the order now of the deities of light, now of those of darkness. Her ambiguous relation to men therefore precipitates the war waged on her account by rival male powers.

thur's rise and fall suggests that Tennyson in the *Idylls* once more transformed woman into an all-embracing Other. The hero in myth and fairy tale, according to Freud, chooses one of three: "One might say that the three inevitable relations man has with woman are here represented [Freud is referring specifically to Lear's final "choice" of Cordelia]: that with the mother who bears him, with the companion of his bed and board, and with the destroyer. Or it is the three forms taken by the mother as life proceeds: the mother herself, the beloved who is chosen after her pattern, and finally the Mother Earth who receives him again." [10] "The Coming of Arthur" presents the three human queens who merely approximate Freud's paradigm: Ygern, Arthur's mother; Bellicent, his sister; and Guinevere, his destructive wife. But in the confluence of the Lady of the Lake, the three phantasmagoric queens, and the three human queens, we sense the emergence of a continuum between the supernatural and natural conceived of as woman. Such a flowing together portends the cosmic female influence of Freud's analysis, a triune female presence through which the high God of the *Idylls* broods over the life of Arthur and the destiny of Camelot. In his adaptation of the Guinevere legend and in Arthur's fatal "choice" of the third Guinevere, Tennyson echoes the theme of "Oenone": even if he is God's surrogate, the hero born of and supported by woman is ultimately doomed to choose the third of his queens, his destroyer.

While Guinevere is Tennyson's most complex evocation of a destructive woman, her very weakness manages to undermine the admiration that Tennyson intends us to have for Arthur either as ideal representative of soul or as long-suffering husband. We can perhaps discount the partisan thrusts of a slanderous Garlon, of a Vivien endowed with the flatness of a medieval vice, of the Red Knight of the North embittered by an allegorical enmity, or of a Tristram who is the thoroughly modern exponent of a base *Realpolitik*. Even their gibes, removed from the malignant texture of their characters, help to define the impossibility of the ideal that Arthur brings into the world. But certainly the errant humanity

[10] "The Theme of the Three Caskets," p. 75.

of Guinevere, poised as she is between Galahad's saintly nun and the serpentine Vivien, contrasts attractively with the rigidity of Arthur's character and of the uncompromising code he enunciates as the foundation of the Round Table.

When Guinevere first comes to Arthur, he seems to her "cold,/ High, self-contained, and passionless" in comparison to the warmblooded Lancelot ("Guinevere," ll. 402–403). This slur is an elaboration of the mean-spirited attack she had visited upon Arthur during her quarrel with Lancelot in "Lancelot and Elaine":

> "Arthur, my lord, Arthur, the faultless King,
> That passionate perfection, my good lord —
> But who can gaze upon the sun in heaven?
> He never spake word of reproach to me,
> He never had a glimpse of mine untruth,
> He cares not for me. Only here to-day
> There gleamed a vague suspicion in his eyes;
> Some meddling rogue has tamper'd with him — else
> Rapt in this fancy of his Table Round,
> And swearing men to vows impossible,
> To make them like himself; but, friend, to me
> He is all fault who hath no fault at all.
> For who loves me must have a touch of earth;
> The low sun makes the color.   (ll. 121–134)

The imagery of Arthur as "the sun in heaven" contrasted with the "low sun" of Lancelot who has a "touch of earth" is extended in Guinevere's self-mortification after she has been raked by Arthur in their final interview. When he has left her, she denounces her "voluptuous pride" that made her refuse to climb the heights which his perfection illumined:

> I thought I could not breathe in that fine air,
> That pure severity of perfect light —
> I yearned for warmth and color which I found
> In Lancelot — now I see thee what thou art,
> Thou art the highest and most human too,
> Not Lancelot, nor another.
>   ("Guinevere," ll. 640–645)

A most articulate modern exposition of the *Idylls* defends her repentance with persuasive logic:

In Guinevere's repentant insight we are . . . given Tennyson's
. . . answer to the naturalistic argument. The vows present the
paradox: The highest is the most human too. A morality which
merely conforms to our nature is based upon less than the highest
possibility of our nature; we are most human when we transcend
our ordinary selves. The ideal must not, like the ascetic ideal, be so
remote that it seems obviously unattainable; nor must it, like the
naturalistic ideal, be so close that it seems obviously attained. But
it is the essence of ethics to be not descriptive, but normative; not
to tell us how we behave, but how we ought to behave. The ethics
of naturalism confuse the prescriptive end of ethics with the descriptive end of science.[11]

But the reader is not wholly convinced. While it is possible to believe in the austere grandeur of Arthur, it is difficult to sense the
warmth and color that Guinevere, so late in life, attributes to him.
When he speaks of his "vast pity that almost makes me die" as he
scourges Guinevere in a sustained invective of one hundred and
fifty-eight lines; when he will show her "even for thy sake" the sin
that she has committed; when he finally forgives her even "as
Eternal God forgives," the most sympathetic reader must concede
a priggishness that has been the scorn of those who see in Tennyson's Arthurian pageant little more than a representatively obnox-
ious document of Victorian male chauvinism. Given Arthur's
premise that the fall of Camelot has been brought about through
Guinevere, we can perhaps digest the diatribe in part, discounting
the more self-righteous cuts and the degraded spectacle of Guinevere at Arthur's feet during the speech. Or we can retreat into the
allegory and assume that we hear not the character Arthur speaking but rather the stylized "voice" of soul or conscience berating
a sense that has brought ruin to them both. In any case it is hard to
appreciate the "warmth and color" of humanity that Guinevere
now attributes to a severe, wrathful Arthur.

Indeed, despite assertions to the contrary in the *Memoir*, it is
hard to believe that Tennyson himself is unreservedly committed
to Arthur's scathing words. For one thing, Guinevere — and Lance-

[11] F. E. L. Priestley, "Tennyson's *Idylls*," *University of Toronto Quarterly*,
XIX (1949), 45–46.

lot with her — are given a concreteness that eludes Arthur. They share the finest dramatic moments in the *Idylls*, such scenes as the quarrel at the beginning of "Lancelot and Elaine." Here we meet the lovers after the affair has passed its first rapture, and we witness the nasty bickering and uneasy reconciliations that cloud its after-glow. The cross purposes of the guilty pair as they attempt to deceive Arthur, the confusions attendant upon the clumsy furtiveness of their adultery are beautifully caught in this scene that prepares Lancelot for the unsullied "maiden passion" of Elaine. Or in a later moment of the same idyll we cannot help admiring a Guinevere whose anguish can generate an intense vitality in even the most insignificant characters that touch her orbit. When Lancelot wishes to present his queen with a crown of "nine-year-fought-for-diamonds" the last of which he has won in disguise while wearing the favor of Elaine, he sends a messenger to arrange an audience with Guinevere. The fellow enters the presence of the queen who knows all about Elaine from the rumors making the circuit of the court. But it is beneath her dignity as queen and woman to let the messenger suspect her disquiet. She accepts Lancelot's request

> With such and so unmoved a majesty
> She might have seem'd a statue, but that he,
> Low-drooping till he wellnigh kiss'd her feet
> For loyal awe, saw with a sidelong eye
> The shadow of some piece of pointed lace,
> In the Queen's shadow, vibrate on the walls,
> And parted, laughing in his courtly heart.
>
> (ll. 1163–1169)

It is a fine moment. The rich counter-deceptions of queen and craven messenger, the clever obsequiousness that unerringly seeks out the shadow of the piece of lace rather than the lace itself, the vindictive laugh of the "courtly heart" — all give to the messenger a memorable individuality that many more fully developed characters in the *Idylls* never attain. We sense, in other words, Tennyson's aesthetic sympathy for the character of Guinevere and her plight that undercuts whatever overt moral judgment he apparently makes. This is nowhere as true as in the scene in which Arthur thunders forth the condemnation of his queen in "Guinevere." For the Guinevere of this idyll is thoroughly credible only in the passage where she says farewell to Lancelot for the last time, each of the lovers accepting the blame for what has happened and exonerating the other. The rest of the convent scene during which a babbling novice unknowingly humiliates Guinevere by continually saying the wrong thing is too patly ironic to be convincing, and Guinevere groveling before Arthur as he fulminates is merely embarrassing. She lives dramatically when we see her acting out the consequences of her adultery, rarely when she is in the moral presence of Arthur. The attractiveness of a sinful Guinevere illustrates the subterranean survival of what Tennyson had presumably suppressed after the 1833 volume, the appeal of a Keatsian eroticism and of the woman who embodies it. The moral and aesthetic confusions of the *Idylls* that have bothered readers have a partial source in this still unresolved war between sense and soul in Tennyson's own mind.

Tennyson apparently insists that it is "Guinevere's sin," more than any other factor, that is responsible for the fall of Camelot. As in the earlier "Oenone" a single forbidden, adulterous love generates the destruction of an entire society. (Both Troy and Camelot, as well as the Thebes of "Tiresias" and "Amphion," are "cities built to music," exemplars of the Tennysonian belief that high civilization has its foundation in the creative processes of art.) The mind may boggle at the Victorian conception of a single woman's power for good or ill, but we are supposed to take with complete seriousness Arthur's accusation ("Guinevere," ll. 484–490) that the "loathsome opposite" of "all" he desired came about "all thro'" his false queen. This stress on Guinevere's culpability is coupled with the gradual extenuation of Lancelot. If the *Idylls* does portray a war between sense and soul, the ravages of that war are most fully described in the character of Lancelot. From this perspective he is the hero of the work. Guinevere's prime responsibility for the adultery with Lancelot is initially made clear in a conversation be-

tween the two that Balin overhears in a bower near Arthur's hall
("Balin and Balan," ll. 235–275), a garden that abounds in the symbolic lily and rose. As the lovers approach each other Guinevere
moves along "a walk of roses" that "ran from door to door" and
Lancelot along "a walk of lilies" that "crost it to the bower." When
they meet in the center of the garden as their diagonal movements
cross, Lancelot describes a dream he has had in which the maiden
Saint Anne had held the "spiritual lily": the purity of this vision
"drew mine eyes — away." To this assertion of the "charm of
stainless maidenhood" Guinevere replies that the "garden rose/
Deep-hued and many folded" is far sweeter to her. By this opposition, first fully stated in "Maud," of a retiring lily and the aggressive garden rose Tennyson implies that Guinevere has been the
prime mover in a carnal passion to which Lancelot has reluctantly
acquiesced. Trapped within the adoration of his queen Lancelot
tries mightily but unsuccessfully to resist the garden rose of sense
she offers in place of the spiritual lily he expects.

Lancelot's defeat in this floral contest reflects one of Tennyson's
major themes in the *Idylls* — the question of whether man, caught
in the throes of an overwhelming passion, can master it. This question Tennyson takes up with reference first to the Lancelot-Guinevere adultery and then again, more obliquely, to its Tristram-Isolt
counterpart.

The guilty love of Guinevere and Lancelot has an antiphonal
voice in Elaine's plea for the love of Lancelot. "Lancelot and
Elaine" pits a Victorian "maiden passion for a maid," presumably
ending in marriage, against the sensual feast of adulterous passion;
and it does so by posing the question of whether Lancelot is free to
choose which of the two, Guinevere or Elaine, he will love or
whether a man driven by passion is at the mercy of a force beyond
human control. The narrator's description of Lancelot's inability
to transfer his love from Guinevere to Elaine certainly does not
suggest much possibility of choice:

> And peradventure had he seen [Elaine] first
> She might have made this and that other world
> Another world for the sick man; but now

The shackles of an old love straiten'd him,
His honor rooted in dishonor stood,
And faith unfaithful kept him false.

(ll. 867–872)

Elaine herself generously testifies to the inefficacy of will in matters of the heart:

it is no more Sir Lancelot's fault
Not to love me than it is mine to love
Him of all men who seems to me the highest.

(ll. 1068–1070)

And finally while Lancelot himself wishes that Elaine could have bound him to her, he insists to Arthur that "free love will not be bound" (l. 1368).

Tennyson certainly manages to constrict Lancelot's choice by burdening it with enormous difficulties. As he attempts in a climactic interview with Arthur to explain his complex motives, Lancelot describes the intertwining of the wholesome and the poisonous flowers of his love. His is not the fall of one who sought to wallow in the "Slime of the ditch"; his corruption followed rather the yielding to one of those temptations that Arthur Hallam had in another context described as "the elevated and less separable desires" which besiege the noble soul, whether artist or lover (see pp. 39–40). "In me," Lancelot tells Arthur,

lived a sin
So strange, of such a kind, that all of pure,
Noble, and knightly in me twined and clung
Round that one sin, until the wholesome flower
And poisonous grew together, each as each,
Not to be pluck'd asunder.

("The Holy Grail," ll. 769–774)

The equivocal nature of his sin, the fact that his adulterous union with Guinevere had sprung from a passionate asceticism, receives an even fuller definition in "Merlin and Vivien." There a wandering minstrel from Camelot brings to the court of King Mark the news of a Lancelot who

worshipt no unmarried girl,
But the great Queen herself, fought in her name,

> Sware by her — vows like theirs that high in heaven
> Love most, but neither marry nor are given
> In marriage, angels of our Lord's report.
>
> (ll. 12–16)

Lancelot in his desire for unearthly perfection has specifically re-nounced the "maiden passion for a maid" like Elaine, which Ar-thur feels to be that most subtle of masters "to keep down the base in man" ("Guinevere," ll. 475–476); he prefers the "wife worship" of courtly love precisely because he believes a noble wife to be more untouchable than a maiden. And Lancelot's example is dis-astrous: model knight that he is, he inspires other

> youths that hold
> It more beseems the perfect virgin knight
> To worship woman as true wife beyond
> All hope of gaining, than as maiden girl.
> They place their pride in Lancelot and the Queen.
> So passionate for an utter purity
> Beyond the limit of their bond are these,
> For Arthur bound them not to singleness.
>
> ("Merlin and Vivien," ll. 21–28)

In Guinevere's refusal of a pedestal, in her preference for the garden rose over Lancelot's spiritual lily, Tennyson dramatizes the transformation of the adulterous devotion of the Provençal trou-badours which was theoretically without physical consummation into the passion that Anglo-Norman *trouvères* such as Chrétien de Troyes and Béroul portray, the physical union with a real woman and therefore a "profanation" of love. (While it is possible to dis-count the mistaken testimony and slanders of various witnesses throughout the *Idylls*, Arthur's indictment of sexual union be-tween Lancelot and Guinevere in "Guinevere," ll. 550–553, has an authorial ring.) Indeed, Tennyson's attack on "the adulterous fin-ger of a time" that gave rise to courtly love anticipates more re-cent Christian evaluations of courtly love as an essentially gnostic "heresy." Thus for Denis De Rougement, the Swiss cultural his-torian, modern eros originates in the "dark passion" of an adulter-ous courtly love. By its grip on the Western imagination as the re-curring Tristan-Iseult myth in its many guises, this love has poisoned the body politic and the soul of the individual man. With its subterranean wellspring in the Albigensian hatred of the senses and of a bodily existence removed from God, courtly passion has as its goal not the person of the beloved, but the idea of love itself. While ostensibly straining toward a physical consummation, the infinite love of Tristan and Iseult really draws the lovers away from each other and from all living things. Ironically, Western romantic love, while seemingly a celebration of life, tends more frequently to be an irrational quest for self-annihilation. The ascetic impulse toward absolute purity may lead either to the *Liebestod* that usually concludes the Tristan and Iseult story or to an uncontrollable carnality.[12] It is this latter fate which marks the progress of Tennyson's Lancelot and of his imitators at Camelot who attempt to become "angels of our Lord's report."

Swinburne, Arnold, Morris, and Tennyson — to name the major Victorian examples — were all drawn to the parallel Lancelot-Guinevere-Arthur and Tristram-Isolt-Mark love triangles. This continuing return to courtly love themes in Victorian poetry owes something to the then newly awakened interest in medievalism generally. But the didactic vigor with which the poets defended and attacked Guinevere and Isolt points to a more specialized interest. The two stories of fatal love are alternate versions of *the* heretical myth in Western literature which incorporates the ecstasies and torments — regardless which side of the barricade one is on — of adulterous passion. Again and again the Victorian poets allude to these two fables which contain the germ of love's dilemma in the nineteenth century in hopes that an incantation of the myth

[12] *Love in the Western World* (Garden City, N.Y., 1957), *passim.* De Rougement's controversial "Albigensian thesis" is substantially indebted to French examinations of Catharism by Déodat Roché (*Le Catharisme*, Paris, 1953), René Nelli (*L'Amour et les mythes du coeur*, Paris, 1952), and Charles Bru, René Nelli, Cannon de Lagger, and Déodat Roché (*Études manichéennes et cathares*, Paris, 1952). The precise origin of Provençal courtly love — and the question of its pervasiveness in Southern France — is of course a matter of scholarly disagreement. Aside from the thesis of Cathar origin, the phenomenon has been traced to sources as various as Bulgarian heresies, Pictish matriarchal customs, social conditions in the South of France such as the shortage of desirable women at feudal courts, the Cult of the Virgin, and the Arab influence in Andalusia.

will exemplify and strengthen their own convictions. Swinburne's "Tristram of Lyonesse," Arnold's "Tristram and Iseult," and Morris' "The Defense of Guinevere" are partisan maneuvers in a recurring Victorian confrontation of soul and sense.

Of the major Victorian poets who have treated the theme of courtly-love adultery, Tennyson is the only one to bring together the parallel adulteries within a single work. "The Last Tournament" spins out the Tristram-Isolt subplot in sordid counterpoint to Lancelot's and Guinevere's betrayal of Arthur. While Malory's *Le Morte d'Arthur* firmly subordinates its Tristram-Isoud-Mark story to its Launcelot-Guenever-Arthur triangle, the *Idylls* accentuates the parallel, primarily through the intermittent destructiveness of Mark and his agents. As early as the second idyll Mark, "a name of evil savour in the land," appears indirectly through his messenger as a malign foil to the noble Arthur; he is introduced again in "Balin and Balan" in connection with Vivien's entrance into the plot — he actually sends Vivien to corrupt Arthur's court at the beginning of "Merlin and Vivien"; and he enters "The Last Tournament" to slay Tristram in "Mark's way" — from behind. Throughout the *Idylls* the court at Lyonesse nourishes those habitual evils that batter at Camelot's stronghold of virtue.

This contrast of Lyonesse and Camelot receives a narrowed focus in the comparable adulteries of Lancelot and Tristram. The difference in the two knights' conception of love accurately measures the moral distance between the courts they represent. No matter how degraded Lancelot's affair has become, it had begun as an impossible pilgrimage toward spiritual purity. A "realist" who does not believe in spirit, Tristram of Lyonesse need not indulge in fanciful crystallizations of his love. In his exultant passion for Isolt, Tristram rejects the idealism of Lancelot in favor of a hedonism he finds appropriate to the dying animal he knows himself to be:

> worldling of the world am I, and know
> The ptarmigan that whitens ere his hour
> Woos his own end; we are not angels here
> Nor shall be. . . .

. . . my soul, we love but while we may.

(ll. 691–696)

Despite this distinction in their origin the two adulteries are drawn together by the changes that Tennyson makes in both the traditional Lancelot-Guinevere and Tristram-Isolt stories of his source.

In Malory, Arthur from the first is not the representative of soul into which Tennyson transforms his hero but is instead a highly fallible lover of battle and blood sports. Glorying in his many wars he throws himself into them with a Celtic gusto. While both Malory and Tennyson portray Modred as the external villain waiting to profit from any weakness Arthur may betray, in the *Le Morte d'Arthur* he is Arthur's own creature, the son of an incestuous union between Arthur and his sister. If Malory implies a cause for the slow decay of Camelot, it is this incest more than the adultery of Launcelot and Guenever. Furthermore, while Tennyson's Arthur seems the last person in Camelot to learn of the adultery, Malory's Arthur is warned by Merlin even *before* the marriage about Guenever's coming liaison with Launcelot.[13] Not only does Arthur fail to take this prophesy seriously, he also seems more afraid of parting with the admired, puissant Launcelot than he is bothered by the adultery when it does occur. Remarkably complacent about the betrayal by his fair queen, he can stand with less equanimity "my good knight's loss." It is presumably such ungracious details that Tennyson disavows in his epilogue to the *Idylls*, "To the Queen," when he distinguishes his Arthur from the king

> Of Geoffrey's book, or him of Malleor's, one
> Touch'd by the adulterous finger of a time
> That hover'd between war and wantonness,
> And crownings and dethronements.

(ll. 42–45)

[13] Sir Thomas Malory, *Le Morte d'Arthur* (London, 1906), III.i.71. Further citations of the *Morte* will refer to this edition and will appear in parentheses within the text. The edition of Malory that Tennyson consulted was the two-volume *The History of Renowned Prince Arthur, King of Britain*, printed for Walker and Edwards (London, 1816). Hallam Tennyson, citing it as the main source for the *Idylls*, says that this edition was "much used by my father" (*Memoir*, I, 156n2).

Considering the almost casual quality of Arthur's love for Guenever, the adultery of Launcelot and Guenever in Malory's work could hardly be expected to shatter an entire civilization, as it does in Tennyson's. And it is important to notice that while Malory's illicit lovers become acquainted only *after* Guenever's marriage to Arthur, Tennyson alludes to premarital meetings between his Lancelot and Guinevere ("Guinevere," ll. 378–384). As in the traditional Tristram story the eros of Tennyson's *Idylls* is initiated during the embassy of the trusted knight as he escorts the bride-to-be to his liege lord. This change from Malory gives added force to the sequence of responsibility that Tennyson's Arthur erects in his denunciation of Guinevere:

> Then came thy shameful sin with Lancelot;
> Then came the sin of Tristram and Isolt;
> Then others, following these my mightiest knights,
> And drawing foul ensample from fair names,
> Sinn'd also. . . .　　　　　　　("Guinevere," ll. 484–488)

Although the Tristram-Isolt passion dominates only one idyll, its significance as the second ripple in a widening circle of destruction is enforced by Tennyson's insistent pairing of adulteries.

Tennyson makes a concomitant change in the Tristram-Isolt plot to bring it in line with his Lancelot-Guinevere story. In the twelfth-century romances which Malory's Tristram story follows, the love potion intended for Mark and Isolt is a central device that renders their violent passion inexorable by placing it beyond the lovers' control.[14] Malory too provides his Tristram and Beal Isoud with a potion whereby "they loved either other so well that never their love departed for weal neither for woe" (VIII.xxiv.273). But Tennyson's Tristram, the carrier of a base naturalism, requires no magical drink to excuse his *carpe diem* philosophy. This absence of a potion draws Tristram's adultery closer to that of Lancelot which traditionally lacks the extenuating potion. Although the sin of

---

[14] De Rougement, *Love in the Western World*, pp. 37–41, sees the potion of the Tristan myth as an "*alibi* for passion" which takes all responsibility from the lovers for the drive toward death that their passion betrays. Thomas, the first twelfth-century writer to minimize the part played by the magic potion, is "the first writer to degrade the myth thereby."

Lancelot and Guinevere plays only a minor role in Tristram's self-justification, he does mollify Isolt's qualms by citing (like Arthur) the exact parallel between the illicit liaison of Lyonesse and its model in Camelot:

> "O my soul, be comforted!
> If this be sweet, to sin in leading strings,
> If here be comfort, and if ours be sin,
> Crown'd warrant had we for the crowning sin
> That made us happy. . . . "
> ("The Last Tournament," ll. 569–573)

Tennyson's removal of the machinery of fate from his Tristram serves to confirm the doctrine of human control that Arthur has defined earlier. When in "Lancelot and Elaine" Lancelot had insisted that "free love will not be bound," Arthur had replied that "Free love, so bound, were freest." The removal of the potion from the Tristram story reasserts this notion of human responsibility: while erotic passion has enormous power and may create the illusion of irresistibility, it is the essence of humanity to cultivate one's passion toward legitimate, creative ends rather than to let it flourish weed-like in whatever direction it will. Insofar as Arthur's doctrine represents Tennyson's own feelings, the seasonal organicism of the *Idylls*, as Jerome Buckley has suggested,[15] foreshadows Toynbee rather than Spengler. Tennyson, like the former and unlike the latter, insists that despite the crush of circumstance civilizations, and individuals like Tristram and Lancelot, are free to shape their destinies. One can, Ulysses-like, assert control over one's life or take refuge in a Lotos-land determinism which can excuse a slack indulgence in the sensual feast.

The *Idylls*, we have seen, carefully balances the false naturalism of Tristram who is certain that "we are not angels here/ Nor shall be" against the misguided aspiration of Lancelot to become one of the "angels of our Lord's report." Tennyson rounds out his complex view of nineteenth-century "angelism"[16] by presenting a ver-

---

[15] *Tennyson*, p. 281n.
[16] This is Allen Tate's term (in "The Symbolic Imagination" and "The Angelic Imagination," *The Man of Letters in the Modern World* [New

sion of it that does not end in sin. If Lancelot's degeneration suggests the impossibility of reaching godhead through erotic devotion, the life of Galahad defines the conditions of the successful
spiritual quest. During his first appearance in Tennyson's 1842 volumes, Galahad hungers to leap beyond the world of sense, to

> muse on joy that will not cease,
> Pure spaces clothed in living beams,
> Pure lilies of eternal peace,
> Whose odors haunt my dreams;
> And, stricken by an angel's hand,
> This mortal armor that I wear,
> This weight and size, this heart and eyes,
> Are touch'd, are turn'd to finest air.
>
> (ll. 65–72)

Even Galahad cannot conceive of etherealization without falling
back on sensuous imagery: his "pure spaces" are "clothed in living
beams"; the "pure lilies" have odors which fill his sleep. His language provides clear evidence of Hallam's thesis (see p. 62) that
Western man has created a religion that insists on a sensuous relation to God.

And the function of woman, God's closest analogue on earth according to Hallam, is to inspire man toward the spiritual city.
"Saint Agnes' Eve," the work that precedes "Sir Galahad" in the
1842 volumes, provides just such an avatar of female perfection to
facilitate a man's ascent. Tennyson conceived of Galahad as the
"male counterpart" [17] of the nun in that poem who disdains her
earthly body and wishes merely for a "spirit pure and clear" with
which to meet her God as quickly as possible.

"The Holy Grail" brings these male and female aspirants toward
pure spirit together, for it is the nun of "Saint Agnes' Eve," trans-

York, 1953], pp. 93–112, 113–131) for the hypertrophy of feeling, will, and
intellect in Edgar Allan Poe's protagonists resulting from the thrust of these
faculties beyond the scale of human action.

Thomas Hardy's Angel Clare in *Tess of the D'Urbervilles* provides a further nineteenth-century instance of the destructive powers of the angelic
imagination.

[17] *Memoir*, I, 142.

formed into Percivale's sister (also a nun), who has the initial vision of the Holy Grail. When Galahad hears of this, his eyes become like her own and he seems to Percivale "himself her brother
more than I." Inflamed by the divine fervor of the nun, Galahad is
able once and for all to leave flesh behind and to enter the spiritual
city, while the other knights who search for the Grail are destined,
as Arthur warns, to follow "wandering fires." True, Bors and Percivale achieve momentary glimpses of the Grail as through a glass
darkly. Lancelot too thinks he sees it "pall'd in crimson samite,"
surrounded by "angels, awful shapes, and wings and eyes." But his
consciousness of his sin and the consequent madness make him
swoon before the veiled apparition: "This quest," he realizes, "is
not for me."

If we compare Arthur's denigration of the quest, the reasons
for Galahad's apotheosis, and the cause of Lancelot's failure, we
see how subtle the dangers are in a paradigmatic Western love (i.e.,
a love inseparable from religious aspiration toward absolute purity
of spirit, an "erotic devotion"). For a representative of soul or
conscience Arthur seems quite practical when he says that his
knights "with strength and will to right the wrong'd, of power/
To lay the sudden head of violence flat" ought to be satisfied with
"the chance of noble deeds" rather than chasing the wandering
fires of spirit. The visions will come of themselves to the man who,
given his allotted field in life, contents himself with plowing it. The
last verse paragraph of "The Holy Grail" in which Arthur coun-
sels such cultivation of one's earthly garden and describes the mystical illuminations that come without vain striving was intended
by Tennyson as the key to the *Idylls*, "the summing up of all in
the highest note by the highest of human men." [18] As an alternative
to the mistaken quest of his knights, Arthur here most directly describes a Christian agape, the grace of the high God that will descend upon the man who is merely open to it. Arthur does of
course insist on a willed idealism in the earthly garden itself, and
his intense sorrow at the frustration of his will is what renders him
believably human at times. He is, however, most clearly the surro-

[18] *Ibid.*, II, 90.

gate of a God of Love as he testifies to the mystical illuminations
that periodically regenerate the man who does not *a*spire, who has
the patience to wait for *in*spiration that comes when God, not
man, wills.

Galahad and Lancelot are driven by another kind of love which,
whatever the authorial force of Arthur's testimony and example, is
more characteristic of Tennyson's heroes, and perhaps of Western
lovers as a whole — the active quest by the dedicated knight for the
City of God. Because Galahad and his nun have a true religious vocation, their pilgrimage toward the Grail is praiseworthy. While
Tennyson had satirized a proud renunciation of the world in "St.
Simeon Stylites" (1842), he had treated religious asceticism sympa-
thetically in "Sir Galahad" and "Saint Agnes' Eve," and was to do
so again in "St. Telemachus" of his 1892 volume. The answer to
Arthur's condemnation of his knights is, after all, that one does
not know whether he is worthy of the quest until he has tried it.
While this may not apply to obviously selfish pilgrims like Gawain,
it does to such marginal cases as Bors, Percivale, and particularly
to the tortured Lancelot.

Lancelot's idealization of Guinevere had been marked by a spiritual intensity scarcely distinguishable from that suffusing Galahad's asceticism. The language used in "Merlin and Vivien" to char-
acterize Lancelot's passion is equally applicable to Galahad's — both
knights are so "passionate for an utter purity" that they wish "neither [to] marry nor [to] be given in marriage." Both cultivate
within themselves the paradoxical humility of absolute spiritual
perfection that will transfigure them into "angels of our Lord's report"; and both are inspired in their heavenly movement by a
woman. As she sends Galahad, wearing her favor, off in search of
the Grail, the nun is as much the lady of courtly love as Guinevere
in the erotic language with which she overwhelms his mere humanity:

> "My knight, my love, my knight of heaven,
> O thou, my love, whose love is one with mine,
> I, maiden, round thee, maiden, bind my belt.
> Go forth, for thou shalt see what I have seen,
> And break thro' all, till one will crown thee king

Far in the spiritual city;" and as she spake
She sent the deathless passion in her eyes
Thro' him, and made him hers, and laid her mind
On him, and he believed in her belief.

("The Holy Grail," ll. 157–165)

And both women are made as impregnable as possible by lovers of divine perfection who use them as agents toward a heavenly flight: Galahad transforms an already inaccessible nun into his "sister," while Lancelot is attracted to Guinevere in large measure because she is a wife (rather than a marriageable maiden) and the queen of a liege lord to whom he has sworn a "deathless vow" of loyalty.

The ability of Galahad to "break thro'" to the spiritual city and the failure of Lancelot's angelism, from this perspective, is determined by the fact that while the nun remains inaccessible Guinevere does not. Man's spiritual destiny, Tennyson implies, depends on the strength of woman to sustain the erotic devotion that man lavishes on her as an analogue of God. When woman can bear the weight of man's devotion and remain a model of purity, she keeps him on the high road toward the spiritual city; when like Guinevere she cannot remain the untouchable object into which man crystallizes her, she turns into the Tennysonian fatal woman who precipitates the destruction of an entire civilization.

Tennyson's disavowal of a poetry of sense tended to reinforce his early belief that love is a thing of pure spirit. But because Tennyson's lovers try to renounce physical union through the agency of the senses — the only way to spirit — the spirit must depend for its thrust toward godhead on the inspirational powers of another spirit. Percivale's sister is the rare woman who can live up to such an extraordinary demand. It is more likely that even the noblest of ladies will betray the knight who asks her for the sake of his quest to deny that she is human, that she is a creature of sense as well as of spirit. Lancelot's angelism — and that of Tennyson and his age — are thus basically responsible for the transformation of Guinevere into a fatal woman "all" through whom Camelot falls. As Allen Tate has generalized about Edgar Allan Poe, another nineteenth-century Platonist whose heroes try to etherealize their women, "If a writer ambiguously exalts the 'spirit' over the 'body,' and the spirit must live wholly upon another spirit, some version of the vampire legend is likely to issue as the symbolic situation." [19]

The weakness of the *Idylls of the King*, a fault more damaging than the generic vacillations that critics have attacked or attempted to justify, is the fact that Tennyson has not sufficiently controlled his divided feelings about the angelic imagination of his protagonists. Offspring of a Platonism, of a Christian gnosticism, of romantic aspiration, of the evangelical revival — of all those forces in his life and in Western thought that encourage the passion for a "fellowship with essence" — Tennyson creates in Arthur an idealized king whose perfection leads men to high deeds that permit them momentarily to reach beyond their routine worldliness. Tennyson's comments in the *Memoir* indicate his unqualified admiration of the Arthurian "Ideal manhood closed in real man." But a reading of the *Idylls* suggests that Arthurian idealism bears the germs of its own corruption. The two ways in which it does so encapsulate the contradiction of a "marriage-war" between Arthur conceived as soul and Guinevere as sense. Most obviously, the angelism of Lancelot undermined by Guinevere sends a destructive sensuality through Camelot. The adultery of Lancelot and Guinevere thereby illustrates and offers a critique of that highly attractive "marriage" of Western love in which the soul does not disengage itself from the senses as it journeys toward the beatific vision of the beloved. More subtly, Galahad's ascetic progress toward the spiritual city implies Tennyson's comment on the competing "war" of Western love in which the soul's upward thrust manages to leave a despised sense behind as it struggles toward a discrete realm of spirit. Galahad's apotheosis is just as disastrous for the existence of Camelot as is Lancelot's frustrated angelism. Galahad has had his vision, has found his spiritual home; and the success of his quest instills a visionary zeal in some of Arthur's other knights. But however exemplary Galahad's journey may be considered in isolation, the futile search for wandering fires it encourages deci-

[19] "Our Cousin, Mr. Poe," *Man of Letters in the Modern World*, p. 140.

mates the Round Table no less surely than Lancelot's and Guinevere's adultery.

As Arthur's radiance plays over the vitality of Guinevere and kindles the idealism of Camelot's worthies, we can sense Tennyson's characteristic movement from a temperamental delight in sensuous beauty, to an obsessive distrust of sensuous abandon, and — doubling back upon himself — to a critique of life-denying asceticism. The *via media* that Tennyson tries to find among these competing impulses is one way of defining the perfection of Camelot, that perilous balance which individuals and societies can win at rare moments from the flux of time. The lasting significance of the *Idylls of the King* is the comprehensive way in which it outlines the most basic of human tragedies, the personal and social dislocations that arise from man's passion to transcend mutability and mortality. Muted in our own sensibility is the extreme aversion to the human body that certain historical periods have stressed in the sense/soul division of both Platonic eros and Christian agape.[20] But man's fleshly nature is still his most persistent reminder of change and death; his heroic drive to elude these twin terrors is as intense as ever; and the certainty of their triumph over his best efforts is as much the occasion of idle tears as it has always been. Whether or not we insist upon translating into a contemporary idiom the Platonic/Christian terminology (a marriage-war between sense and soul) in which Tennyson couches these themes, we cannot escape the continuing relevance for our restless, questing selves of Tennyson's vast Arthurian tapestry.

[20] For a neo-Freudian attack on the Platonic and Christian positions, see Norman O. Brown, *Life against Death: The Psychoanalytical Meaning of History* (New York, 1959). Brown distinguishes the positive, self-centered eros of Freud from Platonic eros and Christian agape, both of which he finds life-denying in their attempt to escape the human body: "From the psychoanalytical point of view, Platonic Eros is inseparable from an aggressive component, Christian Agape from a masochistic component. Freud's doctrine of the narcissistic essence of love seems to lay the groundwork for transcending the by now exhausted debate between Eros and Agape and to pose the proper question, at least for our time, which is to develop a love based neither on self-hatred nor the need to appropriate, but on self-acceptance, self-activity, self-enjoyment. And the Freudian (and Spinozistic) recognition of the bodily nature of all self-enjoyment indicates the obstacle that prevents both Platonist and Christian from accepting the self — the human body" (p. 49).

CHAPTER XI

Conclusion

E MIGHT well begin a summary of what is valuable in Tennyson's view of love by conceding its failures of insight and nerve that this study has tended to slight. The fairest way to assess such limitations is to measure Tennyson against his contemporaries — to describe the effects of which they were capable and that eluded him, to locate the areas that they explored but that were closed to him or that he preferred to ignore.

The Victorian period certainly gave rise to more sophisticated explorations of love than Tennyson was able to manage. The novels, say, of George Eliot and George Meredith contain a more subtle treatment of the moral springs of love than do Tennyson's idealized affairs pitted in strict division against scenes of degraded grovelings in sin. Even if we limit ourselves to Victorian poetry, there exist more penetrating, less polarized investigations of the variegated human puzzle. Except for attenuated hints in his treatment of Lancelot and Guinevere, Tennyson can approach neither Robert Browning's insight into the psychological turns of a complicated passion nor his celebration of the irresistible, if illicit, affinities of impulsive lovers. Though Tennysonian love is tinged by a Christian Platonism, the theoretical Platonism so crucial to the history of romantic love receives its only full Victorian adaptation in the poetry of Dante Rossetti. Tennyson's exposition of a dark carnality, while he can summon up a convincing horror of Dionysian wildness, rarely touches the verve — admittedly sensational, self-conscious, and derivative — of Swinburne.

Nor can Tennyson follow with Arthur Hugh Clough the constantly shifting motivations and the serio-comic attitudes that lovers assume in the social game of love. Tennyson's narrative poems rarely show a believable impingement of class differences upon the private entanglements of his lovers — what he gives us instead are the broad, melodramatic familial oppositions of "The Miller's Daughter," "Locksley Hall," "Edwin Morris," or "Maud." Perhaps novelistic social realism is not what one requires from a poet (though in such poems on love and marriage as Clough's *The Bothie of Tober-na-Vuolich*, Coventry Patmore's *The Angel in the House*, Elizabeth Barrett Browning's *Aurora Leigh*, as well as Tennyson's own *The Princess*, the Victorian poet seems to be reaching for the narrative range of the novel form). At any rate Clough alone among the Victorian poets consistently works for verisimilitude of manner in his characters. Of the period's many extended love poems, his *Amours de Voyage* comes closest to capturing the "buzz of social implication" (Lionel Trilling's phrase) that one hears in the Victorian novel. And, finally, nowhere does Tennyson sound the tragic depths of *Modern Love*. In Meredith's great work a husband and wife, superbly alive to their fatal propensity for mutual destructiveness, are yet unable to extricate themselves from their self-woven doom. In feeding upon each other they voice Meredith's conviction that in the failure of most human intimacies

> The wrong is mixed. In tragic life, God wot,
> No villain need be! Passions spin the plot:
> We are betrayed by what is false within.
>
> (XLIII)

Compared to such knowledge, Tennyson's attribution of simple greed, lust, pride, or timorousness (frequently to one of the partners as opposed to the untarnished virtue of the other) appears simplistic.

But when one has let Tennyson's contemporaries define the inadequacies in his statement of a major Victorian theme, a substantial residue of value remains to indicate why Tennyson is *the* exemplary poet of Victorian love. The heritage which confronted the youthful Tennyson was an impracticable mixture, the nineteenth-century version of an ancient Western dualism. While he was faced on the one side with the Romantic exaltation of sensuousness and passionate love, the evangelical Christianity of his age taught him on the other to fear sensuous and sensual extravagance. In his consequent vacillation between the knowledge that he was quite naturally a "lord of the five senses" and the knowledge that the responsible artist must scout the dangers of erotic indulgence, Tennyson moved as on a strange diagonal between a Dantesque conception of love in which the soul and sense are inseparable and a Platonic one in which the highest kind of spiritual love has disencumbered itself of sense. The apparent drift in Tennyson's poetry is toward a "spiritual" love that takes several complementary forms — the celebration of a bloodless Victorian marriage and of the decorous "maiden passion for a maid" as well as a revulsion against adultery and excessively erotic drives of any sort. The uncertain quality of this moral commitment, however, emerges in the lifelong attractiveness of a sensuousness that he can never wholly control, in, for instance, the aesthetic dynamism with which Lancelot and Guinevere, caught in the toils of their adulterous passion, dominate the *Idylls of the King*.

Typically the Victorian poet in his treatment of love had to accommodate himself to the same dual heritage as Tennyson. The elective affinities of Browning, Patmore's apotheosis of marriage based on erotic love, Rossetti's adaptation of a Dantesque Neoplatonism, Arnold's fastidious turning away from "Marguerite," all can with only slight exaggeration be described as various responses to the same cultural dilemma. Those poets who, yoking the hostile conceptions of love together, denied that there *was* a dilemma were rarely convincing: the assertion in the works of Kingsley and Patmore that the limitless passion of the Romantics could flourish within a spiritualized (and contractual) Victorian marriage usually led to a sentimental moralism that does not ring true. At his worst Tennyson did not escape a like facile optimism grounded in a simplification of his dual heritage and in a dismissal of human complexity.

But no other Victorian poet possessed of a major talent exhibits quite his representative blending of romantic eroticism and sentimental pietism. If romantic marriage does become a secular religion in the nineteenth century, as commentators have suggested, Tennyson most paradigmatically combines the two strains while at the same time betraying the extent to which they are irreconcilable. In his most moving poetry the very intractability of his anomalous heritage found a creative catalyst in his melancholy temperament, in his mourning for an irrecoverable past. While Tennyson tried to celebrate the virtues of an ordered domesticity, his best work mourns a lost or unrealized love in a personal or legendary past ("Tears, Idle Tears," *In Memoriam*, "Mariana," "The Lady of Shalott"), the failure of married love (the *Idylls*), or a serene married love viewed by a spectator who cannot participate in it ("The Two Voices"). The "infant crying in the night" though he or she may aspire to the warmth of the spiritual hearth is a deserted specter floating through a bleak, concretely sensuous landscape.

The sublime effects Tennyson can achieve arise from his sustained ability to translate an overriding personal sense of love's inability to stave off the terrors of decay and abandonment into a cosmic principle. With unsurpassed aural mastery and in an abundant variety of forms he evokes the *lacrimae rerum* of speakers who come to realize the traps implicit in the divided nature of love. Among the major poets in English he is unique in the restricted impulse behind his best poetry, the obscure childhood experience of abandonment that has never been adequately explained but that one feels to be at the core of the Virgilian sorrow. Out of this amorphous and unlocalized sadness, leavened as it was by his personal losses and by the impossible dualism of traditional Western love, Tennyson was able to forge a large body of highly disciplined, beautifully wrought, and far-ranging verse.

SELECTED BIBLIOGRAPHY
AND INDEX

Selected Bibliography

Works of Tennyson

The Devil and the Lady, ed. Charles Tennyson. London, 1930.
The Poetic and Dramatic Works of Alfred Lord Tennyson, ed. W. J. Rolfe. Boston and New York, 1898. Cambridge Edition.
Unpublished Early Poems, ed. Charles Tennyson. London, 1931.
The Works of Alfred Lord Tennyson. London and New York, 1892. Macmillan Edition.
The Works of Tennyson, ed. Hallam Tennyson. 6 vols. London and New York, 1908. Eversley Edition.

Books and Chapters of Books on Tennyson and His Age

Altick, Richard. *The English Common Reader: A Social History of the Mass Reading Public, 1800–1900.* Chicago, 1957.
Auden, W. H. Introduction to *A Selection from the Poems of Alfred Lord Tennyson.* Garden City, N.Y., 1944.
Bagehot, Walter. "Wordsworth, Tennyson, and Browning; or Pure, Ornate, and Grotesque Art in English Poetry," in *Literary Studies*, ed. Richard Holt Hutton, Vol. II. London, 1895.
Basler, Roy P. "Tennyson the Psychologist," in *Sex, Symbolism and Psychology in Literature.* New Brunswick, N.J., 1948.
Baum, Paull F. *Tennyson Sixty Years After.* Chapel Hill, N.C., 1948.
Benson, Arthur. *Fasti Etonensus: A Biographical History of Eton.* Elton, 1899.
Boas, Frederick S. "Tennyson and the Arthurian Legend," in *From Richardson to Pinero.* New York, 1937.
Bradley, A. C. *A Commentary on Tennyson's "In Memoriam."* London, 1915.
Brookfield, Frances M. *The Cambridge "Apostles."* New York, 1906.
Brooks, Cleanth. "The Motivation of Tennyson's Weeper," in *The Well Wrought Urn.* New York, 1947.

Buckley, Jerome H. *Tennyson: The Growth of a Poet.* Cambridge, Mass., 1960.

Bush, Douglas. "Tennyson," in *Mythology and the Romantic Tradition in English Poetry.* Cambridge, Mass., 1937.

Canby, Henry Seidel. *American Memoir.* Boston, 1947.

Carlyle, Jane Welsh. *Jane Welsh Carlyle: A New Selection of Her Letters,* ed. Trudy Bliss. New York, 1950.

Carlyle, Thomas. *The Life of John Sterling.* London, 1870.

Edison, John O. *Tennyson in America: His Reputation and Influence from 1827 to 1858.* Athens, Ga., 1943.

Eliot, T. S. "In Memoriam," in *Essays Ancient and Modern.* New York, 1936.

Fausset, Hugh l'Anson. *Tennyson: A Modern Portrait.* New York, 1923.

Fitzgerald, Edward. *Edward Fitzgerald and Bernard Barton: Letters Written by Fitzgerald,* ed. F. R. Barton. London and New York, 1924.

———. *Letters and Literary Remains of Edward Fitzgerald,* ed. William Aldis Wright. 2 vols. London and New York, 1889.

———. *More Letters of Edward Fitzgerald,* ed. William Aldis Wright. London and New York, 1901.

Ford, George. *Keats and the Victorians: A Study in His Influence and Rise to Fame, 1821–1895.* New Haven, 1944.

Gaskell, James Milnes. *An Eton Boy, Being the Letters of James Milnes Gaskell from Eton and Oxford, 1820–1830,* ed. Charles Milnes Gaskell. London, 1939.

Hallam, Arthur Henry. *The Writings of Arthur Hallam,* ed. T. H. Vail Motter. New York and London, 1943.

Hopkins, Gerard Manley. *Further Letters of Gerard Manley Hopkins,* ed. C. C. Abbott. London, 1938.

Houghton, Walter. *The Victorian Frame of Mind, 1830–1870.* New Haven, 1957.

Johnson, E. D. H. *The Alien Vision of Victorian Poetry.* Princeton, 1952.

Jones, Richard F. *The Growth of "The Idylls of the King."* Philadelphia, 1895.

Killham, John, ed. *Critical Essays on the Poetry of Tennyson.* London, 1960.

———. *Tennyson and "The Princess": Reflections of an Age.* London, 1958.

MacCallum, M. W. *Tennyson's Idylls of the King and Arthurian Story from the Sixteenth Century.* Glasgow, 1894.

Mallarmé, Stéphane. "Tennyson vu d'ici," in *Divigations.* Paris, 1922.

Marshall, George O., Jr. *A Tennyson Handbook.* New York, 1963.

Masterman, C. F. G. *Tennyson as a Religious Teacher.* London, 1900.

Mattes, Eleanor Bustin. *"In Memoriam": The Way of a Soul.* New York, 1951.

Maurice, Frederick Denison. *The Life of Frederick Denison Maurice,* ed. Frederick Maurice. 2 vols. New York, 1884.

Merivale, Charles. *Autobiography and Letters of Charles Merivale,* ed. Judith Anne Merivale. Oxford, 1898.

Mustard, W. P. *Classical Echoes in Tennyson.* New York, 1904.

Nelson, James. *The Sublime Puritan: Milton and the Victorians.* Madison, Wisc., 1963.

Nicolson, Harold. *Tennyson: Aspects of His Life, Character, and Poetry.* London, 1923.

Paden, W. D. *Tennyson in Egypt: A Study of the Imagery in His Earlier Work.* Lawrence, Kans., 1942.

Pitt, Valerie. *Tennyson Laureate.* Toronto, 1962.

Quinlan, Maurice J. *Victorian Prelude: A History of English Manners 1700–1830.* New York, 1941.

Rader, Ralph Wilson. *Tennyson's "Maud": The Biographical Genesis.* Berkeley, 1963.

Reid, T. Wemyss. *The Life, Letters, and Friendships of Richard Monckton Milnes, First Lord Houghton.* 2 vols. New York, 1892.

Ritchie, Anne Thackeray. *Records of Tennyson, Ruskin and Browning.* New York, 1892.

Ruskin, John. "Of Queens' Gardens," in *Sesame and Lilies* (1865), *Works,* ed. E. T. Cook and A. D. O. Wedderburn, Vol. XVIII. London, 1902–1912.

Ryals, Clyde de L. *From the Great Deep: Essays on "Idylls of the King."* Athens, Ohio, 1967.

———. *Theme and Symbol in Tennyson's Poems to 1850.* Philadelphia, 1964.

Shannon, Edgar F., Jr. *Tennyson and the Reviewers: A Study of His Literary Reputation and of the Influence of the Critics upon His Poetry.* Cambridge, Mass., 1952.

Smith, Elton. *The Two Voices: A Tennyson Study.* Lincoln, Neb., 1964.

Stevenson, Lionel. *Darwin among the Poets.* Chicago, 1932.

Swinburne, A. C. "Tennyson and Musset," in *Miscellanies.* London, 1886.

———. *Under the Microscope.* Portland, Me., 1872.

Taylor, Henry. *Philip Van Artevelde.* London, 1834.

Tennyson, Sir Charles. *Alfred Tennyson.* London and New York, 1949.

———. *Six Tennyson Essays.* London, 1954.

Tennyson, Frederick. *Letters to Frederick Tennyson,* ed. Hugh J. Schonfield. London, 1930.

Tennyson, Hallam. *Alfred Lord Tennyson: A Memoir by His Son.* 2 vols. London and New York, 1897.

———, ed. *Tennyson and His Friends.* London, 1911.

Tillotson, Kathleen. "Tennyson's Serial Poem," in *Mid-Victorian Studies.* London, 1965.

Trench, Richard Chevenix. *Richard Chevenix Trench: Letters and Memorials,* ed. Maria Trench. 2 vols. London, 1888.

Van Dyke, Henry. *The Poetry of Tennyson.* New York, 1902.

Warren, T. Herbert. "Tennyson and Dante," in *Essays of Poets and Poetry, Ancient and Modern.* London, 1909.

Young, G. M. "The Age of Tennyson," in *Proceedings of the British Academy,* Vol. XXV. London, 1939.

Background Works

"Agape," "Chastity," "Marriage," in *Encyclopedia of Religion and Ethics,* ed. James Hastings, new ed. New York, 1951.

"Aphrodite," "Venus," in *Harper's Dictionary of Classical Literature and Antiquities,* ed. Harry Thurston Peck. New York, 1963.

Arnold, Matthew. *Essays in Criticism,* 2nd series (1888). London, 1891.

———. "Numbers," in *Discourses in America.* London, 1885.

St. Augustine. *The City of God.* Garden City, N.Y., 1958.

Bodkin, Maud. "The Image of Woman," in *Archetypal Patterns in Poetry*. London, 1934.

Brown, Norman O. *Life against Death: The Psychoanalytical Meaning of History.* New York, 1959.

Carlyle, Thomas. *Latter-Day Pamphlets* (1850), *Works*, Centenary Edition. London, 1897.

———. *Past and Present* (1843), *Works*, Centenary Edition. London, 1897.

Caudwell, Christopher. "Love," in *Studies in a Dying Culture*. New York, 1938.

D'Arcy, Martin C., S.J. *The Mind and Heart of Love.* New York, 1947.

Denomy, Father Alexander J. "Fin'Amors: The Pure Love of the Troubadours," in *Medieval Studies*, Vol. VII. New York, 1945.

———. *The Heresy of Courtly Love.* New York, 1947.

De Rougement, Denis. *Love Declared: Essays on the Myths of Love.* New York, 1964.

———. *Love in the Western World*, trans. Montgomery Belgion (originally pub. in French [1939] as *L'Amour et L'Occident*; revised and augmented in 1956). Garden City, N.Y., 1957.

Eliot-Binns, L. E. *The Evangelical Movement in the English Church.* London, 1928.

———. *Religion in the Victorian Era.* London, 1936.

Frazer, Sir James. *The Golden Bough: A Study in Magic and Religion.* 12 vols. London, 1911–1915.

Freud, Sigmund. *On Creativity and the Unconscious: Papers on the Psychology of Art, Literature, Love, and Religion*, ed. Benjamin Nelson. New York, 1958.

Frye, Northrop. *Anatomy of Criticism.* Princeton, 1957.

———. "The Argument of Comedy," in *English Institute Essays*. New York, 1948.

Harrison, Jane. *Prolegomena to the Study of Greek Religion.* New York, 1955.

Jones, Ernest. *Hamlet and Oedipus.* Garden City, N.Y., 1949.

Keats, John. *The Complete Works of John Keats*, ed. H. B. Forman. 5 vols. Glasgow, 1900–1901.

———. *The Letters of John Keats*, ed. M. B. Forman, 4th ed. London, 1952.

Knox, Ronald. *Enthusiasm.* Oxford, 1950.

Krutch, Joseph Wood. "Love — or the Life and Death of a Value," in *The Modern Temper*. New York, 1929.

Lewis, C. S. *The Allegory of Love.* London, 1938.

Lucretius. *On the Nature of Things*, trans. W. E. Leonard. London, 1921.

Lunn, Arnold. *John Wesley.* London, 1929.

MacKail, J. W. *Lectures on Greek Poetry.* London, 1910.

Malory, Sir Thomas. *Le Morte d'Arthur*, ed. John Rhys. 2 vols. London, 1906.

Marcus, Stephen. *The Other Victorians.* New York, 1966.

Marcuse, Herbert. *Eros and Civilization.* Boston, 1955.

Masterman, C. F. G. *The Condition of England.* London, 1909.

More, Hannah. "Unprofitable Reading," in *The Works of Hannah More*, Vol. XI. London, 1853.

Nelli, René. *L'Amour et les mythes du coeur.* Paris, 1952.

Nygren, Anders. *Agape and Eros*, trans. Philip S. Watson (orig. pub. in 2 vols: Part I, 1932; Part II, vol. I, 1938; Part II, vol. II, 1939; rev. in part, retrans. and pub. in one volume, 1953). Philadelphia, 1953.

Pater, Walter. *The Renaissance*. London, 1910.
Patmore, Coventry. *Poems*, ed. F. Page. London, 1949.
Plato. *Five Great Dialogues*, trans. B. Jowett. Roslyn, N.Y., 1942.
Praz, Mario. *The Romantic Agony*. New York, 1956.
Shelley, Percy Bysshe. *The Complete Poetical Works of Percy Bysshe Shelley*, ed. Thomas Hutchinson. London, 1961.
Stange, G. Robert. "The Idea of Love," in *Matthew Arnold: The Poet as Humanist*. Princeton, 1967.
Stendhal (Marie Henri Beyle). *On Love*. New York, 1957.
Tate, Allen. *The Man of Letters in the Modern World*. New York, 1953.
Taylor, A. E. *Plato: The Man and His Work*. New York, 1952.
Tillyard, E. M. W. "The Personal Heresy," in *The Modern Critical Spectrum*, ed. Gerald and Nancy Goldberg. Englewood Cliffs, N.J., 1962.
Vyvyan, John. *Shakespeare and Platonic Beauty*. London, 1961.
———. *Shakespeare and the Rose of Love*. London, 1960.
Watt, Ian. "Love and the Novel: *Pamela*," in *The Rise of the Novel*. Berkeley, 1959.
Williams, Raymond. *Culture and Society 1790–1950*. Garden City, N.Y., 1959.

Articles in Periodicals

Assad, Thomas J. "Tennyson's 'Tears, Idle Tears,'" *Tulane Studies in English*, XIII (1963), 71–83.
Benton, John F. "The Court of Champagne as a Literary Center," *Speculum*, XXXVI (1961), 511–591.
Buchanan, Robert. "The Fleshly School of Poetry: Mr. D. G. Rossetti," *Contemporary Review*, XVIII (Oct. 18, 1871), 334–350.
Burchell, S. C. "Tennyson's 'Allegory in the Distance,'" *PMLA*, LXVIII (1953), 418–424.
Carr, Arthur. "Tennyson as a Modern Poet," *University of Toronto Quarterly*, XIX (1950), 361–382.
Cross, Tom Peete. "Alfred Tennyson as a Celticist." *Modern Philology*, XVIII (1921), 485–492.
Dahl, Curtis. "A Double Frame for Tennyson's Demeter?" *Victorian Studies*, I (1958), 356–362.
Danzig, Allan. "The Contraries: A Central Concept in Tennyson's Poetry," *PMLA*, LXXVII (1962), 577–585.
———. "Tennyson's *The Princess*: A Definition of Love," *Victorian Poetry*, IV (1966), 83–89.
Donahue, Mary Joan. "Tennyson's *Hail Briton!* and *Tithon* in the Heath Manuscript," *PMLA*, LXIV (1949), 385–416.
Green, Joyce. "Tennyson's Development during the 'Ten Years' Silence (1832–1842)," *PMLA*, LXVI (1951), 662–697.
Hough, Graham. "Tears, Idle Tears," *Hopkins Review*, IV (1951), 31–36.
Johnson, E. D. H. "'In Memoriam': The Way of the Poet," *Victorian Studies*, II (1958), 139–148.
———. "The Lily and the Rose: Symbolic Meaning in Tennyson's *Maud*," *PMLA*, LXIV (1949), 1222–1227.
Johnson, W. Stacy. "The Theme of Marriage in Tennyson," *Victorian Newsletter*, No. 12 (1957), 6–10.

Killham, John. "Tennyson and the Sinful Queen – A Corrected Impression," *Notes and Queries*, V (1958), 507–511.

Kissane, James. "Tennyson: The Passion of the Past and the Curse of Time," *Journal of English Literary History*, XXXII (1965), 85–109.

————. "Victorian Mythology," *Victorian Studies*, VI (1962), 5–28.

Knowles, James. "Aspects of Tennyson, II: A Personal Reminiscence," *The Nineteenth Century*, XXXIII (1893), 170–182.

MacLaren, Malcolm. "Tennyson's Epicurean Lotos-Eaters," *Classical Journal* (March 1960), 259–267.

Marshall, George O., Jr. "Tennyson's 'Oh! that 'twere possible': A Link between *In Memoriam* and 'Maud,'" *PMLA*, LXXVIII (1963), 225–229.

Miller, Betty. "Tennyson and the Sinful Queen," *Twentieth Century*, CLVIII (1955), 355–363.

Paden, W. D. "Tennyson's 'The Poet,'" *The Explicator*, II (1944), Items 5, 6.

Priestley, F. E. L. "Tennyson's *Idylls*," *University of Toronto Quarterly*, XIX (1949), 35–49.

————. "Tennyson," *University of Toronto Quarterly*, XXXII (1962–1963), 102–106.

Rader, Ralph Wilson. "Tennyson in the Year of Hallam's Death," *PMLA*, LXXVII (1962), 419–424.

Ricks, Christopher. "Tennyson's 'Maud,'" letter to the *London Times Literary Supplement*, Dec. 31, 1964.

Ryals, Clyde de L. "The 'Fatal Woman' Symbol in Tennyson," *PMLA*, LXXIV (1951), 438–443.

————. "The 'Weird Seizures' in *The Princess*," *Texas Studies in Literature and Language*, IV (1962), 268–275.

Sanders, Charles. "Tennyson and the Human Hand," *Victorian Newsletter*, No. 11 (1957), 5–13.

Shannon, Edgar F., and W. H. Bond. "Literary Manuscripts of Alfred Tennyson in the Harvard College Library," *Harvard Library Bulletin*, X (1956), 254–274.

Solomon, Stanley J. "Tennyson's Paradoxical King," *Victorian Poetry*, I (1963), 258–271.

Spitzer, Leo. "'Tears, Idle Tears' Again," *Hopkins Review*, V (1952), 71–80.

Stange, G. Robert. "Tennyson's Garden of Art: A Study of *The Hesperides*," *PMLA*, LXVII (1952), 732–743.

————. "Tennyson's Mythology: A Study of *Demeter and Persephone*," *Journal of English Literary History*, XXI (1954), 67–80.

Stevenson, Lionel. "The 'High-Born Maiden' Symbol in Tennyson," *PMLA*, LXIII (1948), 234–243.

Summers, Joseph. "The Masks of *Twelfth Night*," *University of Kansas City Review*, XXII (1955), 25–32.

Tennyson, Sir Charles. "The Idylls of the King," *Twentieth Century*, CLXI (1957), 277–286.

————. "Tennyson Papers: II. J. M. Heath's 'Commonplace Book,'" *Cornhill Magazine*, CLIII (1936), 426–449.

————. "Tennyson Papers: IV. The Making of *The Princess*," *Cornhill Magazine*, CLIII (1936), 672–680.

Van Dyke, Henry. "The Voice of Tennyson," *Century Magazine*, XLV (1893), 540–541.

Index